Praise for

fathermothergod

"*fathermothergod* is a heart-wrenching coming-of-age memoir about the implosion of a family when Christian Science dogma encounters a mother's grave illness. It's impossible to read this and not put yourself in the author's shoes—this will take your breath away."

—LEE WOODRUFF, AUTHOR OF
PERFECTLY IMPERFECT AND *IN AN INSTANT*

"A riveting and heartrending memoir, *fathermothergod: My Journey Out of Christian Science* exposes the monstrous feats of neglect fostered by this strange American manifestation of religious fanaticism. Tracing her mother's decline and its lacerating consequences, Lucia Greenhouse knows the truth about Christian Science, and she tells it with passionate, righteous indignation.

—CAROLINE FRASER, AUTHOR OF *GOD'S PERFECT CHILD:
LIVING AND DYING IN THE CHRISTIAN SCIENCE CHURCH*

"Lucia Greenhouse's book is a heartbreaking reminder of how nefarious religious zealotry can be. Her story drew me in and blew me away. This is an important addition to the genre of memoirs by children who escaped religious hucksterism and are now bravely exposing it."

—JULIA SCHEERES, AUTHOR OF *JESUS LAND*

"Courageous and finely crafted."

—*STAR TRIBUNE* (MINNEAPOLIS)

"[A] powerfully affecting memoir . . . Greenhouse's skill in rendering family relationships under the intersecting stresses of illness and conflicting beliefs makes the book worthwhile reading. Wrenchingly courageous."

—*KIRKUS REVIEWS*

"Through this memoir, readers will see how even those closest to us can remain a mystery."

—*LIBRARY JOURNAL*

"A touching book that puts a human face on Christian Science."

—*BOOKLIST*

"Rather than a journey out of a faith, this is the story of one woman's questioning and anguish over her parents' choices. . . . Teens wondering about their own faith, their parents' expectations, and how to marry the two will find that this book resonates with them. It will also appeal to anyone wanting to know what it's like to grow up in Christian Science. . . . Suggest that readers have tissues close at hand."

—*SCHOOL LIBRARY JOURNAL*

"[*fathermothergod*] resonates with anyone wanting to understand another's beliefs, or trying to understand his or her own."

—*LAS VEGAS REVIEW-JOURNAL*

"*fathermothergod* tells a uniquely complex tale of a family torn apart, disastrously so, by a startlingly dangerous faith. . . . A captivating, heartbreaking work that will leave readers wondering what else they don't know about the hidden pockets of the faithful world."

—*TWIN CITIES DAILY PLANET*

fathermothergod

My Journey Out of Christian Science

Lucia Greenhouse

Broadway Paperbacks
New York

For Olivia and Sherman

Copyright © 2011 by Lucia P. Ewing

All rights reserved.
Published in the United States by Broadway Paperbacks, an imprint of the
Crown Publishing Group, a division of Random House, Inc., New York.
www.crownpublishing.com

BROADWAY PAPERBACKS and its logo, a letter B
bisected on the diagonal, are trademarks of Random House, Inc.

Originally published in hardcover in the United States by Crown Publishers,
an imprint of the Crown Publishing Group, a division of Random House, Inc.,
New York, in 2011.

Library of Congress Cataloging-in-Publication Data
Greenhouse, Lucia.
Fathermothergod: my journey out of Christian Science/by Lucia Greenhouse.
p. cm.
1. Greenhouse, Lucia.   2. Christian Scientists—United States—
Biography.   3. Christian Science—Controversial literature.
I. Title.   II. Title: Father, mother, God.
BX6996.G74A3 2011
289.5092—dc22
[B]   2011001059

ISBN 978-0-307-72093-1
eISBN 978-0-307-72094-8

Book design by Lauren Dong
Jacket photography courtesy of the author

First Broadway Paperbacks Edition

146122990

This book is about my experiences, told to the best of my recollection. To create a readable story of manageable length it was necessary to condense and combine some events and characters, and some things have been omitted to protect the privacy of those involved. Dialogue is re-created to the best of my memory; others may remember or interpret certain events and conversations differently, but I've tried to remain true to the way I remember them.

To succeed in healing, you must conquer your own fears
as well as those of your patients, and
rise into higher and holier consciousness.

—MARY BAKER EDDY,
Science and Health with Key to the Scriptures

part one

One afternoon a couple of weeks before my eighth birthday, my five-year-old brother, Sherman, and I scramble out of the school bus and race each other home up the steep hill, which we only do—and always do—on Wednesdays. Wednesday is Caramel Apple Day, because on Wednesday mornings, Mom volunteers at the Christian Science Reading Room, and on the way home she stops at the Excelsior bakery for their caramel apple special. We drop our books in the front hall and dart into the kitchen to find not only the white square cardboard bakery box sitting, as usual, on the lazy Susan in the middle of the table but also our older sister, Olivia, asleep on the tattered red and white love seat, with a blanket up to her chin. Her long brown hair is pulled back in a ponytail. Her chin, cheeks, nose, forehead, and both hands are covered in little red spots.

"Hi!" Sherman says.

Olivia opens her eyes.

"Chicken pox," she says miserably.

"Do they hurt?" I ask.

"They really itch," she says, wincing.

Satisfied with her answer, our eyes turn to the caramel apples.

"You want one?" Sherman asks.

Olivia shakes her head no.

Mom appears as we help ourselves to the bakery box.

"Olivia has chicken pox?" I ask.

Mom doesn't answer.

"Mom? Chicken po—"

"In Christian Science," she reminds us gently, "we know that there is no illness. No disease. No contagion. Olivia is not sick. She is God's perfect child. We are all going to work very hard to keep our thoughts elevated."

"Does that mean she doesn't have to go to school?" I ask Mom.

"It means I *can't*," Olivia says.

"No fair!" Sherman protests. "How come?"

"Well, even though we know Olivia isn't sick—can't be sick," our mother says, "we need to follow the school's policy on certain… matters."

"I can't go back to school until the chicken—I mean, until… they…crust over," Olivia says.

We know from Sunday school that we're not supposed to name illness, because by naming something, we are giving in to *the lie* about it. Mary Baker Eddy tells us to "stand porter at the door of thought."

For the next several days, life at our house is unbearably dull. My brother and I go to school; our sister doesn't, until her spots crust over. After school, our friends don't come to play kickball or ride bikes in our driveway. We are told it's because of *contagion*, a scary thing other people worry about but we Christian Scientists don't believe in. We know that contagion is about germs spreading; we also know that *prevailing thought* (something we can tell is bad just from the way our parents and other Christian Scientists say it) claims that chicken pox is contagious. But we have learned in Sunday school that there's no such thing as germs.

Before we go to bed, Olivia, Sherman, and I pile into our parents' bed and listen as they read aloud various passages from the Bible and *Science and Health*.

" 'We weep because others weep, we yawn because they yawn,' " my mother recites. Curiously, I find myself yawning.

" 'And we have smallpox because others have it; but mortal mind, not matter, contains and carries the infection.' "

I think to myself that I'd rather hear the next chapter of *Little House in the Big Woods,* the book Mom was reading to us before Olivia got spots.

They read aloud for almost an hour. Snuggled under the soft comforter and between warm bodies, we fall asleep; soon we are carried, half-awake, to our own beds.

"Am I going to get"—I hesitate groggily—"chicken pox?" My father has just brought me a drink of water.

"Let's talk about what you're learning in Sunday school," he says gently. "Is sickness real?"

I shake my head no.

"Are you God's child?"

I nod yes.

"Can you be anything but perfect?"

"Nope."

"Mary Baker Eddy says we must put on *the panoply of Love.* Do you remember what *panoply* means?"

Even though I've heard the word a lot in Sunday school, I can never remember what it means. I make a face that tells my dad I've forgotten.

"A *panoply* is a full suit of armor," he says. "So if we think of God's love as a suit of armor, protecting us, we can never be hurt or sick."

"Well," I ask, "how come Olivia has . . . spots?"

"That's just *erroneous belief—error,*" my dad says, "which we all must guard against. She may have the *appearance* of *error,* but we know it's a lie, an illusion."

My Sunday school teacher talks a lot about *error* too, and I remember what that is: sin, disease, and death. She tells us that error is like a mirage in the desert: the vision of a pool of water where there is nothing but sand. So when my dad says Olivia's spots are the *appearance of error,* I understand that he means the spots are not real. But I don't *exactly* understand how that can be; it seems like everything that Christian Science says is *unreal* is *real,* and vice versa. I guess when I'm older it'll make more sense, but for now, it is comforting enough to know that, as Mom and Dad and Sunday school have taught me, Christian Science is a *science that works.*

"Okay, Loosh," Dad says, and I know it is time for bedtime prayers, and he will give me a choice.

"Daily Prayer?"

I shake my head no.

"Fathermothergod," I say.

Together, we recite the Children's Prayer, written by Mary Baker Eddy.

Father-Mother God,
Loving me,—
Guard me while I sleep;
Guide my little feet
Up to Thee.

I kick the covers off my bed and levitate my feet toward my canopy.

"Good night, Dad," I say, giggling at our silliness. I pull the covers back up to my chin.

My father gives me a kiss on the forehead, and I wonder if he has just done the same to my sister, who is now asleep in the next room. My sister has gotten to skip four days of school already and hang out in our parents' bedroom watching TV and eating cinnamon buttered toast. As appealing as that sounds, my birthday is only days away. If I get spots, I know I won't be able to have my party.

The next morning, I wake up and my pajamas are damp and cold, and I'm shaking. I crawl out of bed and walk over to the mirror on my wall to see if I have red spots like Olivia. I have only a flushed face (it looks like I'm wearing Grandma's rouge) and bright red ears. My throat stings when I swallow, my head hurts a little bit, and I feel really tired. I return to bed and yell, *"Mo-om?"*

Moments later she enters my room.

"I don't feel good," I say.

She sits down beside me, tenderly pushes my bangs out of the way, and places her hand on my forehead. I know from TV that this is how you check for fever, but I have never seen my mom do this. Fever, I know, is *error.* Then she presses her lips against my forehead, which should feel like a kiss, but I wonder if she's doing something else.

"Hmm, I think we'll give Mrs. Hannah a call," Mom says.

Mrs. Hannah is our Christian Science practitioner. We call her when we are sick—I mean, when we have a problem—and she prays for us. She is also the superintendent of our Sunday school. She leads us each week in singing hymns and reciting the Lord's Prayer with its spiritual interpretation by Mary Baker Eddy. She is not much taller than me, and she is round. She needs to stand on a stool when she's behind the *lectern,* and even then, we can't see her face, only the top of her head and her arms. Sometimes I squint, and her arms look like they're attached to the sides of the tall desk.

I hear my brother, Sherman, calling from down the hall. My mother gets up and goes to his room. I fall back asleep, and when I wake up, my sister has already left for school with Dad (her spots have crusted over), and Mom has brought me a tray with cinnamon toast and orange juice. I don't want to eat it.

"How would you and Sherman like to go to Grandma's today?" my mother says, as she sits down beside me again.

Grandma's house could be my favorite place in the whole world. From the moment I walk through the front door, and feel the pleasant warmth of the house my mom grew up in, I experience something magical. The kitchen smells of coffee, and Grandma keeps a candy dish of lemon drops next to her ashtray on the small round kitchen table. In the powder room off the front hall, set on the shelf of the toilet tank, there's a basket of miniature lipsticks, ranging from Siren Red to Pearly Pink, several little rouge compacts, each with its own brush, and a dozen tiny bottles of perfume samples. Next to this basket is a jar of Jergens lotion. I love that smell too. My cousin Mimi and I can spend hours in the powder room, making each other up, and then we climb the steep stairs to the attic, which smells of mothballs, where there are boxes and boxes of costumes, ballet tutus, and our moms' old prom dresses, as well as my grandfather's old black leather doctor's bag filled with his tools. My grandmother's nurse uniform and cap from when she was younger are there too.

But today, I don't want to go anywhere.

"I want to stay home, Mom," I say.

"C'mon," she says. And so we go. Mom lets us each bring a blanket and pillow for the twenty-minute car ride. I close my eyes and try to get comfortable, but now I ache all over. I wonder to myself why Mom's making us get out of bed and drive to Grandma's. When we arrive, Grandma greets us at the door with her soft-cheeked hug and the warm squeeze of her hand on my arm. I love the way her charm bracelet jingles.

"Here, let's get you settled. Would you like to watch TV in my bed?"

Normally, when Grandma asks if I want to sleep in her room during a sleepover, I say no, politely, because Grandma snores, but today, it will be just Sherman and me in the room. I nod yes.

My brother and I climb under the covers and face each other, wondering what to make of today. We should be in school, but instead we'll get to watch *Bewitched* and *Let's Make a Deal*. Grandma brings us a tray, with two tiny glasses of orange juice, two bowls of Lipton instant chicken noodle soup (my favorite), cinnamon toast cut into triangles, and two bowls of applesauce.

I frown. I hate applesauce.

"Go on, have some," Grandma says. "It tastes good when you're under the weather." She spoons it into each of our mouths as though we are toddlers.

I'm not sure what's going on. Olivia just had chicken pox (or *the erroneous belief in chicken pox*), and we've spent the last week praying a lot and not seeing friends. Now, my brother and I *don't* have spots but we're "under the weather" and Mom has called Mrs. Hannah, who is praying for us. Instead of going to school we have come to Grandma's, where we are being spoon-fed applesauce, which has what looks to me like teeny bits of chalk in it and leaves a taste in my mouth that is yucky and bitter. The cinnamon toast fixes that.

Mom comes into the bedroom, Grandma goes downstairs, and together we—Mom, Sherman, and I—sing "Mother's Evening Prayer," one of the hymns by Mary Baker Eddy that we know by heart. I don't know why, but when I sing it, my eyes tear.

O gentle presence, peace and joy and power;
O, Life divine, that owns each waiting hour,
Thou Love that guards the nestling's faltering flight!

My throat tightens, and when the tune climbs upward on "nestling's faltering flight," I start to cry. I just want to feel better.

Keep Thou my child on upward wing to-night...

Mom rubs my back, my nose gets all runny, and my voice sort of wobbles through the remaining four verses.

After we're done with the hymn, we recite the Scientific Statement of Being, just like we do at the end of Sunday school every week:

There is no life, truth, intelligence, nor substance in matter. All is infinite Mind and its infinite manifestation, for God is All-in-all. Spirit is immortal Truth; matter is mortal error. Spirit is the real and eternal; matter is the unreal and temporal. Spirit is God, and Man is His image and likeness. Therefore man is not material; he is spiritual.

Although the words skip over my tongue as easily as the Pledge of Allegiance, I don't really understand what they all mean, separately or together. But we say the Scientific Statement of Being so often in our house that it just sounds to my ears like the words should make sense.

We stay at Grandma's until two-thirty, when we have to hurry home before Olivia gets back from school. By then, I feel fine.

A few days later, Sherman and I both wake up with red spots. My brother counts eleven on his face, and more on his tummy, back, and arms. I have only two on my face and three on each hand, so I figure I've done a better job of praying than Sherman has. Still, we both stay home from school until the spots crust over. "The school has certain rules we have to obey," my father reminds us. Neither of us asks why.

THANKSGIVING 1970

I am sitting in the backseat of my dad's old red Mercedes sedan, smushed between Olivia and Sherman. In the trunk of the car are three pies—apple, pumpkin, and pecan—and a loaf of banana nut bread, hot out of the oven. The warm, spicy smell is seeping into the back of the car, making me hungry. It is 10:45 A.M., the beginning of what will be a long day; we will not be home again until late tonight. We are rushing to church, and then to Ammie and Grandpa's for the Thanksgiving feast. Earlier this morning, the thermometer outside our kitchen dipped below freezing.

I can see my breath until the car's heat kicks in. Dad is singing "Oh, What a Beautiful Morning" and driving a bit too fast, because we are running late. Mom is perched on the front passenger seat, applying bright pink lipstick to her mouth with the help of a tiny mirror in the makeup compact she keeps in her purse. People say it's *uncanny* how my parents look *just like* Angie Dickinson and Burt Bacharach. I have no idea who they are, but the way people say it, I know it's a compliment. My mom is blond and pretty and slender, with brown eyes. My father is handsome with thick, dark hair and deep-set blue eyes.

Under our heavy jackets, we are wearing our Sunday best. Olivia and I are in matching plaid dresses, which she hates but I don't mind. My brown hair is neatly parted down the middle, and I have two tight braids. Olivia refused the braids this morning, so beneath a pom-pom ski hat, her hair hangs in her face. Sherman is wearing gray slacks, a blue blazer, and a collared shirt with a tie. Already the tails of his shirt are untucked, the tie is crooked, and his blond hair looks like a rag mop, even though I watched Dad pull a comb through it just ten minutes earlier. Mom is wearing dressy brown leather boots with a skirt and matching blazer. Our father is in a suit.

This is the first time I have been in our church since the renovation. On the walls I see the familiar quotes:

God is Love.
—Christ Jesus

Divine Love always has met and always will meet every human need.
—Mary Baker Eddy

We are sitting in a pew toward the front of the church. We have our choice of seats because Dad likes to get here early, even though we rarely do. Usually, when Dad shaves on Sunday mornings before church, we can hear him whistling in the steamy bathroom. Getting ready for church puts him in a good mood. Mom has to make sure we kids are appropriately dressed, so she has less time for a relaxed *ablution.* (I like that word; it sounds like it has my name in it.) Almost always, the hot rollers are still in her hair when Dad calls from the bottom of the stairs, with a combination of disappointment and eagerness in his voice, "Honey, we're going to be late!"

Mom's sister, my aunt Kay, likes to say to Mom, "Well, Jo, if you're always late for church, maybe subconsciously you'd rather not go." Dad says Kay likes to be controversial.

I love the new wooden pews of our church, even if they are hard and uncomfortable. Churches are supposed to have pews. Before the renovation, the First Church of Christ, Scientist, in Excelsior, Minnesota, had rows of plastic molded chairs with shiny metal legs like you see in a classroom or at Baskin-Robbins. Now our church looks more like the Lutherans' and the Episcopalians'. I had hoped we'd get a crucifix and stained glass windows too, like they have at Grandma's Mount Olivet, or Ammie's St. Martin's-by-the-Lake, but Dad says that's *idolatry;* Christian Science is *metaphysical.*

I'm not sure what he means by that, but in the Commandments, Moses says,

> Thou shalt not make unto thee any graven image, or any like-
> ness of any thing that is in heaven above, or that is in the earth
> beneath, or that is in the water under the earth.

Even though I don't know exactly what *graven image* means, I do know from Sunday school that stained glass windows and cruci-fixes are graven images, and we are following the Commandments by having plain windows in our church and nothing fancy like pic-tures of Jesus on the cross.

At First Church of Christ, Scientist, Excelsior, Minnesota, the walls are bare, except for the two quotations and the posted hymn numbers. Where other churches have an altar and a minister in pretty robes, we have a platform with a double-wide lectern for the First and Second Readers, who are democratically elected by the church members and are frequently practitioners.

I turn around in the pew to watch as the church fills. I see my friend Lisa from Sunday school sitting with her parents and younger brother; we wave to each other. The organist starts to play some soft music to signal that the service is about to begin. Suddenly, I am nervous. The butterflies are flitting in my stomach, my heart races, and even though I just went to the bathroom, I know I could go again.

On Thanksgiving Day, everyone is invited to stand during the service and give a brief testimony. I have never spoken in church, or in front of any audience for that matter, but I've decided today is the day. I know the order of service well. Because it's Thanksgiving, the First Reader will read the Thanksgiving Day Proclamation from President Nixon. Then there will be a hymn and readings from the Bible and *Science and Health,* which the First and Second Readers will alternate. Then we make a silent prayer and sing another hymn and recite the Lord's Prayer with its spiritual interpretation by Mary Baker Eddy. Then, it's time for the soloist. (We don't have a choir. I really wish we had a cherub choir like Mount Olivet, where the Lutheran kids get to wear gowns and sing holding candles.)

The soloist is always a problem for us. My brother and I are strategically placed at opposite ends of our pew, with our sister exactly in the middle, so that when the lady opens her mouth and the big song comes wobbling out, we can be *managed:* Sherman next to Mom next to Olivia next to Dad next to me. We tend to have trouble with giggles, and if we kids sit next to each other, it gets really bad. It never fails: we are perfectly well behaved until—and we know to hold our breath and pinch our lips between our teeth—the lady with the chins sings. There is almost nothing we can do to stop giggling. We close our eyes so we are not tempted to look at her. We sit on our hands. We play hangman with the back of the tiny envelope and the golf-size pencil, but the singing gets louder, louder, **louder,** and I start thinking of Tarzan swinging through the jungle. Sometimes, the lady doesn't quite hit the high note right, and we almost pee in our pants it's so funny. Today, I wish I had gotten to sit at the other end of our row because Mom doesn't glare at us like Dad does when we giggle. And sometimes she almost snickers herself.

Finally, the First Reader will announce: "We welcome brief testimonies of Christian Science healing, as well as words acknowledging the power and efficacy of Christian Science in our daily lives. To accommodate everyone who would like to speak, please limit your comments to under two minutes."

I know this invitation, because I've heard it—I've waited for it—every Thanksgiving Day for as long as I can remember. But I've always chickened out.

Today the service starts with the hymn "O Gentle Presence." We sang it a lot when we had the chicken pox. I proudly close my hymnal, because even though there are five verses, I know all the words by heart.

During the reading of President Nixon's proclamation, I start to think about what I will say when I stand up. If this were a Wednesday evening testimony meeting, I could tell about a healing (or a *demonstration,* which is what Christian Scientists call healings). At the moment I can't think of a single healing I've had. I know my brother had a healing of asthma and weak ankles when he was a toddler. And my sister had her ski accident. But those were their healings, not mine. I guess I can mention the chicken pox, since I only had eight spots.

I am so nervous about what I'm going to say that I completely miss the silent prayer, the readings from the Bible and *Science and Health,* and everything else before the soloist stands up, holding her black music folder in front of her. She breathes in through her nose so loudly that it whistles, and then she opens her mouth. I glance at my brother and sister; they have been trying to get my attention. My mother pokes my brother and sister gently in the ribs, and they look down at their shoes. The lady sings, and luckily we do not laugh.

And now the congregation waits for the first testimony. The long, seemingly endless stretches of quiet—while members of the congregation listen for their own divine inspiration, or for someone else's—are the signature of Wednesday evening testimony meetings. During the Thanksgiving service, however, there are fewer silent gaps because there are more people in attendance, and therefore more speakers. I gaze around the room, looking for any obvious takers. My sister? My brother? No. They're playing hangman. Am

I the only kid who plans to stand up? What about my friend Lisa? I turn around and find her. We catch eyes, and with raised eyebrows and a dip of her head, I know she is asking if I am going to stand up. I shrug my shoulders and grin a maybe. She shakes her head, a definite no.

Although we wait less than a minute, it feels like a long time before the first person stands up. It is Mrs. Warner, a dignified woman who has seven children and a husband who is not a Christian Scientist. She has a huge house, where every year she holds a carol sing with a piano player and a long buffet table with lots of Christmas cookies and spiced hot apple cider.

"I am so *very* grateful to Mary Baker Eddy for Christian Science, and the way our family has been so *beautifully* protected each and every day."

Mrs. Warner sits down, and lots of people nod in agreement. (She says the same thing every year, and I think: With all those kids and that big mansion, it sure is true.)

The First Reader nods and says, "Thank you."

I look around the church again. Another couple of minutes pass, and Mrs. Hannah, our practitioner, stands up. She has a sugary voice with rounded *o*'s and lots of nose. Whenever I see her, I think of the teapot song.

" 'To th**o**se leaning on the sustaining infinite, to-day is big with blessings!' " Mrs. Hannah starts.

I've heard this before too. My Sunday school teacher opens class with the sentence practically every week. She continues, " 'Th**ee**se are the **oh**-pening words of Mrs. Eddy's textbook, *Science and Heath with Key to the Scriptures*—and **oh,** how true, how precious they are! We are s**oh** blessed to be living at a time, and in a pl**ay**ce, where we are free to practice our faith, the *Science of Christian healing*. I am s**oh** very, *very* grateful for Christian Science."

The First Reader nods again and says, "Thank you."

Mrs. Hannah sits down. Over the next ten minutes, more people stand, including my dad. I think his testimony is the best. He is not nervous at all. He stands with his hands in his pockets, jingling his keys or some change. Every once in a while he pauses and rocks up on his toes when he is saying something important.

"When I was a child," my father begins, "I was plagued with a persistent stammer. I couldn't say words that started with *p* without getting stuck. But when I found Science—or, I should say"—he goes up on his toes here—"*it* found *me,* I decided to do something about it. I called a Christian Science practitioner, who guided me toward a prayerful solution to my problem. She helped me to see my true, God-given perfection. I learned that if I am speaking God's words, and living God's love, I simply cannot"—Dad goes up on his toes again—"have a stammer. Within a week, my problem with *p*'s literally vanished! I am so grateful for Christian Science, and its healing power."

Dad sits down, and the First Reader says, "Thank you."

That was a lot of *p*'s! I remember when my dad used to talk like that: P-p-pumpkin p-p-pie. I smile up at him. He smiles back.

The church is silent again. I look at the First Reader, who glances at his watch. I can tell there are only a few minutes left for me to say anything. Now my hands are really sweating.

But I stand up. Or rather, all of a sudden, I realize I *am* standing up! I open my mouth and take a deep breath. I try to speak loudly and clearly, but my words come out barely above a whisper. I race through "IamverygratefulforChristianScienceandandandandShepherdShowMeismyfavoritehymn" and sit down. I realize that a man stood up at exactly the same time as I did, and he is still giving a testimony. My brother and sister snicker, and I think to myself that I would like to disappear, be invisible. I've never been so embarrassed in my life. I try to pretend that nothing's wrong: I bend down and purposefully yank my tights at each knee, even though they're not falling down. The man giving the testimony finally sits, and then the First Reader nods to him.

"Thank you," he says. "And now, hymn number 253."

I want to stay there, hiding under the pew. I kind of hate the First Reader for not noticing me. But then I think, maybe nobody in the church—other than my family—heard me. Maybe it's not as bad as I think. As we all stand up to sing the closing hymn, my father leans in toward me, puts his arm around me, and whispers, "You did good, Loosh."

His little hug and gentle voice are supposed to make me feel better, but they don't. I wish I could fall through a trapdoor into the basement of the church.

Later that night, after the Thanksgiving feast at Ammie and Grandpa's with the Morrison cousins, we are back at home. It is bedtime. I am waiting as usual, way down under the covers near the foot of my pretty, canopied trundle bed, for our bedtime prayer ritual, even though at eight and a half, I've begun to wonder if I am getting too old for this. As always I have asked my father for a drink of water. When he returns with Dixie cup in hand, he has *no idea* where I am. He sits on my bed. "Lucia? Loosh?" he calls out. "Where are you?" And he pats down the bedding with his hands. "Well, I feel a bunch of pillows in here, but no Lucia! Hmm." He scratches his head. "I guess she's gone out for the night," he says. He walks toward the door, turns off the light, and I scamper out from under the covers and say, "I'm here!" The light goes back on, and I take a sip of water and set the cup on my bedside table.

"Fathermothergod?" Dad asks.

I fold my hands, and he covers mine with his, and we pray in unison, eyes closed.

My father pauses.

"I was very proud of you today, Loosh."

I smile, but I'm doubtful.

"No one even heard me," I say.

"*I* heard you," he says. "And God heard you."

"Well, it wasn't about a healing. I haven't even *had* a healing."

"Oh, yes you have!" my father says.

"No I haven't," I persist.

"Don't you suppose that your good health is sufficient proof of God's healing power? Christian Science has protected you so well, you've never even been sick!"

"Except for chicken pox," I correct him.

"And that's something to be grateful for, isn't it?"

I nod.

After my dad leaves the room, I think to myself that I've outgrown our lights-out ritual. I'm also curious. He said because of Christian Science I haven't needed healings. But how can he even say *that* if there's no such thing as sickness? If there's no such thing as sickness, there should be no need for healings.

JUNE 1972

I am ten years old. Sherman, who is still seven, is bouncing with me on the trampoline in our backyard, while Mom prepares dinner and helps Olivia study her vocab words. It is the first really warm day of the summer, and Sherman and I are soaking wet. We've spent the last half hour chasing each other through the sprinklers. Now, as we jump up and down, my long, wet hair makes a slapping noise as it hits my back, and the water from our sopping clothes drips onto the trampoline's canvas. Each time we land, the water shoots upward from the canvas, spraying us again.

Sherman jumps high and doesn't worry about his landings, but I worry about mine. I keep thinking about the time last fall when we were jumping on Aunt Kay's trampoline, when some junior high kids launched me overhead and I landed right on my ankle, *crrk*. It hurt so much that immediately I started to sweat, and my eyes filled with tears. I couldn't scooch off the trampoline because the big kids kept bouncing. Suddenly the air around me was too hot and I thought I might throw up. I lowered myself quietly to the ground and crawled across the lawn favoring my left side; fortunately none

of the big kids noticed. Halfway to the house, I had to stop and rest
against the trunk of the big oak tree. I prayed the woozy feeling and
the awful throb in my ankle would stop. As I watched it swell, I
wondered if maybe it was sprained or even broken. I groaned. Then
I whispered, trying not to cry, "There is no life, truth, intelligence,
nor substance in matter."

Please, Mom, I thought to myself, please look out the window
and see me and take me home.

"All is infinite Mind and its infinite manifestation, for God is
All-in-all."

Mom was sitting at the kitchen table with her two sisters. She
didn't look up—Aunt Kay was showing Mom and Aunt Mary plans
for the new house—until I had crawled all the way down the lawn
and into the kitchen, and was standing in the doorway. I motioned
to her to come to me, and my eyes started welling up again. She
stood up and excused herself. I held it together until we got into the
car, and then I sobbed all the way home.

I guess that was a real healing, since now, nine months later, I
notice it doesn't hurt a bit. My ankle was huge, but I only missed
two days of school, and I didn't get to use crutches or even an Ace
bandage, obviously, which was kind of disappointing.

It was a long time before I would even sit on the edge of our trampoline again. But now I will jump as high as any of my friends, and
I can land a backflip with a half twist every time.

All of a sudden Chipsie, our shaggy mutt, trots up beside the
trampoline. She frequently carries a stick or an old sock in her
mouth, but today we know to stop and take a closer look. Just yesterday, she brought home a very small, white, dead kitten. Today,
like yesterday, Chipsie's tail is not wagging; she is cowering. Sherman
and I jump off the trampoline, and as we approach her, she backs
up slowly and goes down on her elbows.

"Look! She's got another one!" I say.

"Maybe this one's still alive," Sherman says. "Drop it, Chips."

Chipsie very gently sets a little black kitten on the ground, and we realize that she is trying to save the poor thing. We kneel down to take a closer look. The kitten appears freshly licked. I can see that its black, downy fur is moist on its underbelly. I gently stroke the kitty with one finger. Its body is warm. I can feel the soft, squishy belly and the corrugated ribs. The kitten's eyes are closed.

"It's alive," Sherman whispers.

"I don't think so," I say. "I think it's dead."

My brother sprints to the house and disappears through the door to the kitchen. He returns with the makeup compact from our mother's purse.

"What are you doing?" I ask.

"Checking for breath," Sherman says. "They do this on TV."

Sherman pinches open the makeup case and holds the mirror to the kitten's tiny nose. No steam.

"Try it again," I whisper, and we move closer, but again, there is no steam.

Sherman's eyes fill with tears.

"It must have just died," I whisper. We wait there, thinking.

"Let's call Mrs. Hannah!" Sherman says.

I look at my brother warily before glancing back down at the kitty. Admittedly, it looks *barely* dead. But as a fourth grader— in one more week I'll be a fifth grader—I am old enough to know that dead is dead and alive is alive. *Common sense* (my fourth-grade teacher Miss Fetterly's favorite term, she uses it daily) tells us that you can't make something that's dead, un-dead. But in Christian Science, there is no such thing as death, just as there is no such thing as illness. I know from Sunday school that this kitten is perfect in God's eyes. We only have to see his perfection to make him *whole* (or un-dead) again.

"No, wait!" Sherman blurts out. "Shouldn't we call Dad? We should call Dad!"

The idea of calling Mrs. Hannah is instinctive, automatic, be- cause she has been our practitioner for so long. Every time there's

been a bump or a scrape, a sore throat or a sprained ankle, we have
called her and asked her to pray for, and with, and about us. And
every time we've called her, we've gotten better. But now we remember that we can call our father instead. Early this spring, one evening before bedtime, our parents sat the three of us down on the
tattered love seat in the kitchen to share some very special news.
The way their eyes sparkled, I had thought Mom and Dad were
going to tell us about a baby on the way, and my mind had rushed
ahead: Would it be a sister? A brother? The announcement—that
Dad had quit his insurance job at Marsh & McLennan and was
going to be a Christian Science practitioner—would draw out many
complicated feelings over time, but at first, the news was merely a
letdown compared to the dashed fantasy of a new baby.

My first reaction to Sherman's suggestion is I doubt even Mrs.
Hannah can heal a dead kitty, and she's journal-listed. Her name is
in the back of *The Christian Science Journal,* under "Practitioners/
Minnesota." (I like that you can leaf through the *Journal*'s back
pages and find churches and practitioners listed from Excelsior,
Minnesota, and Boston, Massachusetts, and Paris, France, or even
places as far away as Nairobi, Kenya, and Tokyo, Japan.) Our father
isn't listed, not yet. He says he has to have a number of *documented*
healings under his belt first.

I know that the *documented* healing of a dead kitten will surely
get my father listed in the back of *The Christian Science Journal,* whose logo, after all, is a cross encircled by a crown, with the
motto

HEAL THE SICK • RAISE THE DEAD • CAST OUT DEMONS •
CLEANSE THE LEPERS

in small lettering around it. Resurrecting a barely dead kitten has to
be—by weight alone—less complicated than healing a dead person.
But I don't know where common sense ends and Christian Science

begins, or if there is any overlap, like those intersecting circles of the Venn diagrams in math class. I decide that the worst that can happen is the kitten remains dead. Then, we'll bury him in a shoe box in a grave next to his sister, in the backyard at the edge of the woods.

We hurry through the kitchen with the dead kitten cupped in Sherman's hands. Our sister, Olivia, who is still sitting at the kitchen table, looks up from her homework long enough to give our mother a bored, knowing, slightly appalled glance. In one more week she'll be an eighth grader. Our mother, on the other hand, appears casually amused, indicating with an elbow where we might find another shoe box. We prepare a Buster Brown box, padding the interior with toilet paper. We stick the kitty inside, march upstairs to our father's study, and put the box, covered with its lid, on his desk.

When Dad gets home and discovers the dead kitten in the box on his desk, he wants to know the meaning of the practical joke. I am confused that he thinks we would joke about something so serious.

"Dad, we put him there so you can *heal* him," I say.

He sighs. "Gee, kids," he says. He is at a loss for more words. He seems uncomfortable.

"Aren't you going to pray for him?" we ask. "Aren't we going to know the Truth?"

Knowing the Truth, we've learned in Sunday school, means acknowledging God-given perfection, refusing to surrender to prevailing mortal mind.

There is a long pause.

"I think probably we should bury . . . him," my father says slowly, tenderly, facing us but looking at the box out of the corner of his eye.

"But Dad," I say, "there's no such thing as death."

"That's right," my father says, squatting on his haunches now so that he is closer to eye level with us. "We can *know* that he—is in—his—right place."

My father isn't even going to try.

Sherman starts crying. "But Dad, he's so young! He's just a baby!" he says.

"I know, kiddo," says Dad, "but this kitten hasn't really died at all. He's just moved on to a higher plane of existence."

From Sherman's confused expression, I can tell he is thinking of flying machines.

I eye my father. I feel angry, but I'm not sure why. Something bigger than disappointment has settled over me.

"You mean," Sherman says hopefully, his eyes widening, "he's still alive?"

"Well...yes," Dad says, somewhat uncertainly. "This kitten has *passed on* to another level. You know we don't talk about death, right? We say *passed on*."

My father seems satisfied with his answer. I'm not.

You can call death whatever you like, a higher plane, or passing on, but the kitten is dead.

CHRISTMAS EVE 1973

It hardly seems fair that we had Sunday school yesterday and have to go to church again today, but that's how the calendar falls this year. At least we are going to Mount Olivet Lutheran Church. Our church has Christmas Eve services only when December 24 falls on a Sunday or a Wednesday. Grandma likes us all together for the holiday, so we go with her to Mount Olivet for the candlelight service.

We are sitting near the front of the enormous church, in two long pews, and everyone is here except the Bowmans, who are late. I'm holding a spot next to me for Mimi, but with the church filling up, I wonder if I'll be able to keep it for her. Down the pew to my left, Sherman and Dad, and Uncle Jack and the Johnson boys—Harry, Sargent, and Steven, who go everywhere as a threesome—are all wearing blue blazers, gray slacks, loafers, and assorted red ties. So are Uncle Bear, Jerry, and Teddy, seated in the pew behind us. Mom and I are in matching floor-length wrap-around skirts, but Olivia flatly refused to wear hers. Now that she's in boarding school, she burns incense in her room and wears whatever she wants, which this evening happens to be a purple beaded dress and a pair of brown suede boots. My cousin Tristin Erickson, who is a year older than Mimi and I, looks like she got her dress from Scheherazade too. Aunt Kay is wearing a silk blouse, a skirt, and patent leather boots and is chewing on a piece of gum. (I wonder what Mom thinks about that!) Aunt Helen is wrapped in a luxurious mink coat, which I'd like to touch except for the fact that it's a dead animal. She always leaves her coat and gloves on for the entire Christmas Eve service. Little Annie Johnson is wearing a green silk taffeta dress and a huge matching bow in her hair. She is sitting on Uncle Jack's lap now. Poor Teddy. He is sitting directly behind Uncle Jack and Annie. What with Uncle Jack's size, and Annie's hair bow, Teddy won't be able to see a thing.

Mount Olivet has thousands of members. I know why. It has an adult choir, a teen choir, a children's choir, and a cherub choir, and youth groups that go on camping trips. At First Church of Christ, Scientist, in Excelsior, Minnesota, we have none of these things. We just have a boring soloist. We don't have candles or kneeling benches either. I would love to kneel down and pretend to pray like a Lutheran right now, but I think Mom and Dad might feel betrayed.

Grandma keeps turning around, searching for the Bowmans. She looks so pretty in her ruby red pantsuit with the beautiful corsage that Uncle Bear pinned on her lapel as we were walking in.

What I don't understand is why Grandma is Lutheran, when nobody else in our family is. We Ewings are Christian Scientists, the Bowmans are Episcopalians, I don't know what Uncle Jack and Aunt Helen are—maybe they go to Wayzata Community Church?— and Aunt Kay told me when I was in second grade that she is agnostic but used to be an atheist. I feel sort of sorry for Grandma that nobody stayed Lutheran. I would switch just to be in one of the choirs.

The sanctuary is filled with hundreds of poinsettias, the ones with the dark red leaves, and everywhere I look I see even more glowing candle flames than plants. This is what a church is supposed to look like at Christmas.

The service starts, and still the Bowmans are nowhere to be found. This would be a lot less painful with Mimi here, fun even, playing hangman or passing each other notes. Last year she scribbled on the collection envelope "Did you know that so-and-so's mom got a boob job instead of going to her Smith reunion???" We got snickering so loudly that Mom and Aunt Mary gave us both the evil eye. Now, Smith reunion, or just plain Smith, is code for boob job. As in, "Did so-and-so go to Smith?" Or "Gee, I think I may go to Smith after high school!"

My favorite part of the candlelight service at Mount Olivet is the cherub choir, the way they all toddle up the center aisle in their little choir robes, some of them singing, a few of them sobbing, most of them looking out into the sea of faces for their parents. After they're done with "Silent Night," I just drift off, thinking about what we'll get for Christmas, and where Mom and Dad have hidden all the presents.

The service is over. Grandma wants us to stand in the long line to shake hands with Pastor Youngdahl—*young* Pastor Youngdahl. His father, the older Pastor Youngdahl, was the minister here when Mom was little. It's hard to believe that this Pastor Youngdahl, in his beautiful vestments with the embroidered wide scarf draped elegantly over his shoulders, used to wear a leather jacket and ride a motorcycle, but that's what Mom says.

"...and this is my fifth granddaughter, Lucia," Grandma says proudly, nudging me toward him. I stick out my hand.

Pastor Youngdahl smiles at Grandma, and nods to Mom and Dad, as though they have done something extraordinary by producing me. I shake his hand and gaze up. He is almost as tall as Uncle Jack. He cups my hand in both of his, and for some reason a line from the Twenty-third Psalm pops into my head.

Thou anointest my head with oil; my cup runneth over.

The robe, the warm hands, and a smile that seems genuinely concerned for his flock feel magical to me. Maybe holy. One day perhaps I'll join a church like this.

Aunt Kay's house has never looked so gorgeous. From the outside, it's bank-like: a big rectangular box, nothing special, and nothing like a *home*. But when you walk inside, your eyes pop. There is a three-story garden with a tropical tree growing right up through the center of the house. In the basement, a rec room with huge windows and sliding glass doors opens to the snow-blanketed back lawn and the frozen lake. The rec room has a fireplace, a yellow Yamaha piano, and a huge projection television. There's even an indoor swimming pool with a gently arched footbridge, and a wall of black lava rock, which is bumpy and sharp if you run your fingers across it. At the shallow end, an enormous hippo sculpture watches over the swimmers.

Hanging on the big wooden double doors in the front entrance are two enormous wreaths, and the tropical tree in the atrium is covered in tiny white lights. Draped on the handrails throughout the house are fragrant pine garlands. Downstairs, a grand Christmas tree stands at attention next to the Yamaha piano, and for tonight's feast, three round tables are elegantly arranged with candles, the good silver, water goblets, and wineglasses. Christmas carols are playing on the hi-fi.

In the kitchen, I help Mom and Aunt Kay put out the hors d'oeuvres. We are stalling, still waiting for the Bowmans. Sherman and the boy cousins are off playing air hockey. Olivia is telling Tristin and Grandma all about boarding school, and Aunt Helen and Annie are looking at the pool.

Dad is a Christian Science practitioner, Uncle Jack is a plastic surgeon, Uncle Bear's family owns a big chain of gas stations and convenience stores, and Uncle Brad doesn't have to work. So when the families get together, the men mostly talk about sports. And hunting and fishing.

At the moment, Uncle Bear is tending bar, talking about this fall's outstanding muskie and deer seasons. Dad listens, holding his glass of tonic water. He's not much of a fisherman—we have a small aluminum outboard that he and Sherman take out maybe twice a summer—and he's never hunted (we don't even own a rifle), so he can't contribute much to the conversation. He looks up at Uncle Bear and Uncle Jack, and I wonder if he feels small standing next to them. Uncle Bear played football in college; he has hands as big as a bear's. And Uncle Jack is practically a giant. Talk invariably turns to the Vikings. Now Dad can join; this year he and Sherman have season tickets. The big question on everyone's mind is: Can Fran Tarkenton finally bring us a Super Bowl victory?

A car's headlights beam through the plate-glass windows by the front doors. The Bowmans are finally here.

"Aaah! Merry Christmas, everyone!" Aunt Mary says, her lyrical voice crescendoing on *kriss,* as she breezes in with a tray of food, the December chill whooshing in behind her. My earliest memory, when I was three and we were living in Chicago, was the arrival of Mary Poppins at Olivia's sixth birthday party in an ankle-length skirt and jacket, lace-up boots, an umbrella, and a cap with flowers in it. I didn't realize that Mary Poppins was actually my aunt Mary until long after Olivia's party guests had left. I still think of this whenever Aunt Mary makes an entrance.

Uncle Brad, Sarah, Bradley—and finally Mimi—appear, each carrying something: full grocery bags, a box of gifts, a huge green salad. Mimi rolls her eyes at me, and I can tell that her family has had a stressful time of it. Their chronic lateness is often a topic of conversation. Nobody quite knows if Aunt Mary or Uncle Brad is the real culprit, although every adult seems to have a strong opinion.

The women hug and chat and linger and laugh. There is something reassuring about seeing the four of them, a mother and her grown daughters all together.

"...we ended up parking half a mile from the church," Uncle Brad grumbles to no one in particular. In appearance, he reminds me of Oscar Madison on *The Odd Couple*. He is a bit of a curmudgeon. Aunt Mary, by contrast, is warm and cheerful.

"It was standing room only, but," Aunt Mary adds gleefully, "we got there in time to see those *adorable* cherubs."

During dinner, the adults are at one table, the thirteen cousins are at the other two. Mimi and I always sit together; so do Olivia and Sarah (Mimi's older sister) and Sherman and Bradley (Mimi's younger brother). We are *twuzzins,* a word I made up in second grade that means "cousins of the same age and sex."

Judging from the noise level, the adults are having more fun than we are, growing increasingly boisterous as the dinner goes on. Every few minutes I hear Aunt Mary's high-pitched *whooooh!* at whatever outrageous thing Aunt Kay is saying at their table. Mom and Dad are laughing along, but it looks to me like maybe they're missing something by not drinking wine. A pretty stemmed glass must be more fun to drink from than a boring old water glass. Some of the grown-ups are holding lit cigarettes. Observing the smokers as they elegantly inhale—making their embers glow, delicately flicking their ashes into the silver ashtrays, and releasing puffy, fleeting clouds—makes me think one day I'll smoke too. And maybe I'll be Episcopalian. *E-pis-co-pa-li-an.* I love how the six syllables skip over my lips.

Dessert is finished, and the seven boys are getting restless. Their ties are pulled loose or missing altogether, and they are sitting on their calves or ankles instead of their butts, playing finger football. Their table has a Coke spilled all over it and eight barely touched plates of Aunt Helen's cranberry pudding, but on the cookie tray, only crumbs are left. At the girls' table, almost everyone has eaten the cranberry pudding and the tablecloth is spotless.

Uncle Brad gets up from his seat and stands with his pipe in his mouth, ponderously puffing. He is the oldest of the uncles, and his stony face could belong to an army general. The room turns quiet.

"Did you hear something?" he says, again to nobody in particular, but everyone is listening now. "I—I could have sworn I heard bells." He squints slightly and gazes off into the distance, his tiny, straight mouth widening ever so slightly into a grin. Little Annie squeals and bounces up and down on Mimi's lap, and Mimi gives her a hug around the waist.

Everyone moves over to the sliding glass doors that face the frozen lake, Annie and Teddy with their noses and hands pressed to the glass. After a minute or two, Santa comes trudging in with a heavy-laden burlap sack, stomping the snow off his boots.

Santa settles into a wingback chair that Uncle Bear and Dad have placed prominently near the fireplace and, one by one, calls the grandchildren up. This year I can tell right away who Santa really is: the tennis pro at Woodhill. Grandma is seated on her own throne off to his right, where she has a good view of everything. There are several cameras with flashbulbs going off (or not going off, accompanied by some audible cursing). Dad fiddles with his light meter, and several minutes pass before he takes a single picture.

After Annie, Teddy, Jerry, Sherman, Brad, Steven, Sargent, and Harry have their mandatory chats with Santa, it's our turn. "Mimi and Lucia!" Santa says. Everyone starts clapping when Santa gestures to his lap. Mimi and I are both thinking we are too old for this, but we walk sheepishly up and take a seat. He hands us each a present, which we rip open: new Lilly Pulitzer bikinis.

It is almost midnight. I am lying in my bed, under the white eyelet canopy, reflecting on the wonderful Christmas Eve we have just had. After Santa left, all the cousins went swimming (except for Olivia, Sarah, and Tristin, who didn't want to put on their new bathing suits) while the grown-ups exchanged family gifts. The boys played Perry Mason—Woodhill Country Club's version of

Marco Polo—and Mimi and I tried to teach Annie how to bump butts underwater, by holding hands and pressing the soles of our feet against each other's. Annie couldn't do it because she needed one hand to hold her nose, so we taught her somersaults instead.

At ten-thirty, Uncle Bear put his thumb and forefinger to his mouth and whistled. "Everybody out. Time to go home. Grandma has something for you!"

There was a commotion while some of us stood, dripping at the side of the pool, shivering and blue-lipped, and waited for the others to get out. Uncle Bear helped Grandma dole out her presents. (I've noticed that he, of the three sons-in-law, is particularly sweet with her.) The identical packages were bulky, soft, wrapped in dark green tissue, and tied with thick, red and white yarn bows. If we weren't all freezing, we might not have appreciated the gifts right away: giant green plush beach towels, with our last names embroidered at one end in block letters. There were three EWINGS, three ERICKSONS, three BOWMANS, and four JOHNSONS.

There is a light rap on my bedroom door, and Olivia pokes her head in. "C'mon, let's go," she whispers. I kick off my covers and hop to the floor. It doesn't seem late enough to go snooping for presents. Mom and Dad might still be awake, but Olivia's timing has always been right in the past.

We tiptoe toward Sherman's room, wearing our matching Christmas flannel nighties, which have that new, sour smell. Olivia is about to knock on Sherman's door when we hear our father's voice, muffled, behind the master bedroom door. Olivia looks at me, her eyes suddenly big. She smiles nervously and covers her mouth with her hand, and I'm afraid I might erupt in giggles and then we'll be caught. Olivia's index finger goes up. "Shhh," she mimes.

Now Mom is talking. I strain to hear her.

"Those weren't *exactly* his words," Mom says in a low voice. I'm not sure what I detect in her voice. Is it a soothing quality? Defensiveness?

"Pretty close," our father snaps back, just above a whisper. Olivia and I stand there. My heart is pounding now. We thought we were going to wake up Sherman and hunt for hidden Christmas presents, but instead, curiosity draws us closer to our parents' bedroom door. Like spies, we are eavesdropping, and it feels dangerous. I go from titillation to fear.

"He called it *quackery*," Dad says bitterly.

Olivia motions to me with her head, and, wasting no time, we return to our end of the dark hallway. Outside my room, I want to ask my sister about what I heard, but she rushes past me to her room and silently closes her door. I go back to my bed and pull the covers up to my chin. All of a sudden, I feel sort of queasy.

I have never heard that word, but I can tell from the way my father said it that it isn't good. *Quackery*. It is an insult, a sharp one, not at all Christmasy. I wonder what it means. I stare at the canopy over my bed and try to commit the word to memory. In the morning, before we head to Ammie and Grandpa's for Christmas Day with Dad's family, I'll want to sneak into Dad's study and find the word in his unabridged Webster's dictionary.

Sleep drifts into my room, surrounding me with warmth. My eyes close, my breathing slows, and with each gentle exhale the word I must remember tiptoes away.

MAY 1974

One Friday afternoon, a week after my twelfth birthday, Sherman and I pile into the backseat of our mother's yellow station wagon.

"Aren't you nervous?" Sherman asks. He is nine.

"No," I lie.

I am about to have my ears pierced by Uncle Jack. He's a plastic surgeon. Mimi says he does lots of boob jobs and nose jobs, but once he reattached a woman's ear after her horse bit it off. Mimi had her ears pierced by Uncle Jack last month, since she's four weeks older than me. Sarah and Olivia had theirs done when they turned twelve. Very soon I will be sitting at my uncle's kitchen table just like they all did.

I know that the five-minute procedure will make me look older a lot faster and more permanently than anything else (short of a boob job, ha-ha), and since I look like twelve-going-on-nine, I'll take all the help I can get. Still, I'm scared. I've never been stuck with a needle, at least not for as long as I can remember. I had vaccinations before I turned three, but none since then, because of the Christian Science exemption. I've even been excused, for religious reasons, from the routine eye exams given by the school nurse. The last time I went to the doctor was before my parents became Christian Scientists, when I was a toddler.

Uncle Jack's house is on the other side of town. Aunt Helen greets us at the front door. She is my godmother, which doesn't really mean anything anymore. She became my godmother when I was born, and she signs my birthday card "with love, your godmother" every May 4. But Christian Scientists don't have godparents, because Christian Scientists don't baptize. I got baptized when we were still regular Christians.

"Are you nervous?" Aunt Helen asks.

"Not really," I lie, my heart pounding. My head is swirling with a new and uncomfortable awareness of the difference between the way my family does things and the way other people do. It strikes me, all of a sudden, as weird, and maybe complicated, that my mother is a Christian Scientist and her brother is a plastic surgeon. Then it dawns on me that maybe *we* are weird. Maybe almost everyone in the world goes to doctors.

I sit on a kitchen stool, shoulders squared. I pull my hair back into a ponytail. Grandma takes my right hand in both of hers, which are warm and powdery soft.

Uncle Jack wraps a towel around my shoulders, like he's a barber. I face straight ahead, but I am watching his every movement, biting my lip.

I feel something wet and cold, first on my right earlobe, then on my left. The cool turns icy. I hold my head totally still.

"What's that, Uncle Jack?" I ask.

"I've just cleaned your ears with rubbing alcohol. They should feel a little cool. Don't worry, I'll let you know when I'm about to do something."

Relieved that the drips aren't blood, I move a bit on the stool, pull away from Grandma's grasp, and sit on both hands.

"Ready?" Uncle Jack asks.

"Yes."

"First, you'll feel a little pinch. That's the Novocain. It takes a few minutes to kick in. Then, I'll pierce the lobes, but you shouldn't feel anything. Your ears will be numb."

Uncle Jack stands six foot seven. Right now, I'm not looking in the mirror. We are eyeball to belt buckle. I feel him tug on one ear, then the other.

"There."

"Are you done?" I ask.

"Take a look in the mirror," Uncle Jack says. I see him wink at Mom and Grandma.

I slide off the stool and approach the mirror on the wall. I see two enormous needles—more like *poles*—sticking through my earlobes. Blood is dripping all over my toweled shoulders. My uncle laughs. I don't. I feel like I'm going to throw up.

I climb back onto the stool. Mom takes a closer look at the needles sticking out of my two ears and says to my uncle that the placement is fine.

"Jo, separate the earrings from the posts, will you, and stick them in the alcohol," Uncle Jack says.

In Sunday school I have learned that there is no such thing as germs. Nevertheless, my mom, like the nurse on *Marcus Welby, M.D.* (forbidden viewing at our house, so I have to be sneaky about watching it), obediently plops the shiny bits of gold into the dish of alcohol, swishing the dish around before handing it to Uncle Jack. In less than a minute, the earrings and their posts are pinched into place. Uncle Jack wipes the blood from my earlobes with another damp cotton ball.

"There," he says, "*now* take a look." He winks at me this time and pats my shoulder.

I hop off the stool again and approach the mirror. This time I see a blood-blotched towel on my shoulders and a pair of pink, puffy lobes with gold ball earrings. My ears are *pierced*. And almost magically, I can't feel them at all.

"Thanks, Uncle Jack."

"Your mom will pick up some rubbing alcohol at the drugstore. I want you to clean your ears every morning when you get up, then after school, and finally before you go to bed at night. Like this."

He picks up a cotton ball and saturates it with alcohol. Then he squeezes the ball gently so that little drops plop into his palm. "Wipe the cotton ball around the back and front of each earlobe. Then tilt your head, and let the alcohol drip right onto the earring, so that it gets through to the puncture. You should do this for two weeks. And twist each earring once around before every cleaning. It will sting a little. Other than that, try not to fiddle with them, or they may get infected. Okay?"

I am still smiling at my reflection, but now I'm sort of worried. What if rubbing alcohol is against Christian Science?

"What if they do?" I ask. "You know, get infected?"

Uncle Jack pauses and looks at Mom. "If you clean them carefully like I showed you, they shouldn't. But if they do, you call me, okay?"

"Okay," I say. I wonder how I will know.

I walk out to the driveway, where all the kids are, relieved that the ear piercing is behind me.

Sherman comes over to inspect my ears, but the cousins don't. They're used to this.

"Do they hurt?" Sherman asks with a squeamish smirk.

"Can't even feel them," I say, running my finger along the edge of one ear, still amazed at the power of Novocain.

Sherman leans the bicycle toward me and asks if I want a turn. I eye the jump, get on the banana-seated, high-handlebarred bicycle, and take a warm-up loop before heading toward the ramp.

I can't figure out why everyone—Grandma, Aunt Helen, Sherman, the cousins—is standing over me. I'm not sure where I am. I feel odd, not *right*, like I'm in the narrowest part of a giant funnel into which everything—the trees, my uncle's house, the driveway—is being poured, speeding by me on all sides.

I can see Uncle Jack squatting beside me. He is holding my wrist, looking at his watch. Mom is kneeling on my other side, squeezing my other hand. Grandma is standing above me, right hand over her mouth. I hear Aunt Helen scolding her boys about the jump. She sounds impossibly far away, but I see that she is right here.

"I think she fainted because of her ears," Sherman says. But Harry tells Uncle Jack that the high handlebars gave way just as I flew into the air, throwing me headfirst over the bicycle and onto the concrete driveway.

"I hope she doesn't have a concussion," Grandma says, speaking softly to my uncle. She looks worried. I've never heard the word *concussion* before. It sounds serious. Tension seems to be hovering over me, like a ghost, around Uncle Jack, Grandma, and Mom.

"I want you to follow my index finger," Uncle Jack says, slowly drawing his hand from right to left in front of my face. "How do you feel, Lucia?"

I don't know how I should answer him. I look up to my mother. I can tell she is praying: her eyes focus on an imaginary point between my face and hers. I feel dizzy.

Uncle Jack looks into my eyes, and his hands move lightly over my scalp. I wince as he finds the far edge of my right eyebrow. Then I feel a sharp ache, mellowing to a throb, somewhere above my hairline.

I look to my uncle, and it occurs to me that maybe they all think I can't hear them, or am too startled to answer. I know how I feel: like I'm being looked at under a microscope. I'm scared, my head hurts, and I think I might get sick. I need to lie back down. The pebbles on the driveway cut into my elbow.

I'm so scared I start to pray. I can't be hurt. I can't be sick. I can't feel pain. I am a child of God, made in God's perfect image. I reflect all of God's qualities: perfection, love, harmony, health. I don't have to be afraid because God is taking care of me.

Still, I am terrified. I know my mother can tell. She squeezes my hand gently.

"Should we go home?" she asks. It's not a question; it's a statement. But I'm wondering to myself if we should go home. Part of me wants to stay here, close to Uncle Jack, who would know how to take care of me.

Mom says, "Here, let's get you to your feet."

Uncle Jack cautions me to get up slowly, to rest for a moment in a sitting position.

Grandma, Uncle Jack, and Aunt Helen walk with us to the station wagon. I wonder what they're thinking. Does Grandma think I have a concussion? Does Uncle Jack think he should take me to the hospital? Does Aunt Helen wonder if maybe my uncle should take charge? I'm sure Mom wishes Dad were here. Sherman self-consciously walks beside me, taking my elbow, and I can tell he is scared too.

Can people die from concussions?

Many times I have imagined something just like this: I have an accident, or get some disease, and everyone feels sorry for me and does nice things, like sending me get-well cards and bringing me stuffed animals. But the very idea of get-well cards is shunned in Christian Science (a get-well card for someone who is already God's perfect child, illness-free?). This isn't fun at all. I feel like I've done something wrong.

On the way home, I sit in the front passenger seat. Mom asks me what we talked about in Sunday school last week. I tell her that accidents are *error,* and that error isn't real and therefore can't happen. I try to say this with certainty, but I start to cry. Are the tears flowing now out of relief that I am going home? Or is it because I'm afraid? Should I be at a hospital right now?

Mom rubs my knee soothingly. "We'll call Dad as soon as we get home," she says, "and he will get straight to work."

We arrive at home, and Mom lets me lie down in her room, on the high, four-poster bed. Then she calls Dad from the phone in his study. I am straining to hear what she says.

"Daddy is on his way home now," she tells me. "Would you like to call Mrs. Hannah?"

I feel myself start to cry all over again. Now that Dad is a practitioner, we call Mrs. Hannah only for really serious problems, like when Sherman's finger got caught in the heavy storm-shelter door in the basement. I don't know why *Mom* is asking *me* if I want to call Mrs. Hannah. I just want Mom to take care of me. I'd rather she call Uncle Jack.

My mother dials Mrs. Hannah's number and hands me the phone. I take a deep breath to try to stop crying. Mrs. Hannah picks up after two rings. Her melodic, gentle voice brings tears to my eyes again. I tell her what happened, leaving out the word *concussion*. We don't believe in concussions.

Mrs. Hannah talks about God. She says that "Love is reflected in Love" and that I am therefore perfect. "'Be ye therefore perfect, even as your Father which is in heaven is perfect,'" Mrs. Hannah says, quoting Jesus in the Sermon on the Mount. Together we sing the hymn "Feed My Sheep," and then she tells my mother we should call her in the morning.

I hear the old red Mercedes turn in to the driveway without the usual *toot-toot* announcing my dad's return. Moments later, he appears in the master bedroom, sets down his briefcase, and takes a seat beside me on the bed. He doesn't ask me how I am feeling—to do so might be giving in to *error*. I want to tell him how it all happened: how I went off the jump and the handlebars gave way. I want to tell him what Grandma said about a concussion. But I don't.

"Do you like my earrings?" I ask.

"They're lovely," Dad says.

"I'm okay, Dad," I say. "I'm just a little tired."

The next morning, I wake up. Something is sore on both sides of my head, and I remember my pierced ears. I twist both earrings and wonder if Mom bought the rubbing alcohol. Then I remember the bicycle jump, and I gently touch my hand to my forehead and find a bump.

At breakfast, my mother asks me, "How do you feel, honey?"

"Fine," I say. All I want to think about is my newly pierced ears and how I look.

But Dad says, "You've had a beautiful demonstration." He is standing behind me, wearing a suit and tie, about to leave for the office, and I am pouring some cereal into a bowl. He squeezes my shoulders gently, affectionately.

"You know, Loosh," he says, "now that you're twelve, you can join the Mother Church."

I'm not sure I want to, but I'm not sure I don't: What if I join the church? Does that mean I can't go to a hospital if I get really sick? I'm scared all over again.

"Can I go with you to church on Wednesday night?" I ask, looking up at Dad and then Mom. I know if they say yes, it will be so that I can give a testimony. I also know I will get to stay up later, and maybe stop at Baskin-Robbins for ice cream on the way home after the service. Mom and Dad both smile broadly and say they think that is a wonderful idea.

SEPTEMBER 1974
SEVENTH GRADE

"The two most important things we can give you kids," Mom says to me one night, "are your education and Christian Science."

I am about to start seventh grade at a new school. Mom has

joined me on my bed, and I am resting with my head in her lap before she turns my lights out.

She combs her fingers through my long hair, making my scalp and the back of my neck tingle. As disappointing as it might be for my parents, I don't look at either Christian Science or my education as precious, and I don't think of them as gifts. Gifts aren't boring.

For years my parents have wanted me to enroll at Northrop Collegiate (Nor-throw-up, we called it), an all-girls school in Minneapolis. Until now, I've successfully resisted their appeals. Every winter I've taken the entrance exam, and I've done well enough to be accepted (proof, I point out, that Deephaven Elementary is doing a fine job). Every April my mother has bought me a pair of navy blue oxfords, somehow thinking the uniform lace-ups might lure me into the private school camp; they never do. But this year, I'm making the switch: sixth grade was the last year of elementary school, and my parents aren't thrilled with the public junior high option.

"It's the *right* activity at the *right* time," my mom coaxes, and even though I'm not looking at her face, I know she is gazing out into an imaginary distance, making a silent prayer. I roll my eyes. (When she catches me reading with a flashlight under my covers at night, it's the *right* activity at the *wrong* time.) I love when she combs my head with her fingernails, but I swear, sometimes she can be so—*ugh—mothery*.

The truth is, I don't need much convincing on the school thing anymore. This fall, three local private schools are merging: Northrop (all girls), Blake (all boys), and Highcroft (coed). They will become the Blake Schools, keeping the three campuses, blending their student bodies. They're giving up uniforms. And I won't have to wear those hideous blue shoes. I'll count among my schoolmates lots of cousins, as well as Mary, my best friend from Deephaven, and many camp friends.

Tomorrow, the entire incoming seventh grade of the newly merged Blake Schools will board buses and head north for a much-anticipated orientation. There will be hiking, a campfire, trust falls, and other activities. We will get to know one another and some of our teachers before school starts. It could be fun.

Mom kisses my forehead, and we say our prayers:

"Thy kingdom come"; let the reign of divine Truth, Life, and Love be established in me, and rule out of me all sin; and may Thy Word enrich the affections of all mankind, and govern them!

The bus ride to the camp is long. At the outset, the Blake Schools' new seventh-grade class behaves admirably, with self-restraint, but by the time we are bumping along the final dirt road to the campground, a number of boys launch the first of many handfuls of Cheetos toward the front of our bus. A quick food fight ensues.

Once the bus stops, we proceed to the bulletin board on the edge of the parking lot, where we'll find our family assignments. There is a confused dash, followed by a nearly spontaneous and unanimous judgment that Family B is the best. It has all the jocks, and all the popular girls. My best friend Mary is in B. My cousin Mimi is in B. I am in D. I recognize a few names on the D list, and some acquaintances, but nobody I can actually claim as a friend. Still, I'm not entirely disappointed. I like getting new school supplies; I figure I'll enjoy making some new friends too. I've already met a nice girl on the bus who will also be in Family D. Her name is Liz.

I am sitting on the ground in a circle with a bunch of kids and a teacher who asks us to introduce ourselves one at a time and share something about ourselves and our families. He starts with me, and I politely decline. He asks the boy to my right to go first instead.

"I'm Tracy Lund," he says, looking down at his hands self-consciously. "I like going to Viking games."

"And what does your father do?" the teacher asks. I stifle a groan. Why did he have to ask that?

"My dad owns grocery stores," Tracy says easily. We all know this. Everyone's mother shops at Lunds.

The person to Tracy's right is Liz, the girl I sat next to on the bus. "... I like to ski, I have a brother named Happy"—we all giggle— "and my dad is a lawyer."

But the teacher hasn't actually asked about her father's occupation, Liz just offered it! So now the pattern is in place, and nobody will likely break it.

How I wish my father worked for General Mills. I have wanted this for as long as I can remember. In second grade, my class went on a field trip to the General Mills test kitchens, courtesy of a classmate's father. *That* was cool. The white-aproned, white-hatted, and latex-gloved ladies there tested recipes using Betty Crocker cake mixes, and not only did we get to help, and taste, but we came home with goody bags stuffed with product samples.

What does your father do?

Whenever I answer this question, and no matter how I inflect it—with a cautious question mark or a bold period—the eight syllables seem to take forever stumbling past my lips.

Chris-tian Sci-ence prac-ti-tion-er. I know my answer will only bring more questions. I can gauge what will come next: if my cross-examiner's eyebrows go up, there soon follows something along the lines of "My grandmother had a friend who..." or "We have a neighbor whose cousin..." The sentence always ends badly, with a broken leg, or a heart attack, or an early, preventable death.

"This is a wonderful opportunity to act as an Ambassador of Truth," my mom says, which means, I suppose, that I can be a spokesman for Christian Science. But the truth is, it feels more like time for a hasty getaway.

The rest of the kids around the circle introduce themselves and announce their fathers' occupations or workplaces: one doctor, two lawyers, Cargill, stockbroker, 3M, Dayton's, Piper Jaffray, Jolly Green Giant. Even Jolly Green Giant can be said without raising eyebrows. Now, it is my turn. Why couldn't my father just sell stocks?

"I'm Lucia Ewing. I have an older sister and a younger brother."

Just then, a teacher walks up to our circle.

"They're ready for us in the mess hall," she says. "Five minutes?"

I'm spared? Amen. I uncross my legs and start to get up. Our teacher gestures for me to take my seat again.

"Whoa, not so fast, everyone. Let's give Lucia a chance to finish telling us about herself."

"I like to water ski and play tennis," I say, "and my father is . . . a minister."

That was easy.

And it worked; there are no further questions. It's close to the truth, I tell myself: an approximation. I can just be Lucia, a minister's daughter, and that feels nearly as Wonder bread normal as being the daughter of a businessman. I am free to spend the rest of the weekend—maybe even the rest of seventh grade?—just like everyone else. I feel almost giddy as I head for the mess hall. I only hope Mimi and Mary don't give me up.

After lunch, I am hanging out with some new friends. We take turns pushing each other on a tire swing. There is a cute boy named James, with blue eyes and golden hair, small like me, and he looks my way whenever I glance in his direction. Liz gets off the swing, and now it is my turn. I pull myself into the tire and grasp the end of the rope, just below where it is securely knotted. James takes hold of the tire and slowly pulls me way, way back. I can't help but smile. He lets go, and I soar through the air. He catches me around the waist and pushes me again. With each push I fly higher, and warm to the possibility that I have a crush, and that maybe it's mutual.

What seems to matter at Blake—more than what Dad does, or the fact that we don't go to doctors—is who my family is. Lucky for me, my family—or not my family but my parents' families—preceded me. When I meet classmates' parents for the first time, they might tell me they knew Mom from Edina High School, or they remember the annual Christmas pageants at Highcroft, when Highcroft was still the name of the house Dad grew up in, not one of the three campuses of Blake Schools. My uncles' younger faces can be spotted in the black-and-white team photos that hang on the school's walls.

OCTOBER 1974

In October, the seventh-grade class parents plan the first Friday night social, a sock hop. James asks Mary to ask me if I'll go with him. The night of the sock hop, James wears blue jeans rolled up above the ankles and a white T-shirt with a pack of fake cigarettes rolled into the sleeve. His blond hair is greased back, and he stashes a peppermint Winston behind one ear. I wear my hair pulled up in a high ponytail, Mom's old poodle skirt from Grandma's attic safety-pinned at the waist, white bobby socks, and a red cardigan put on backward, buttoned up the back. At the party, everyone dances as a group to oldies like "The Loco-Motion," and "Rock Around the Clock." When the Johnny Mathis song "Misty" comes over the loudspeaker, James's hands go timidly to my waist, and I tentatively place mine on his shoulders. I look around the dance floor and see that others have paired off too, but I won't look anyone in the eye, especially my mom. She is chaperoning. Mary and her friend Jay float past James and me, and she gives me the thumbs-up. I chew my upper lip nervously, trying not to smile too obviously.

James and I win a prize for best costumes.

The next morning Mary calls me on the phone as I am eating breakfast, watching Saturday cartoons with Sherman and Dad.

"So?" she says. "Are you going together?"

"*I* dough-no!"

"You're going together," she declares.

I grin.

THANKSGIVING 1974

On the day before Thanksgiving, Mom, Dad, Grandma, Sherman, and I drive to the airport to pick up Olivia. She is now a tenth grader at Principia, a Christian Science boarding school near St. Louis, Missouri.

Each time we meet Olivia's plane, I harbor a vague feeling that I won't recognize my own sister, but there she is, walking down the jetway. A sense of relief washes over me. Only two things about Olivia look different: She has a long, tiny braid on either side of her face. And now she's taller than Mom. She drops her backpack to give us each a hug. I wonder briefly if I'll ever catch up to her.

Late Wednesday night, after everyone else has gone to bed, I sit with Olivia on her bed, and she makes two tiny braids for me while we listen to her new Stevie Wonder album. We don't talk much. She plays "Heaven Is 10 Zillion Light Years Away," on low volume, lifting the needle delicately and setting it back precisely on the wide groove at the beginning of the song, over and over again. Olivia knows every word, and her voice is rich and low, and I wish I could sing like she does. I hear the unhurried rhythm, and Stevie Wonder's voice overlaid with hers, and even though the song is about God and the cosmos and being black, to me it voices a universal sorrow and—somehow—my own unexpected, blurry longing.

We page through the Principia yearbook together, and Olivia points out all her friends; I can almost see their faces beneath the loopy, smudged ballpoint scrawl and scratch of various hands, the *i*'s with tiny circles or hearts for dots. A lot of them are seniors now; Olivia has always preferred the company of older people. She calls most of Mom's and Dad's friends by their first names, not Mr. and Mrs. the way Sherman and I do.

Sometimes when Olivia talks about life at Principia, I try to insert myself into the picture, but I'm not sure boarding school is for me.

In the morning, we go to church, where Dad leads the service, because now he is the First Reader, which is sort of a big deal. (Everybody knows us now, which is annoying. Sherman, Olivia, and I have to shake hands with people after church, and it takes twice as long to get to the car and go home.) When Dad invites the congregation to stand and testify, I watch Olivia move to the edge of her seat a couple of times, putting both of her hands on the pew in front of her. Has she had a healing at Principia that I don't know about? She lingers there for moment, and then she eases back into a slouch. After several minutes, she winks at me and I realize she is just fooling around.

My stomach growls loudly. Sherman snickers, and Mom bites her upper lip.

We are greeted at Ammie and Grandpa's front door first by Uncle Truck, Aunt Adrienne, and their two kids, Mimi and Truckie, who are visiting from St. Louis. Then there is a huge, happy ruckus as everyone else squeezes into the entry hall: Ammie, Grandpa, Mom, Dad, Aunt Laurie and Uncle Nick, and their six kids, Jane, Ted, Sage, Sasha, and the twins, Tib and Cal.

All the grandchildren except Olivia (who is the oldest and chooses to stay upstairs with the grown-ups) retreat to Ammie and Grandpa's basement—the girls to play with Ammie's old dollhouse from her childhood, the boys to Grandpa's workshop. The dollhouse stands five feet tall, with real electric chandeliers and wallpaper, miniature Oriental rugs, and tiny plates and silverware. When we play with it, it is easy to imagine Ammie's life in the olden days. From old photographs, and the stories we've heard, Highcroft was a magical place where fancy balls and Christmas pageants took place attended by ladies in ball gowns and gentlemen wearing tuxedos and monocles, in rooms that probably looked something like those in the dollhouse.

Across the hall, Sherman and Ted hammer nails into a work-bench and saw two-by-fours in half. There is never a speck of saw-dust anywhere, on the floor or the benches or the equipment, until the boys spill their hard-earned shavings on the concrete floor.

"There's two tables in the dining room," Ted says through gritted teeth, without looking up. Jane and I have strolled in, our interest in the dollhouse exhausted. Ted is pounding a thick nail into the work-bench, with a spare one sticking out of the left side of his mouth.

"*You're* sitting at the *other* table," he adds, indicating with his eyes that *you* means Sherman and me.

Sherman stops hammering.

"Why?" I ask, puzzled.

"Because you're Ewings," Ted says matter-of-factly. The edge of his mouth turns up in a satisfied smile.

"What are you *talking* about, Ted?" Jane says. She looks at me and blushes.

"It was a *joke*," he says. "*Jeez.*"

Jane grabs my elbow and whisks me away. Sherman seems fine, he resumes his hammering, but I am unnerved, even if I don't show it. I know it was a joke—but it felt like a jolt. Grandpa is Dad's stepfather, and Uncle Nick and Uncle Truck are Dad's half brothers. Still, I have always felt fully my grandpa's granddaughter. That we are Ewings and not Morrisons has never, until now, been pointed out.

We march up to the dining room, where there are, in fact, two tables set. The big table has place cards for all the grown-ups, plus Olivia. The lower table is for the rest of us, and there is no division along last names. Jane rearranges the place cards at our table so that we can sit together. I feel only slightly relieved.

In the living room, a fire crackles and blazes. I survey the room and allow its familiarity to soothe me because I am suddenly feeling like I'd rather not be here. On one wall hangs the gilded portrait of Grandpa as a younger man, clad in a khaki-colored military jacket, complete with medals and badges, sitting erect with his arms folded on his desk, peering discerningly right into my eyes.

You are my Grandpa too, I think.

Yes, I am, he seems to be saying.

Jane and I plop down on one of the sofas by the fire. On the coffee table, we spot the small, familiar photo album, in aged brown leather, with HIGHCROFT embossed on it in gold. We nestle together and hold the book between us, poring over the yellowing black-and-white photos encased in crisp cellophane sleeves. Ammie's maiden name was Heffelfinger, and her grandparents built Highcroft. I used to laugh at the funny-sounding name, and poor Olivia was teased mercilessly for it when grade school classmates discovered it was her middle name. But over the years I've heard enough stories, and seen enough pictures, to know that Heffelfinger is a name my family takes pride in. When people say "She's a Heffelfinger"—and they actually do—even though it's not my name, I feel connected, anchored.

The first photograph shows the front of Highcroft, buried in several feet of snow. From the size of the trees flanking the brick house, and the Classical entrance, it looks like an important house, and even though it was torn down several years before I was born, the picture fills me with a satisfying pride. Another picture shows the same view in summer. Each window is shaded by an awning, the kind I have seen at country clubs. I count twenty awnings on the front of the house alone, not including the third-floor windows, which are bare. A third picture shows the back of the house from a distance, with a three-story colonnade partially shaded by two tall trees. In the foreground is a sprawling lawn.

I prefer the pictures of the outside of the house to the ones of the inside. The interior pictures remain lifeless, gray, and cluttered. We skip over these to find our favorite picture: the summer gardens, with huge swaths of well-tended flowers, which I visualize as pink and white.

In the buffet line, Mom and the aunts serve food from chafing dishes set up on the sideboard. Everyone knows to stand behind his or her assigned place and wait for Grandpa's nod to be seated. Then, in silence, with bowed heads, we hold hands and listen to Grandpa's soft, commanding voice: "Bless this food to our use, and us to Thy service. Amen."

Then he raises his glass. "Here's to family, to those of us who are here"—Grandpa pauses. Gazing over the room, his eyes fall on each of us (including the Ewings)—"and to those of us who cannot be here."

In my head, I count those missing: Uncle Sherm, Dad's brother who is a rancher in Calgary; his wife, Aunt Claire; and their three grown kids. Dad's sister Aunt Nan, who lives in Greenwich, Connecticut, with Uncle Dave. They have six kids, three in college, one in boarding school, two still at home. And Dad's other sister, Aunt Lucia, who lives in New Hampshire and is divorced. She has three, all grown. That makes twelve more cousins, twenty-three grand-children in all.

I think Grandpa has two more children—and maybe they have children?—from before he married Ammie, but I've never met them.

For a commanding officer, Grandpa is quiet by nature. He sits at the head of the table, his posture board-straight, and chews his food deliberately, rarely speaking between mouthfuls. When someone says something funny—if Uncle Truck boasts about being the only person in the world to have gotten kicked out of Dartmouth twice, and accepted *thrice*—Grandpa's laugh is nearly mute, his face turns crimson, and he holds a napkin to the corner of his eye to wipe away a tear.

"Here he goes!" someone will say.

Grandpa looks down in his lap, so we can see his gleaming bald head, and transfers his napkin to his opposite hand to wipe the corner of his other eye.

Ammie is a natural storyteller. She keeps us on the edges of our seats with her tales of life at Highcroft: the Christmas pageants in which all the kids—including grandchildren and second cousins and the help's children and grandchildren—acted in the Nativity play; rites of passage, like learning to drive, and carving one's initials in the old Ford's dashboard upon mastery.

Invariably, someone mentions Mr. D, the butler, and then someone else hollers "the pervert!" and then everyone laughs some more.

I don't know why that's funny.

Once in a while, but not today, someone tells about the time little Heff (Dad) threw a chair at Grandpa. I have always laughed along with everyone else, thinking this was hilarious, but now I'm not so sure.

On Thanksgiving night, we are back at home and I am in bed. Dad brings me a glass of water and tucks me in.

"How come our house doesn't have a name?" I ask.

Dad smiles and pats my knee, a bony knob beneath the covers.

"You know, like Highcroft," I say, "and Many Pines" (Ammie and Grandpa's place up north), "and...what's Hickory Hill again?"

"That's where I was born," Dad says, "in Pleasantville, New York."

"Oh," I say.

Dad doesn't offer an answer, but I don't really give him time to before I've moved on to my next question.

"And why do you call Grandpa *Unc*?"

At this, Dad pauses.

"Well...," he says, "it's short for Uncle Terry. When I was little, I could only say Unc, so it stuck, and I've called him that ever since."

"But he's not your uncle," I say.

"No, he's not. He's my stepfather."

"Oh."

"You knew that, though, didn't you," Dad says, not as a question but as a statement.

"Of course!" I say. I feel embarrassed, somehow, for having asked.

After Dad kisses me good night, Mom comes in and sits on the bed between Dad and me, so that we are all three together. "Good night, sweetheart," she says. She pushes my hair out of my face and kisses my forehead. Dad puts his arm lovingly on Mom's shoulder, and they gaze at me like I'm some sort of miracle, which, even at twelve years old, still feels wonderful. I'm glad they are both my real parents, no steps.

Together, we say prayers.

SPRING 1975

Several of my friends at school start going to Perkins Cake & Steak for breakfast on Thursday mornings with Bill, a youth leader for Young Life, a Christian organization. I plead with my parents to let me join this group ("All they do is eat breakfast, it's not like they're going to convert me or anything"), and when I point out that our church doesn't have a youth group—no camping trips, not even a choir—Mom and Dad give in.

My first Thursday morning, Bill's old station wagon pulls up to our house. I see Mimi, Mary, and James among the faces peering through the car windows, ballooning their cheeks with their mouths on the glass. Bill walks up to our front door and rings the bell. He has clean, shoulder-length hair and dresses sort of like a hippie, in a wrinkled shirt and baggy white painter's pants.

Mom and I answer the door together. She introduces herself as Joanne, and then me, and shakes Bill's hand.

"Have fun!" she says, and I feel myself cringing as Bill and I walk down the path.

"Is that your sister?" Bill asks.

"That's my *mom*," I say, mortified.

"Wow, she's not bad looking."

I climb into the backseat, say hi to my friends, and try to erase Bill's comment from my head.

Every Thursday at Perkins, I order the same thing: French toast with bacon. I love the golden ovals of spongy French bread with the powdered sugar sprinkled on top and the mini-scoop of whipped butter.

"Dear Lord," Bill says, as we are about to dig in. We follow his lead and bow our heads, smiling self-consciously and checking in with one another out of the corners of our eyes. "Bless this meal, and be a comforting presence for these friends who have gathered in Your Name. Teach them what it means to have a deep personal relationship with You. Amen."

Even without a text in front of me, I am sufficiently literate in religious matters to know which of Bill's words should be capitalized. But having a "relationship with Christ"—like He's a person—is something I've never considered. In our church, God has never felt personal. I've been taught to think of God as the Father-Mother, but God has always felt inanimate, more like the three-letter word *air* than the three-letter word *Him*.

Bill's blessing is the only reference to religion at breakfast. After the grace, we dig in. James and I usually sit across from or next to each other, and occasionally make eye contact or smile. Throughout the meal, there is much laughter and the occasional tossing of food before we pool our dollars to pay the check. We get back into Bill's car for the drive to school. At the first red light, we jump out, chase one another once around the car, and pile back in before the light turns green. Arriving at the school's front entrance just in time for the first bell, I feel like I am—by dint of sheer luck—part of quite possibly the coolest group at school.

One Thursday, as Bill drives us to school after the weekly breakfast, I become aware, very quickly, that I don't feel well. My stomach is uncomfortably full, and a queasy sensation starts making its way from my belly up toward my throat. During the Chinese fire drill I stay put, while my friends climb over me to make their dash around the outside of the car. As everyone piles back into the car, fortunately oblivious to me, I elbow my way to the window seat and pray that, first, I don't barf right then and there; second, I am not forced to ask Bill to stop the car; and, finally, I can make it to school without anybody noticing me. I don't know if this desire for privacy is a function of being a seventh grader and not wanting to stand out at all, in any way, or if everything I've learned from Mom and Dad and Sunday school is kicking in.

> When thou prayest, enter into thy closet, and when thou hast shut thy door, pray to thy Father which is in secret; and thy Father which seeth in secret, shall reward thee openly.

God, please don't let me barf.

I crank down the window for some air and pray pray pray.

The car pulls up to the traffic circle at the school's entrance. I run to the bathroom, lock the stall door, and vomit my French toast. I made it. Thank you, God. I try to hold back my hair the way Mom does when I throw up. I wish she were here. Once I've emptied my stomach, I curl up cold and clammy on the tile floor and stay there for a while.

Eventually, I get up and walk down the hall to the nurse's office, a room I've never had to visit. "My goodness, dear, you don't look so good," the nurse says, hands on her hips, before taking my arm and leading me to the cot against one wall.

She asks me my name, and I wonder if she knows I'm a Christian Scientist.

"Can I call your mom? Would you like to go home?"

I nod.

She dials our number, but there is no answer. I remember that Mom plays tennis on Thursday mornings and there is no way to reach her, so the nurse looks up something in my file and tells me she is calling Dad at the office.

"... she is white as a ghost," the nurse explains when he answers. "Sure, she's right here."

The nurse looks over at me and tilts her head sweetly. "Would you like to talk to your dad?"

I get up and move to her desk.

"Hi, Dad," I say.

"Hi, kiddo."

"I threw up."

"Would you like me to pray for you?"

I look at the nurse.

"Can I go home?" I ask Dad. I want him to say yes.

"That might not be necessary," he says. "Lucia, you, as God's perfect creation, cannot be sick. You are the perfect reflection of God."

"Can you come get me?" I whisper.

I stare at the floor, because I know the nurse is looking at me.

He goes on. "Mrs. Eddy says, 'Let unselfishness, goodness, mercy, justice, health, holiness, love—the kingdom of heaven— reign within us, and sin, disease, and death will diminish until they finally disappear.'"

There is silence now, and I am trying to concentrate on what Dad is saying, about disease disappearing if I fill my thoughts with goodness, health, and love, but my eyes are filling with unwelcome tears. My fingers fiddle with the phone cord. I'm embarrassed that the nurse is listening, and Dad is not offering to come get me.

"...you needn't give in to the erroneous suggestions of mortal mind. You *cannot* be sick, Lucia. Jesus said, 'Be ye therefore perfect, even as your Father which is in heaven is perfect.'"

I wipe my eyes with my sleeve.

"Loosh?" Dad asks. "Do you think you'd like to go back to class?"

"Yes," I say. But what I'd really like is to be in my bed. At home. With Mom.

"That's wonderful," Dad says. "I know you're going to feel fine."

I say good-bye and hand the phone to the nurse.

"My dad's going to call my mom again and she'll come get me," I tell her.

"Hmm," the nurse says, an hour later. "Do you want to try her again?"

She dials the number and hands me the phone. I count six rings, seven, eight, and am about to hang up when Mom answers.

"Mom, I'm at the nurse's office. I threw up. Can you come get me?"

"Of course, sweetheart," Mom says. "I'm on my way."

I feel such relief.

JUNE 1975

I am thirteen years old, nearing the end of my seventh-grade year, with one week to go before school lets out for the summer. Olivia has just returned from Principia. She is now officially an eleventh grader. Her steamer trunk stands on end just inside the door leading from the kitchen to the garage. As I set the table for our first family dinner in months, my sister and mom chat in the kitchen. Olivia is showing her how to make something called guacamole, which sounds to me like something stuck in your throat. It looks even worse than it sounds. Still, I feel curious and a bit resentful at this proof of my sister's maturity—that she is actually in a position to teach Mom something about cooking. I've gotten used to being the oldest kid here, but now Olivia has returned with another Stevie Wonder album, and guacamole, and tales of dormitory life, all pointing to the differences between her exciting world and mine.

Dad is standing in the backyard grilling steaks, wearing an apron and his goofy chef's toque. Chipsie and Moptoe, our two dogs, are hovering nearby, tongues hanging out, hoping for scraps. Sherman is playing a solo game of tetherball. As Dad turns the steaks, and swats away the smoke, he sings an old favorite song called "George Jones," which dates back to his own boarding school days. I figure he must be happy to have my sister home again, and all of us under one roof.

"Five minutes!" he hollers.

We sit down to eat at the table in the screened porch off the dining room. I get to light candles, which I know signifies a special occasion. My mother sits at one end of the glass table, my father at the other. Olivia and I take our places at one of the long sides of the table, with Olivia next to Dad, me next to Mom. Sherman sits on the opposite side, facing us. We bow our heads and hold hands around the table to say grace. I squeeze my sister's hand: welcome back.

> *'Tis by thy Truth, O Lord, we're fed*
> *Thy Love our every need doth fill.*
> *Give us this day our daily bread,*
> *The grace to know and do Thy will. Amen.*

My brother and I replace the word *doth* with *death* and peek up from bowed heads, smiling at our usual joke.

Steak. Salad. Baked potatoes. Green beans. Sliced tomatoes with vinegar and sugar: our standard menu for Friday family dinner. We all drink milk.

For dessert, Mom has baked a rhubarb crisp, served warm with vanilla ice cream.

The meal is winding down, everyone spooning up the last mouthfuls of melting, sweet ice cream and tangy, soft fruit.

"Your mother and I have something important to tell you," Dad says.

Our parents' eyes meet, and they both smile. The last time they said this, Dad announced his decision to become a Christian Science practitioner. I exchange glances with my sister and brother.

"What?" we all ask in unison.

"We-ell," our father says in a jovial, teasing way, enjoying the moment of suspense, "you've all learned the metric system at school, right? You may want to brush up on it."

Family trip abroad this summer? Might be fun. But I'd rather go back to camp.

"You remember when your mother and I flew to London in April?"

I sense something ominous. I set down my spoon and look again at Sherman and Olivia.

"Well, while we were there, we visited two terrific schools. There's a Christian Science boarding school for girls called Claremont. There's also a Christian Science boarding school for boys nearby called Fan Court."

Olivia, Sherman, and I sit there, dumbstruck.

Eventually, my sister speaks. "What are you *saying*?" she asks in an uncharacteristically low voice.

"We're moving to London!" my father says.

Dead silence. Utter disbelief on Olivia's face. Absolutely nothing on Sherman's. Our parents smile at each other.

Some intangible, shatterproof thing has shattered.

My father starts talking again, but only shards of his run-on sentences register with me. "...an opportunity for all of us...," he says.

"What about our friends?" I ask.

"Mom can pursue Christian Science nursing...," he adds.

"What about Grandma? And Ammie and Grandpa?" Olivia asks.

"...at a place called Hawthorne House, and I can take my practice *anywhere*," he says.

"What about our friends?" I press, more urgently.

"You'll make new friends," he finally answers, casually. "We'll get to travel..."

"What about our house?" Olivia asks. I feel frantic.

"We'll sell the house.... We've found a nice duplex in Hampstead ... right near the Heath ... you'll love your new schools ... right outside London."

What? *What?*

"*I* don't want to go to boarding school!" I yell.

"Can't I stay at Principia?" Olivia pleads.

"Is there hockey?" Sherman asks. "What about hockey?"

"No, there's no hockey, kiddo," my father says gently. Seeing my brother's eyes overflow with tears, he adds, "But they have soccer. And they don't have football, but they have something like it called rugby."

"I don't play soccer," Sherman says. "Or rugby." He looks dazed.

"What about eighth grade? What about Chipsie? And Moptoe? And the cats?" I ask.

"It will be wonderful," my dad says, plowing over my questions. "You'll love London. It's a real European city. And there's no language barrier—"

"I'm not *going* to boarding school," I announce.

"Why can't I stay at Prin——?" Olivia asks again.

"But ... hockey," my brother murmurs.

My mother leaves the table and reappears moments later with two brochures in her hand and a stack of photographs. "This," she says, handing Olivia and me one brochure, "is Claremont. And this is Fan Court. I also have pictures of our new house in Hampstead. It's right across from John Keats's house."

That she took these photos with her Instamatic camera way back in April feels like a worse betrayal than the brochures themselves.

"Who the heck is John Keats?" I ask, my voice rising again, cracking. *And who cares?*

My mother slides her chair over to Sherman's side and sits down next to him to show him the brochure of the boys' school. It takes me all of twenty seconds to see enough of Claremont—a big mansion with white columns, and images of ruddy-cheeked girls wearing uniform everything: beige socks; brown shoes; beige skirts;

white blouses; maroon blazers; maroon, brown, and pink striped *neckties.*

I get up from the table.

"I'm not doing this," I announce, and I rush from the screened porch and head for my bedroom. If I close the door, and bury my face in my pillow, maybe it will go away.

London? Boarding school? When I think of England, I see Mary Poppins, Oliver Twist, and Simon, the whimpering, pasty-faced kid down the street who wears belted, pleated shorts on the school bus, even in November, frequently without underwear, his little jigglies there for everyone to see.

There is a knock at my door.

"Loosh?"

"Don't come in," I say, lying flat out on my bed.

My dad enters anyway.

"Listen, I know this comes as a surprise. And I know that change can be difficult, but sometimes it is for the best."

"But why? What's wrong with Minnesota?"

"Nothing's *wrong* with Minnesota. It's just that we have an opportunity to give you kids something really special."

"But what if we don't want it?"

"Well, you have to trust that we are doing the right thing. We've given this a lot of prayerful thought. We've been led to the right decision. Things have fallen into place so beautifully. I just know we are being divinely guided."

I don't really have an argument. I'm never good at debate when the moment calls for it, so my dad's viewpoint goes unchallenged. Later that night, waiting to fall asleep, I come up with a response: Nothing has fallen into place, any more than shrapnel falls into place.

"Would you please come downstairs, so we can finish our discussion?" he asks.

"I need to splash my face," I say, not disguising my bitterness.

When I go to the bathroom, I find my sister, fuming.

"This is unbelievable," she says, shaking her head. I'm not sure if she's talking to me or to her reflection in the mirror. "They throw this fait accompli at us" (like guacamole, it's another new term for me) "the day I get home. I can't even say good-bye to my friends! Could they have let me know last week even?"

Now she looks at me, and I think she wants an answer.

"Don't you think maybe we can change their minds?" I ask. "I mean, they can't *make* us go. Can they? You wouldn't have gone to Principia if you hadn't wanted to. Right?"

"Lucia," my sister says. "We're going. It's done."

Sherman is still sitting at the table when we return. Mom's arm is draped over his shoulder as he stares silently at the Fan Court brochure. He's not yet eleven, which seems really young for boarding school. I think maybe Dad was sent away to boarding school when he was even younger. But I never knew my parents intended to shove us down the same path.

"Listen, kids, maybe we should have eased you into the idea," my father says. "And maybe this warrants some further explanation. Your mother and I have always said that the two most important things we can give you are Christian Science and your education. With this move, we can give you both. This is a real gift, believe you me."

"And we have been so blessed in Science," Mom adds. "This is an opportunity for us to give back. With your dad's practice, and my goal of becoming a Christian Science nurse, we can really support the movement. As a *family*," she emphasizes, "we can support the movement."

"What do you mean, as a family?" I ask skeptically.

"Well, for one thing, by praying about this, by really *embracing* this new...adventure"—my father says *adventure* with ridiculous enthusiasm—"you are in a sense doing your part for the Cause. There is a real need for Christian Science worldwide, and this is one way you can play a part. An important part."

"So, you're saying the need in London is greater than here?" I ask.

"Are you being flip, young lady?" my father snaps.

My eyebrows rise up in defiance, but I know to keep my mouth shut.

"So, here's how it will work. We're going to put our house on the market in a couple of weeks. We'll be here until the beginning of August. Then, before we fly to London and get you settled in schools, we'll spend some time on the East Coast, starting in Boston, traveling as far south as Williamsburg, Virginia, with stops in New York and Washington. A pre-Bicentennial tour, if you will . . ."

We'll miss our country's big party, the two hundredth birthday we've been talking about in school for the last year?

". . . we'll have a wonderful time and you'll learn a thing or two about this great country. You'll get to see the Mother Church. The Statue of Liberty. The White House."

Normally, I'd be excited to see the Statue of Liberty and the White House, and even the Mother Church.

"Does Grandma know?" Olivia asks. Her tone is more worried than accusing, as though she's already surrendered.

"Not yet. We wanted to tell you first."

Thanks.

"And," Dad continues, "because we are still ironing out the details, we expect you to keep this hush for a while, to guard against malpractice."

Not too long ago, our homework assignment for Sunday school was to memorize Mary Baker Eddy's definition of *mental malpractice:* "the injurious action of one mortal mind controlling another from wrong motives . . . practised either with a mistaken or a wicked purpose."

What the *hell*?

My eyes well up again, and for the first time in my life I understand the meaning of *overwhelmed*.

"How long?" we ask in unison.

"Well, until we put the house on the market, anyway. We all need to do our protective work. As Mrs. Eddy says, we must 'stand porter at the door of thought.'"

"What's protective work?" Sherman asks, bewildered.

He hasn't learned about mental malpractice yet, or the need to do protective work.

"We have to keep our thoughts elevated, to know the Truth: that this is part of God's perfect plan—" Dad says.

"But what if it *isn't*?" I ask.

My father glares at me. "—so until we've dotted our *i*'s and crossed our *t*'s," he continues, "we're not going to discuss this with anyone."

"Anyone? Not even Grandma?" Sherman asks, his voice now at a panic-ridden, high pitch.

"Not even Grandma," Mom says and pauses. "There are those out there—not Grandma, just...people," she adds, but she sounds uncomfortable with her words, "who might wish us, and the Church, ill. We need to protect this *right idea*, like a mother protects her newborn child."

It is late at night. I am restless, unable to sleep. My head hurts. I have been sobbing, silently, for hours through gritted teeth. I take shallow breaths through my mouth because my nose is stuffed up. I am so angry, but I am determined to stifle the crying; I don't want to be heard. The last people in the world I would want to be comforted by are the two responsible for this.

I keep asking myself, *Why?*

At dinner our father's patience was quickly exhausted, and he was left to deal with our total lack of enthusiasm. "It wouldn't be any different if I worked for Cargill, or Exxon, or the State Department," he said, annoyed. "People get relocated all the time. Families *adapt*."

But he doesn't work for Cargill. And he's not being relocated. He's doing this *to* us.

I wonder how we can even afford a move like this. It has to

be expensive, and there's no Exxon paying for it. Several years back, when Dad and Mom announced that he was going into the practice, they warned us (enthusiastically) that there might be some changes, some belt-tightening. We might have to give up summer camps. Or family trips. But we never did.

"How come we haven't tightened our belts?" I had asked Dad once before bed. He smiled sort of awkwardly.

"Do you make a lot of money as a practitioner?" I pressed.

My dad looked searchingly into my eyes, and then his eyes twinkled tenderly. I thought for a second he was going to tell me something extraordinarily wonderful.

But, gently patting my knee, he shook his head. "No, Loosh. Practitioners do not make a lot of money."

"Well, then...how...?" I started to ask.

"Do you know what a dividend is?" he said.

One day soon a moving truck will come to take everything. Some of my things will be given away, some will be shipped to England, and some will be put into storage, because, Dad said tonight, "shipping everything to London makes no sense."

But nothing makes sense.

Choices will be made, things will be culled, but they will not be my choices.

The trampoline? My bicycle? Our three cats? My dollhouse, which, even though I never play with anymore, I'm not ready to give up. It's *mine*.

Will I see my grandparents again? They're getting older.

When I think of the possibility of never seeing them again, the pain I feel is sudden, sharp, like all three of them have just died.

Will we ever come back to Minnesota? What about Mimi and Mary? Will they still be my friends?

At the dinner table Mom said they could be my pen pals, and I scowled at her. The suggestion was like a knife to my stomach. Pen pals are never friends...

I'll have no friends.

"You'll make new ones," Mom said.

Like friends are replaceable. And what about James?

Even my canopied trundle bed is going to be taken apart, boxed, and hauled off to storage, which sounds to my ears cold and soulless and unprotected.

In my mind's eye, I see Mrs. Lurton, my Sunday school teacher. A stern, brainy woman in her mid-forties, the mother of my friend Jenny, Mrs. Lurton walks with the aid of crutches, has an angular face and perfectly manicured nails at the ends of her knotty fingers. A couple of times I've asked Mom what's wrong with Mrs. Lurton, and she has said, "You know, Lucia, in Science we don't put labels on . . . problems we're working out."

I see myself sitting, along with Jenny and the rest of our class, at a round table in the Sunday school, where we are memorizing passages from the Christian Science textbook. Mrs. Lurton points a gnarled index finger with its elegant nail at her leather-bound copy of *Science and Health,* opened to page 451: "Mental malpractice is . . . ?" she prompts, and we recite, " 'the injurious action of one mortal mind controlling another . . .' "

We say the words, over and over, tripping and stumbling semi-rhythmically, until we have committed them to memory. We have done the same drill with the Scientific Statement of Being, Mary Baker Eddy's definition of God, the Lord's Prayer, and the Twenty-third Psalm, but they sound more fluid.

I memorized the definition of *mental malpractice* because I was told to. I was assured that the words would be helpful at some point in my life when I needed God.

If there were ever a time I needed God, it would be now.

But I *hate* God.

And I hate my parents.

I wake up the next morning, remembering. London. Boarding school.

Girls' boarding school. Christian Science girls' boarding school. My face hurts, my head hurts, a reminder that I fell asleep sobbing into my pillow. We're moving. I will have to say good-bye to everyone I know and everything familiar. My parents' new house won't be *home*. At least Olivia and I will be at the same school. For Sherman, it's even worse: he will be alone at Fan Court. We'll see him only once a week after Sunday school.

But today, Saturday, there is an immediate pressure: I am spending the day with my friend Annie at the Lafayette Club, and I mustn't breathe a word about England to her. I want to scream it.

Until last night I had looked forward to swimming in the indoor pool and staying for lunch, but now, I dread it. Outside, it is cold and rainy, and that is just how I feel on the inside. When Annie and her parents pick me up in their red Pacer with the wide rear window, my mother exchanges totally phony, empty words with Mrs. Goan. As the car pulls away, and my mother waves good-bye, she makes meaningful eye contact with me that I can see even through the raindrops on the rear window. The lump in my throat aches.

In the ladies' locker room, Annie and I change into our bathing suits in separate cubicles, seventh-grade modest. We jump into the pool and swim and splash to warm up, then race to the deep end. Approaching the far wall, I feel like I'm taking the swimming test at camp, trying to tread water fully clothed, and my boots are filling with water. I panic. I begin to sob, and as I gasp for air, my mouth fills with the pool water and I start to choke, and then I'm coughing and the chlorinated water fills my nostrils and burns them.

Annie thinks I am struggling to swim, even though I'm pretty sure I am only working to fight back the tears. She grabs me at the elbow and pulls me to the side of the pool. "What's wrong? You okay?" Annie asks.

I take a deep breath and try to inhale evenly, but my chest stutters.

"Annie, I'm not supposed to tell you."

It is Saturday morning, and I am riding the train from Esher to Waterloo Station. I've been excused from Prep and am heading home for an unspecified weekend leave. Normally, I'm not allowed to do this, since I'm a full boarder, but Mom called the school for special permission. A surprise of some sort, Mrs. Williams said. Olivia isn't coming. She has to study for A levels.

I ride the Northern Line from Waterloo to our stop, Hampstead. I don't mind the walk from the tube station to Keats Grove. Sometimes I stop at the newsagent to get sweets, but not today. I turn down the High Street and take a left on Downshire Hill, past the church, and then fork right onto Keats Grove. The trees lining the street are beginning to sprout little green leaves.

I pull open the heavy wooden door with the broken hinge that leads to our small, enclosed garden. Dad's moped is blocking the footpath; I go around it. I walk up the front steps and bang on the door before I remember it's *my* house; I don't need to knock. I push the door open and walk in.

There, standing in the doorway, is Ham.

He gives me a huge hug, lifting me up in the air, my chest to his. It is great to see him, but I wonder if he realizes that, almost fifteen, I'm a bit old for this type of greeting.

Ham, or Bum, is tall and a bit stiff in his back. He has a ruddy face, with a long chin and a square jaw, a big beak of a nose, and thick reddish blond hair that he combs back with Jamaican bay rum. Ham is I guess what you'd call a favorite uncle, except that we're not really related. His mom is Dad's stepmother's sister. (I think.) He's also our only Christian Science relative. The last time I saw him was in New York, right before we moved to London. As a send-off gift, he gave me a red Panasonic Toot-a-Loop radio, which I still listen to clandestinely every night after lights-out. Sometimes a song will come on that makes me homesick for Minnesota, like Rod Stewart's "Sailing," and even though hearing it brings on tears, I don't let on to my roommates, who are listening to radios under their own pillows. Something about the longing feels good.

Standing behind Ham, inside the front hall, are Mom and Dad, smiling. Ham backs up slowly and turns the corner into the sitting room, and when he's about to bump into the sofa, he bends down with some effort, leans backward, picks something up, and hands it to me. It's a gift, wrapped in crumpled purple tissue paper. I open it and find a gray suede skirt, very hip. He always brings cool stuff.

"Thanks, Ham. I love it." I turn to Mom and Dad. "Where's Sherm?"

I can tell by their faces that he's not coming home. Mom explains that he has a rugby match. I'm disappointed.

"How long can you stay?" I ask Ham.

"How long can you sta-ay?" Ham repeats, and he hugs me again. I don't have a British accent, but sometimes what I say comes out more British than American.

"I'm just here for the afternoon," he says.

My mood sinks further.

"I'm en route to Geneva. My sister is in the hospital."

His sister's not a Scientist. Ham converted because of Dad.

Ham asks if I'd like to come with Mom and him to Camden Market, but it doesn't sound like much fun. I grimace.

"Afterward," Mom adds, "we can have tea at Fortnum & Mason."

"What about you, Dad?" I ask.

"Oh, gee, I need to do some work," he says, his hands clenching in his pockets. He seems satisfied with his plan, but there's no room in it for me. He is always working, praying for his patients, even when we come home for the weekend. Sometimes I wonder if it isn't just an excuse to close the door and be alone.

"All right," I say to Ham. There's nothing else to do.

The three of us walk down to the bottom of Hampstead Heath

and catch the 24, a double-decker, near the Royal Free Hospital. At Camden Market, Mom and Ham rummage through stacks of antique china. I'd rather be anywhere but here, but the depressing truth is that I have few options. None actually. I could still be at Claremont, which I pretty much hate, or 15 Keats Grove, where Dad's holed up in his study. I don't know a soul in Hampstead.

If Sherm were here, we could at least see a movie.

I wish I were back in Minnesota.

We take a black London taxi to Fortnum & Mason. In the tearoom, the three of us squeeze around a table for two.

"So, my dear," Ham says (it comes out *dee-eh*), "tell me. How's Claremont?"

"It's okay. I guess."

I look at Mom, who is eyeing me while she removes the cozy and pours the tea into the three cups. She's gotten really into the tea thing. Right now she's wondering if I'm going to be glum or up. She doesn't like glum, and I'll hear about it later if I'm not up. Several months after we moved here, feeling very depressed and homesick, I wrote a letter to my friend Diana back home. Word of it went from Diana to her mom to her grandma to my grandma to Mom, and then I got an earful.

"How can Dad successfully pursue his practice, and I my nursing, with this kind of...betrayal?"

I didn't answer her, but I felt that it was I, not Mom or Dad or the Church, that had been betrayed.

I'm supposed to be *up,* like, all the time, or at least fake it.

"Do you like your roommate?" Ham asks. He is spreading a scone with Devonshire cream.

"I have five."

"Five?"

I smile.

"Six of you in one room? Good God! Do you like your teachers?"

"They're all doddery old spinsters."

Ham grins, leaning his head back stiffly. He thinks I'm being funny, but I'm totally serious. He slaps the café table with his hand, spilling the tea into the saucers.

It feels good, I guess, to be in bed, in my own room at the top of this house. Sometimes at Claremont, after lights-out, I close my eyes and imagine that I am back in my canopied bed in Minnesota. I try to picture my grandma, and Ammie and Grandpa; Mimi, Diana, Mary. And James. I get so homesick that my chest tightens and my throat aches and I feel like I'm going to cry. But usually I don't. One time my housemother, Mrs. Williams, sat on the edge of my bed and rubbed my back after she caught me crying. She told me that God is my true Father and Mother; I am always in God's presence, and therefore always *at home.* I try to remind myself of this, and sometimes it works.

Despite what I said to Ham today, I don't hate England anymore, at least not all the time. In some ways it's easier being here than in Minnesota, although I would never admit that to my parents. Here, I never have awkward conversations about what Dad does. Everybody already *knows* what a Christian Science practitioner does. In fact, when Dad comes to Claremont for meetings—he sits on the social committee—he gets treated with a certain reverence. Not exactly guru status but almost VIP. Maybe it's because he's American, like Mary Baker Eddy. Or maybe it's because the sight of any man at Claremont, where Mr. Fox is the lone male teacher, elicits awe.

It's better now too, since I'm no longer the dumbest girl in my form. Commendations are posted on the notice board in the front hall at the bottom of the grand staircase for everyone to see. For the first four school terms, I didn't get a single commendation. This term I received five, as many as Alice Arnold, which shocked everyone, especially me: English Lit, Geography, Scripture, Math, and French. I had to run my finger from my name across the commendations list to make sure I wasn't seeing things.

But I remind myself what Jesus said: "I can of mine own self do nothing." I have to give credit where credit is due. I prayed. A lot. Every morning after breakfast, during Quiet Time (when we all sat in the common room to read the Lesson), I would highlight anything in *Science and Health* with the word *Mind* in it. And every night before lights-out, I would go into the Quiet Room (our school's own little version of a Christian Science Reading Room) and find something from *Science and Health* or the Bible, opening to a random page. Sometimes it was weird how relevant stuff was. Like, once:

> *If the student adheres strictly to the teachings of Christian Science and ventures not to break its rules, he cannot fail of success in healing.*
> —MARY BAKER EDDY, *Science and Health*

Another time, I found this:

> *Trust in the Lord with all thine heart; and lean not unto thine own understanding. In all thy ways acknowledge him, and he shall direct thy paths.*
> —PROVERBS 3:5, 6

Of course, sometimes you open to the Old Testament and get verse after verse of who begat whom.

I look at my alarm clock. It is after midnight. Unable to sleep, I tiptoe down to Dad's study to do some dialing. I never actually talk to anyone. Dad says long-distance charges are prohibitive. I just dial the long series of numbers, and wait for the familiar single ring tone, which is how I know I've reached the States. I let it ring a couple of times, and then I hang up. Sometimes when I call, it's morning in London and the middle of the night in Minnesota, and someone will pick up before I can replace the phone on the hook. I hear a voice—that of Grandma, or Mimi—and I feel a surge of excitement, knowing that I am *connected.*

Tonight, I dial James's number, James from seventh grade, and when the phone starts to ring, I can picture him, with his blond hair and blue eyes. If he picks up the phone, I'll want to say "Hi, James, it's me! Lucia!" I'll want to reminisce about the sock hop, or the breakfasts at Perkins. The phone keeps ringing, and I remember the thrill of him holding me at the waist to pull the tire swing way back.

It just keeps ringing. He must be out. I hang up, disappointed.

Next I dial Mimi. I count twenty rings. No answer. I wonder what she's doing tonight, Saturday. She—and everyone—must be at some party.

Finally, I dial Grandma, and she picks up after the first ring.

"Hyello."

I am caught off guard.

"Hyello?" Her lovely voice sounds so close, like I could almost squeeze her hand. *Grandma, it's me! Lucia!*

But then I remember: Dad will kill me. So I hang up. The adrenaline wanes, the excitement deflates. I am no longer connected.

It's Sunday morning. I don't want to go back to Claremont. I haven't done my homework, and I have three tests tomorrow.

Mom has already left for Hawthorne House to work her shift. She'll be gone all day, and I may or may not see her before I leave for the train. I wonder what she does, exactly, after she puts on her white nurse's uniform and heads out the door. I've never set foot in Hawthorne House, a redbrick building near the highest point in Hampstead. I wonder if people ever die there, or if they all get healed. I wonder if any of the guests are kids.

Dad and I are supposed to go to Sunday school because he teaches the sixth formers—Olivia's age-group—at Eleventh Church. I don't want to go there either. I hate Sunday school; it's so boring.

I hear Dad climb the stairs to the third floor, where Olivia's and my bedrooms both are, to see if I'm ready to go. I am still in bed.

"C'mon! Up'n at 'em, madam," he says, clapping his hands like he used to when I still lived at home.

I tell him I'm not feeling well. He tries to entice me with an offer of burgers at the Great American Disaster after church, but I don't take the bait.

"Dad, I feel gross," I say and groan.

He sits down at the edge of my bed and asks if I'd like him to do some protective work.

"Sure," I say and roll over. Protective work is praying.

We sit there in silence for a while, and I wonder if he can tell I'm faking it.

"Mrs. Eddy says, 'Every sort of sickness is error,—that is, sickness is loss of harmony,'" my father quotes.

I writhe, just a bit. "Dad, my stomach hurts."

"I want you to hold fast to that thought," he says, patting my leg. "Let's try to think about ways to find harmony in Life. *Harmony,* really, is another word for balance. Sickness is imbalance, discord."

"I feel like I'm going to barf," I say, just above a whisper.

"Hmm . . . maybe you *should* stay home this morning," he says.

I'm glad he can't see my face.

"But I do have to teach Sunday school. I'll be back in a couple of hours. I'll give it some good thought"—another term for praying—"and if you need anything, you can call Mom at Hawthorne House. She's not off until this evening, but I'm sure she can come home early, if need be."

After I hear Dad leave, I feel almost giddy at the success of my ploy. I have at least two hours to study and do my homework. But first, I go down to the second floor, to my parents' bedroom, and turn on the TV.

I fall asleep in my parents' bed and don't wake up until I hear Dad.

"Loosh?" he hollers from the front door.

Oh no. I look at the clock on the bedside table. I've been asleep for almost three hours.

"Lucia?"

"I'm in here," I yell back. "I'm in your room."

I haven't done my homework or studied for my tests. I can't go back to Claremont.

"How are you doing?" Dad says and sits down on the end of the bed. "Are you feeling any better?"

"Not really. My stomach hurts." I wince and close my eyes. What am I going to do?

I think back to last December in Egypt. Mom got sick. *Really* sick. We had to stay in Luxor an extra day—Christmas Day—and Sherman, Olivia, and I waited, frightened and stunned, in an adjoining room while Mom and Dad prayed. (Or Dad prayed; Mom couldn't.) Nobody in our family had ever been sick before, not really. From our side of the thin wall, all we could hear was groaning. Mom shivered with such intensity that the sound of the accompanying moans undulated like an old woman's wails, even from where we were in our room. We sat on the beds, or stood at the window or with one ear to the wall. We could make out only that Mom was at times freezing and then, almost immediately, too hot. The complete lack of communication from Dad, except for when he asked for our blankets, heightened our fear.

Two of us would walk down to the hotel restaurant to order grilled chicken, bread, and Cokes, while the other remained in the room. As scary as it was to be holed up in the hotel room, leaving it was even more frightening.

The only other sound we heard was the haunting, periodic call to worship from the nearby mosque, which made us feel all the more displaced and isolated. As the hours slowly crept, our fear grew to terror. Was Mom getting worse? How long would this go on?

After a day and a half, we decided that Olivia should talk to Dad. She knocked gently on the door, and eventually he opened it, barely.

"Would it be okay—if maybe—we called a doctor?" Olivia asked tentatively.

"No," Dad said vehemently, clenching his teeth, the door wedged open just enough to show the middle third of his face. "No. Your mom is going to be fine."

He knew from our faces that we doubted him.

"Mom needs each of us to do our part," he said.

"Please, Dad?" we said, unified. He lowered his gaze and shook his head no.

"Besides," he said, "look where we are. Luxor isn't London. I'm not sure we'd want to go to a hospital here anyway, even if we weren't Scientists."

"Oh, Heff," Mom moaned again from the bed, "that's . . . too much . . . light."

Dad closed the door, and we faced one another. I wished we could have at least gotten a glimpse of our mom. With no other options, we resolved through tears to sing some hymns, the Mary Baker Eddy ones.

Shepherd, show me how to go
O'er the hillside steep,
How to gather, how to sow,—
How to feed Thy sheep;
I will listen for Thy voice,
Lest my footsteps stray;
I will follow and rejoice
All the rugged way.

Amazingly, Mom got better. On our fourth morning in Luxor, she emerged from their room thinner and famished but otherwise fine, and we resumed our tour of Egypt. I more or less forgot about the healing until March, when Mom wrote me a letter to say she'd given a testimony about it at church.

"Uuugh," I say to my dad.

I pull the covers around me. I shiver—just a bit—tensing the muscles in my rib cage and squeezing my elbows into my sides. I wonder: If Mom had gotten sick here in London, instead of in Luxor, would Dad have brought her to a hospital? I open my eyes enough to see that Dad's eyes are closed, and his head is bobbing. He does this sometimes when he is deep in prayer.

If I play this right, maybe I can stay home one more night. Go back to Claremont late.

"Dad, would you get me another blanket?" I ask. "I'm chilled."

He goes to Sherman's room, which is next to theirs, pulls the comforter off the bed, and brings it to me. I feel sort of bad, how he's spreading it out so gently, tucking it in around the sides to make a contour of my shivering, curled-up body.

"Thanks, Dad," I say and roll over again. He leaves the room.

I lie there, feeling fine, almost baffled at my brilliance, and wonder how long I should wait before I call him in again. I decide thirty-five minutes.

Thirty-five minutes is a very long time to lie in bed feeling totally okay with nothing to do: I can't watch television (even if there *were* something good on, but this is the BBC, not American TV, which is why I fell asleep in the first place); I can't study, because my books are upstairs. All I can do is lie here, thinking about Dad in the next room, at his desk, doing his protective work for me. *Is he scared? Does he worry that, unlike in Luxor, maybe this time he won't be effective?* I stare at the alarm clock on his bedside table, willing the hands to move faster. My friends at Claremont are probably just leaving the dining hall.

I make it to twenty-five minutes.

"Da-ad!" I yell sort of weakly, suggesting great pain.

He comes in right away.

"It's not getting...better," I moan.

Together we recite the Scientific Statement of Being: "There is no life, truth, intelligence, nor substance in matter..."

And then the Beatitudes: "Blessed are the meek: for they shall inherit the earth..."

Somehow, I don't think this is what Jesus had in mind. I know that what I'm doing is wrong. It's hard to believe my father is falling for it. But I can't dwell on it too much while he's in the room with me, or I might crack a smile. Instead, I shiver again, just slightly, and ask if he wouldn't mind closing the window.

This is an incredible waste of time, lying in my parents' bed all afternoon, when I know I have to study for my tests. I get up twice to "try" to use the loo, semi-buckled over, wrapped in Sherman's comforter.

I hear the front door open downstairs and realize that Mom has come home early. When I hear my parents whispering in Dad's study, I start to feel guilty. Dad is worried enough that he called Mom home. The initial giddiness and subsequent boredom of my ruse have vanished. Now there's a fleeting but not altogether unpleasant surprise at their concern, which is quickly replaced by the visceral fear of being found out.

My parents' room is very warm. The radiator hisses because earlier I told Dad I was *freezing* and asked him to open the valve. Now I am roasting. When Mom comes in and feels my forehead, it is totally sweaty. She asks if I'd like something to eat, chicken broth or buttered toast. The buttered toast sounds delicious—I'm starving—but I say no, I'm nauseous, so I don't blow my cover.

I wonder if Mom offers chicken broth and buttered toast to Hawthorne House's guests, or patients, or clients—or whatever they call them. Does she press a cool, damp cloth to someone's feverish forehead? Wouldn't that gesture of kindness—an acknowledgment of the existence of fever—be forbidden?

After another hour, it is time to execute a beautiful, gradual healing. It takes about forty-five minutes, two full intervals of my parents' checking in on me. I time it perfectly so that I can miss my train, stay the night, and delay returning to Claremont. Mom lets me sleep in and study for my tests in the morning, and makes me Swedish pancakes, before riding the train with me all the way back to Claremont.

GOD. *The great I AM; the all-knowing, all-seeing, all-acting, all-wise, all-loving, and eternal; Principle; Mind; Soul; Spirit; Life; Truth; Love; all substance; intelligence.*
—MARY BAKER EDDY, *Science and Health,* Glossary

Susie and I are in the dorm; everyone else has gone down to dinner. I am changing out of my school uniform, and she is lolling on her bed next to mine. The bell announcing dinner rang almost ten minutes ago. Susie will miss the headmistress's grace, and her penalty may be kitchen duty, but she doesn't care. She's more of a rule breaker than I am. During Quiet Time in the morning, when we are supposed to be reading a section of the Bible Lesson, she fills out magazine questionnaires about personality type, carnal knowledge, and boyfriends, which she keeps folded up in the pages of her *Science and Health.* On Saturday afternoons, when we walk along Esher High Street, she wears thick black Mary Quant eyeliner and tight jeans and smokes cigarettes with equanimity, while I am nervously on the lookout for teachers.

"What's the occasion?" she asks, and I shrug my shoulders, but I'm not feeling as casual as the gesture implies.

Mrs. Williams found me this afternoon in the library to say that Mum was coming to take me out for dinner, which is odd. It's a school night. And it's not my birthday—not that *that* would justify special dispensation at Claremont; Mary Baker Eddy says, "Man in Science is neither young nor old. He has neither birth nor death," so birthdays are downplayed. What is most unsettling is the fact that Mrs. Williams didn't say anything about Dad coming. Mom and Dad never come to see me separately. And they never visit without a clear purpose.

I wait alone in the marble entrance hall, and my mind keeps returning to the reason for Mom's visit. As I sit on my hands on the windowsill, I assume nothing good. *It's Dad. Maybe he's sick. Or maybe they're getting divorced.* It's hard to picture either possibility, because I never see Mom and Dad fighting, and Dad never gets sick.

Of course, I hardly see them, period, so how would I know? Maybe he *is* sick.

Then, I correct myself: *Am I going to allow mortal mind to whisper to me of evil?*

I think of a passage in *Science and Health*: "When the illusion of sickness or sin tempts you, cling steadfastly to God and His idea."

I tell myself that in God's kingdom, there can be no disease (dis-ease). There is only perfection.

Right at six-thirty, Mom drives up in her Volkswagen Golf, and when I descend the school's majestic front steps, she is out of the car, enveloping me with a big hug. Her embrace feels like a warning, but it reveals nothing right away. Our conversation during the short drive to the restaurant is nonspecific. Over fish and chips at the pub, Mom asks me about school, and whether the girls in our dorm are getting along better. She says that Dad's sorry he couldn't come; he's working. Sherman won his rugby match yesterday. Olivia called the other day and likes Sarah Lawrence College. Whenever there is a lull in the conversation, Mom fills the void with a question about my studies.

For dessert, we order trifle, with two spoons, and after a few bites, she puts her spoon down.

"There is something I need to tell you."

My stomach knots up. Worry is all over her face.

"Aunt Mary called this morning."

As my mother struggles to find the words for whatever it is she must tell me, my mind races ahead: *Something's happened to Grandma, or Aunt Kay, or one of my uncles. Or Grandpa or Ammie.*

"It's about your friend James," she says softly.

For some reason, before my mother utters another word, my face flushes with emotion. I don't know if it's fear, anger, dread, or betrayal. My mother is on the verge of tears.

"I—he—" Mom attempts, looking down in her lap and then again up at me. "Aunt Mary called to tell me that—he—is dead." Mom shakes her head, correcting herself. "He's passed on, Lucia."

"What?"

I shake my head. James is fifteen, like me.

I have letters from him. I see the handwriting—the *young* handwriting and misspelled words—of the cards he has sent me. I still picture him twelve, the age we were when we first met, when he pulled me back, back, back on the tire swing, and let go.

Lowering her voice, my mother says that he has taken his own life.

I cannot breathe.

I feel like I've been pinned against the back of the booth.

Mom reaches for my hand, but I pull it back.

"What?" I say. I am angry. I am confused.

We sit there in silence.

"What?" I say again.

The pub feels too small, the wood-paneled walls too close. Mom says nothing. I want information, but she gives me none. She can't—or won't—bring herself to tell me anything more.

"Lucia, what we have to remember," she finally says, now grabbing my hand against my will, "and really hold on to, is what Mary Baker Eddy tells us about death: 'The belief in sin and death is destroyed by the law of God, which is the law of Life instead of death, of harmony instead of discord, of Spirit instead of the flesh.'"

Mom drops me off after dinner, and Susie is waiting for me. She can see that I have been crying, but when she asks me what's wrong, what happened at dinner with Mum, I don't feel sadness, or grief. I feel nothing, as in no sensation. In my mind, I hear, *there is no sensation in matter,* and I know it's from *Science and Health* and/or Sunday school. Monotone, I tell Susie that James killed himself. Her eyes grow wide and her face turns white, and all of a sudden she is sobbing, and clutching me, horrified, and I'm hugging her back, but everything seems strangely backward.

* * *

March 1978

Dear Ammie,

By the time you receive this letter, you will be back from Arlington.

I just want to say I am sorry about Grandpa. I wish I could be there with you and everyone else. I loved Grandpa. (Of course, I still do!) I still do! I always will! He was sweet and funny, and I love how his eyes always cried when he laughed. I remember the time he gave me $5 when I got a pixie cut that I hated because it made me look like a boy. He told me I could keep the money if I kept the pixie cut. He knew that would cheer me up!

I will always think of the purple jock strap story (remember that weird man at the hotel at Disney Land?!!) and everything else that happened on the granddaughters' trip. Not many grandpas take seven granddaughters to Disney Land, but I think he liked being outnumbered like that, don't you?

I hope I can see you soon, and if you get lonely — Call me! (I can't call you because it's too expensive.) Please come visit us in London! I miss you. so much.

Love,
Lucia

It is eleven-thirty at night. I'm down the hall in the Quiet Room, because I can't sleep. I'm uneasy about what I should say in this condolence letter, but I think what I wrote probably turned out okay. I take the Liquid Paper from my pencil box and dab the crossed-out words until they disappear. I crossed out "so much" because I don't want Ammie to worry about me. And I crossed out "and if you get lonely" because mentioning it might make her feel even worse. She and Grandpa were married for forty years, and now she'll be alone.

I fold the aerogram into thirds, then lick the adhesive edges and seal it up. I write Ammie's name and address on the front. I have to remind myself not to write "Gen. and Mrs. H. Terry Morrison." That Grandpa could be—is—dead doesn't seem possible.

The last time I saw Grandpa was three months ago, when we flew to Minnesota for Christmas. (But first we visited boarding schools on the East Coast because, at the end of this year, we are moving. Another of Mom and Dad's classic out-of-the-blue announcements. They said we were "moving back," and I brightened for about a millisecond, imagining a return to our old house, our old life. But we are moving to New Jersey. *New Jersey?*)

We were at Ammie and Grandpa's for Christmas dinner. After the meal Grandpa tried to get up and sort of stumbled, and reached for the sideboard to steady himself. I thought he was going to fall down, but Ammie was right there beside him. I didn't know he was sick (Mom and Dad never told me), but I remember feeling scared that something bigger was going on than just a misstep.

Last night Mom and Dad called me from Hampstead to say that Grandpa had passed on, and they were flying to Minnesota and would be back in a week. Dad told me I shouldn't be sad: *Grandpa's passing wasn't unexpected. He lived a happy, long life.*

But it was unexpected for me! I didn't even really know he was sick. I only found out that Grandpa wasn't well because Ammie mentioned it in a letter. And I *am* sad. How could I not be? I'll never see him again.

Mostly, I'm angry that I can't go back for the funeral. Mom and Dad said it's too expensive, and Sherman and I would miss too much school. But *they're* going. It's not our fault we live here, so far away; it's *theirs*. They should bring us. The other grandchildren—all twenty-one of them—are going to be at the service, and then everyone is flying to Washington, D.C., for the burial at Arlington cemetery.

First James. Now Grandpa.

Dad reminded me what Mary Baker Eddy said about death: "'Death is but a mortal illusion, for to the real man and the real universe there is no death-process.'"

In some ways, death *does* feel like an illusion. From here, being so far away, it's easy to think that James and Grandpa are still alive. Even the letters from Mimi and Mary, which described James's memorial service, seem unreal. They are not the letters I choose to reread. James's are.

I don't know how Sherman's taking the news about Grandpa. I haven't talked to him, and I won't see him until Sunday school. I can't call him because I don't have coins for the pay phone, and I can't reverse the charges like I do when I call Mom and Dad. Either Sherman is feeling really lonely or else he's not feeling much at all. Like me.

*   *   *

One Tuesday morning, my roommates and I head down to the common room for Quiet Time like we always do before school, to find that Mr. and Mrs. Williams's door is closed. The door to their quarters is always open, except on their day off, which is Monday. Mrs. Williams always proctors Quiet Time, but today, the matron, Mrs. Mills, does.

"Where's Mrs. Williams?" we all ask. "Why is their door closed?"

Mrs. Mills looks up from her *Science and Health,* then down at her plump hands. She purses her lips and in her Welsh accent says that the Williamses are taking a brief leave.

"Why?" we ask. "Where are they going?"

"They're not going anywhere. But we ought to be mindful of their needs. And respectful of their privacy. We should try to keep the noise to a minimum."

We all look at one another, puzzled.

Over the next few days, the Williamses' door remains shut, and rumors fly. Mrs. Williams is sick. Mr. Williams is sick. Their daughter who lives in Australia is sick. They've been terminated.

The only rumor we know to be false is that they've been terminated. Mrs. Williams is a good housemother, if a bit stern, balancing order, discipline, humor, and kindness. When I first arrived at Claremont, she terrified me. She was solemn and formal, and I never saw her smile. Eventually, I came to see that her smile is a subtle, British sort, which doesn't raise the edges of her mouth or make her eyes twinkle but pulls her chin down toward her neck and makes her gaunt cheeks sink deeper. She discreetly parcels out affection to those who need it most, with a pat on the back during lights-out or an extra biscuit at teatime. If she delivers the post in the morning, and someone's got a letter from a chap, Mrs. Williams's chin goes down, and her eyebrows go up, and she takes great pleasure in keeping everyone in suspense. On the rare occasion that she laughs openly, her chuckle feels worth waiting for.

Mr. Williams isn't paid to be a houseparent, and he has no duties per se; he is our housefather by marriage. A dapper gentleman, balding with a silver mustache, he wears three-piece suits and looks as though he might smoke a pipe, or at least hold one, were it not for Christian Science. If Mrs. Williams evokes stern, formal propriety most of the time, Mr. Williams is jovial and charming always, adored by everyone. One Saturday early on, when I was feeling particularly homesick, he invited me to bring a friend for high tea at his favorite spot in Esher. I felt like a beloved granddaughter.

After several days of official silence and collective speculation, the mood among the boarders is somber, worry-laden. We still have not seen Mr. and Mrs. Williams, and nobody has told us anything. One morning during Quiet Time, while Mrs. Mills sits in one corner of the common room reading from her *Science and Health,* a lower-fifth former scribbles something on a piece of paper and passes it to another girl, who is sitting next to her. She reads it and passes it to Susie, who passes it to me.

It's Mr. Williams and it's serious.

After Quiet Time we learn from the lower-fifth former that in the middle of the night she woke up hungry, so she snuck down to the kitchen that we use for afternoon tea and last laps. There, she found Mrs. Williams alone at the small table, drinking a cup of hot milk and Horlicks. Mrs. Williams told her that Mr. Williams was working out a problem in Science and that their daughter was on her way home to lend support.

She says Mrs. Williams looks awful.

Later in the day, Mary Williams arrives by taxi while we are having our tea, and she goes directly into her parents' quarters and shuts the door.

The next morning, an ambulance arrives at the school, and a stretcher is carried by two men up the front steps and the grand staircase and wheeled into the Williamses' quarters. Several of us are milling about nearby, and Mrs. Mills emerges from her office and tells us to go to our rooms. Minutes later, peering out the windows, we see a very old-looking, motionless Mr. Williams being transferred to the ambulance. Mrs. Williams disappears in the ambulance with him, and Mary follows behind in her parents' car.

For the rest of the day, we speculate more. We conclude that Mr. Williams must have had a stroke, or maybe a heart attack, because one day he was fine, and the next he wasn't. We wonder aloud where the ambulance has taken him: to a hospital? or maybe Hawthorne House? Nobody says so, but we are all wondering if we will see him again. I find myself thinking about Grandpa. For the first time his death feels very real, and immediate, as though it happened today, here. I cry on and off all afternoon.

At dinner that night, the headmistress, Miss Doran, says grace as usual.

"Good evening, girls," Miss Doran says. "Before we sit down to our meal, I know that Mr. Williams is on everyone's mind. Mrs. Williams has asked me to assure you that he is doing well, and that he is in good care. We can keep the Williamses in our prayers, and hold fast to our understanding of man's perfection..."

I look around the dining room and see that several other girls are crying. "...Mrs. Eddy states in *Science and Health* that 'Divine Love always has met and always will meet every human need.' But do you know what she says next? 'It is not well to imagine that Jesus demonstrated the divine power to heal only for a select number or for a limited period of time, since to all mankind and in every hour, divine Love supplies all good.'

"And now, shall we bow our heads? For what we are about to receive, may the Lord make us truly thankful."

"Amen," we all say.

"Please be seated."

I pick at my dinner and, afterward, go back to the dorm and call home, reversing the charges. Mom answers the phone. I want to know if Mr. Williams is at Hawthorne House.

"Lucia, I can't tell you that."

"I want to know if he's okay," I demand.

"I can't tell you where he is, but I can tell you—and you know this—that Mr. Williams is the perfect reflection of God. He cannot be sick."

"Is he going to get better? Did he have a stroke?" I ask this frantically, angrily, not knowing exactly what a stroke is but understanding fully that such a question will not be answered. After a long silence, Mom replies with a familiar Sunday school question:

"Lucia," she says, "are sin, disease, and death real?"

"Mom! Stop!" I scream.

"Lucia?" The louder I am, the quieter she is.

I am sobbing now.

"Would you like to speak to Dad?" she asks calmly.

"No!"

She waits silently. She is probably praying.

"Mom: James is *dead*! Grandpa is *dead*! Mr. Williams is *sick*."

"Mrs. Eddy says..." My mother pauses, perhaps searching for the exact quote. "'Sin, disease, and death have no foundations in Truth.'"

"Mom, I have to go."

Two days later, Miss Doran comes to the common room for our Quiet Time—a first. I know, in my bones, why she is here. We stand when she enters the room.

"Good morning, everyone." Her voice is lower than usual.

"Good morning, Miss Doran," we say in unison.

"Please, be seated. Last evening, Mr. Williams passed on. For the next several days, Mrs. Williams will not be working in the capacity of housemother, but if you see her, you may offer her some kind words. In the meantime, Mrs. Mills will carry on with house-parenting duties."

Miss Doran leaves the common room.

There is no memorial service. After several days Mrs. Williams is back at work. I don't know what to say to her, so I say nothing. Death is not an illusion. It is real.

SPRING 1978
BACK IN THE STATES

My parents' new home is a two-hundred-year-old farmhouse in Hopewell, New Jersey, the next town over from Princeton, where there is a Christian Science care facility called Tenacre Foundation. There, Mom plans to continue the nurse's training that she started at Hawthorne House, and I suppose Dad's practice will have a ready supply of patients. He will also commute to Manhattan twice a week to share an office close to Grand Central Terminal with some other practitioners.

I don't know why they have decided to move again, and why

now; whether happiness—or even the exchange rate, which Dad was always checking in the *Financial Times*—has anything to do with it. If they've been less than satisfied with our schooling, they've never let on. Maybe they want to be closer to "home" but not too close?

Sherman and I finish the school year in England before joining them; Sherman enrolls in Princeton Day School, which cannot accommodate me in their eleventh-grade class. So I am sent to the Emma Willard School, a girls' boarding school in upstate New York. I don't ask why Sherman and I are being allowed to attend non–Christian Science schools. The decision feels to me like a stroke of luck.

JANUARY 1979
EMMA WILLARD SCHOOL

"I'm having trouble seeing the blackboard," I say to my mother during one of our usual Sunday evening checking-in telephone calls. I'm midway through my first year at Emma Willard.

"Do you want to talk to Dad?" Mom asks. It is a quick, natural assumption for her, but that is not why I am calling.

"No," I say cautiously. I swallow hard. My mouth is suddenly dry. "I think maybe I should go to an eye doctor."

There is silence at the other end of the line. I realize I am holding my breath.

I can tell that my mom's hand is covering the mouthpiece of the phone. There is mumbling, then my mother hands the telephone to my father. My resolve weakens a bit. I'm not sure I can do this.

"Hi, Loosh," Dad says sweetly. "What's up?"

"Well, I'm having trouble seeing the board during math class. My teacher thinks maybe I need glasses. And last week, when I took the SATs, I got a really bad headache. After the exam, everything was totally blurry. So . . . I thought I'd make an appointment with an eye doctor."

I thought I'd . . . For a brief moment this casually mentioned plan convinces me that Dad will view it as reasonable. But there is another long silence.

I sit down on the wooden bench in the phone booth. I'm glad I didn't bring this up face-to-face during the Christmas break. The two-hundred-mile distance between school and home is a comfort.

"Don't you want to give Science a chance?" my dad asks tenderly. He isn't angry. He sounds hurt, and I realize I have disappointed him. I feel sort of bad that I am letting him down, but not bad enough to give in. I *am* getting headaches, and the equations on the blackboard *are* fuzzy. But it is also true—and I keep this to myself—that I have always secretly wanted glasses. My best friend in fourth grade had glasses, and braces, and a dad who worked at General Mills, and I coveted all three. And now maybe I actually need them.

"I've already tried praying about it," I say to my father. This is a lie.

"Well, why don't you give it another shot?" he asks, as though I have double-faulted on the tennis court. "Do you know what Mrs. Eddy says about vision?"

I can picture the framed print of an ageless Mrs. Eddy, a Victorian New England Everygrandmother, on the wall of my father's study, in three-quarter view, with a somber expression and deep-set brown eyes gazing—not squinting—into the distance.

"She says that eyes are 'spiritual discernment,—not material but mental.' If you think about your vision as a God-given ability to see Truth, and if you *focus* on seeing that perfection in everything, then you will understand that clarity must come from your thoughts... not from a pair of glasses. Perhaps it's your mental outlook that needs correction."

My father says this delicately, as I imagine he might if he were talking to one of his patients. I concede to myself that he may have a point, and yet I am unswayed.

"I *have* prayed," I repeat, "the board's still blurry. And choosing Christian Science," I remind him, "is up to the individual."

"You haven't really tried," he says firmly, just above a whisper.

"Yes, I *have*."

"Not really," he coaxes.

"I just think maybe I should get glasses," I say, holding my ground.

There is a long pause now.

"What do you want to do *that* for?" he blurts out.

"So that I can read without squinting. So that I don't get headaches." I brace myself. I know that mentioning these imperfections is taboo.

"You're not getting headaches!" he spits out contemptuously, as though the very possibility is ridiculous. I won't tell him that the headaches are tolerable.

"You're just giving in to prevailing erroneous thought!"

His accusation feels disproportionate. It's not like I've been smoking pot, or otherwise caving to peer pressure.

"No, I'm not, Dad," I say, like I'm bored. But my heart is pounding. I don't want him to know that his anger is affecting me.

"Now it's glasses, but next it will be aspirin. And then? Are you going to start taking pills every time you have a problem?"

I think back to England two years before. I was on my way home from Claremont for the weekend, and I stopped at the pharmacy on Hampstead's High Street and bought a bottle of aspirin, out of curiosity. Heading down the hill toward home, I popped two tablets in my mouth, without water, and nearly gagged on the bitter, powdery taste that stuck tenaciously to the back of my tongue. And then I waited for something mysterious to happen. It didn't. I am quite sure—even if Dad isn't—that it is highly unlikely I will take aspirin again anytime soon.

"No, I just think I need glasses. That's all," I say, still acting calm, although below the surface I am seething.

"Well, if that's what you want, go right ahead. But don't expect me to pay for the doctor, or the glasses!"

"What?" I say, outraged. "How else will I pay for them?"

"Don't you realize that your going to a doctor is like stabbing me in the back? Do you have any regard for my practice? For the movement? For what I'm dedicating my life to?"

My father's voice is booming down the phone now. Maybe he's right, that I don't have any regard for his practice—but is that indifference such a crime? My pending SAT results feel relevant, so does last night's dance at Deerfield; and my essay on the Federalist Papers—which isn't finished but has to be turned in tomorrow morning—feels all too relevant.

"It's that school, isn't it? It's poisoning your thoughts!" my father hisses, and I snort reflexively, which just makes him angrier. "You should have stayed at Claremont!"

My father slams the phone down, and I hear the click of the receiver, then a dial tone. He has hung up on Olivia before, but never on me. I remain in the phone booth, holding the handset. I realize I am shaking. I feel certain that I am right and my father is wrong, so why am I crying? I gently return the handset to its cradle and debate whether to call him back. Reversing the charges, which is how I always call home, feels for the first time demeaning to me. Should I apologize? Have I actually done anything that requires an apology? And his last words sting: that he wishes I were still in England feels more like his desire for greater distance than it does concern for my spiritual well-being.

While I am standing there shaking, unable to decide on a course of action, the phone rings.

I answer it and hear my mother's voice.

"Your father is very upset," she says evenly. I can't read much in her tone.

"I'm not doing this to upset him, Mom. I just think I should go to an eye doctor."

"Well, when you're old enough to be making this decision, you can go to all the doctors you like," she says, turning indignant, "but for the time being, I think we deserve some support and respect from you."

I am stunned. For years, my parents have said that faith is a personal choice. Now, I'm trying to choose my path, and they're setting up roadblocks.

"So, what do I do in the meantime, go blind?" I ask, instantly regretting the *go blind* part. But my mother doesn't react to it.

"Do you realize that people depend on your father? Do you realize that he has some very serious cases right now? The last thing he needs is to have you calling him and getting him upset. He has phone calls at all hours of the day and night from patients who count on him!"

This is more information than I've ever gotten about my father's practice. The last time I was home, I heard, more than once, his end of a phone conversation with a patient.

"Elise, Elise, *Elise!*" I would hear my father plead, and then, exasperated, he'd say, "You are giving in to mortal mind! Mrs. Eddy says..."

"If you'd stop thinking about yourself for once," my mother goes on, "and show a little consideration for your father—"

"Mom, it's about a stupid, lousy pair of glasses," I say. I am both emboldened and fatigued by my mother's imposition of guilt, but while I say it's about stupid glasses, I know it's about who I am, and who I am not. It's a battle for my well-being. We're talking about my eyes right now, but we might just as well be talking, theoretically, about my appendix.

If my teacher thinks I need glasses, who are my parents to say I don't?

"Fine," she says. "Pay for them out of your allowance."

"Fine," I reply, and we exchange terse good-byes.

Two days later, I sign out from the dorm and walk apprehensively several blocks from campus to an ophthalmologist's office that I have found in the yellow pages. I'm worried, for starters, that I won't know the proper way to *be* in a doctor's office. I'm nervous too that I might not have enough cash to pay for the appointment. And what if the doctor hurts me? The only other time I remember going to a doctor's office was when we were living in London, and we were legally required to obtain smallpox vaccinations before our trip to Egypt. There was no exemption for Christian Scientists. After watching the needle slide into my arm, and feeling the sting, burn, and charley-horse ache, the next thing I knew I was flat-out on my back on the cold linoleum floor, the doctor on one side of me, taking my pulse, and my father on the other side of me, eyes closed, deep in prayer. I had no idea where I was, but I had a fuzzy sense of déjà vu.

If I faint again, I will be three for three, if you count the incident at Uncle Jack's when I was twelve.

Most of all, though, I'm afraid that, in the end, the doctor will say there is nothing wrong with my eyes, and I will have to report back home sheepishly that the whole episode was a waste. My father will have been right, and I will have been wrong.

After a quick and pain-free examination, the kind doctor removes his own glasses, folds them, and stuffs them into his shirt pocket. "Well, my dear, you are astigmatic in both eyes."

My heart is in my throat; I'm clearly agitated. The diagnosis sounds life-threatening to me. But the doctor pats my shoulder comfortingly and laughs warmly at my nerves.

"It's nothing serious," he tells me, shaking his head. "Your corneas are a little bit warped, is all. You'll need glasses."

The diagnosis is a relief: my blurry vision and headaches are real. And, fortunately, I have enough cash to pay him. He sends me on my way with a scribbled slip of paper: my first prescription.

A few weeks later, I ride the train home for a long weekend. Normally this is a beautiful, soothing trip south along the Hudson River. But I am nervous about seeing my father. We have not spoken since he hung up on me, and I worry that he will redouble his criticism of my position on eyeglasses. Or maybe he won't even meet me.

But he is waiting for me under the clock at Grand Central, and I feel relieved. My father's hug doesn't feel quite as robust as usual. Together we head over to Penn Station, where we board

New Jersey Transit to ride out to Princeton Junction. The subject of eyeglasses doesn't come up, but it is dangling there, between us.

Sherman and Mom meet us at Princeton Junction, and we all go to the Great Wall in Princeton for dinner. Sherman looks at me across the table in utter disbelief: Can it be that Lucia has done something...wrong?...controversial? Perfect Lucia? I've always been something of a rule-following goody-goody in his eyes. I can tell he knows about the whole battle—he probably overheard the phone call that Sunday evening—but he says nothing. The four of us eat our food in relative silence.

Later that night, Mom and Dad have turned in and Sherman and I are watching TV. "So," he asks, "did you get glasses?"

"No," I say, "but I have a prescription."

"Man, was Dad on a tirade after your call. You sure it was worth it?"

The next day, Mom and I go shopping at the mall. We look at shoes. She buys me a sweater. Over donuts, we talk about school. As we're heading back to the parking lot, my mother stops in front of the display window at an optician's shop.

"Do you need a pair?" she asks.

I nod. I have the prescription in my wallet. I follow her into the store, and together we look at several frames. One pair, tortoiseshell, are the nicest ones I try, and more expensive than I can afford. Even if I were to set aside my entire allowance each week, I would have to save up for a long time to buy them.

"They look good on you," Mom says, pulling a credit card from her purse.

Afterward we find the car in the parking lot. My mother puts the key in the ignition but doesn't start the car. She turns to me.

"Christian Science works," she says.

I look out the passenger window. I don't really care if it works. It's not for me.

"And your father is very good at what he does."

I have to resist the urge to roll my eyes. I don't know exactly why I'm so angry, so skeptical. The truth is, in my three years at Claremont, nobody ever really got sick or injured, aside from a brief bout of flu, or a cold. That's an amazing record for any school. But I feel like Christian Science is being crammed down my throat.

"Christian Science has proven itself to your father and me over and over again. That is *why* we are devoting our lives to it. But your faith has never been tested, Lucia, at least not until now. You could have turned to the Bible and *Science and Health* and seen for yourself the efficacy of *C.S.*"

I remain silent.

"If only you'd given it a chance. Well," she adds lightly, "all in good time. You'll come around."

I'm not sure what to make of my Eyeglasses Rebellion, but I decide, out of respect for my dad, not to wear my glasses at home. I am the victor, I suppose, but my father and I are adversaries now, and his goal is to win both the contest and me back to his side, while Mom is the cheerleader who tends to favor the underdog.

part two

*O*n *December 24, 1985,* we gather in Hopewell for what we assume will be our traditional holiday celebration. I am a year out of college, a graduate of Brown University, working in Manhattan at Condé Nast, in the New York office of German *Vogue.* Sherman is a senior at Columbia. Olivia is a newlywed; she and her husband got married in March, so this will be our first Christmas as a family of six. Olivia and Terry met shortly after she moved to Minneapolis, post-college. We all took an immediate liking to him. A Native American who grew up on Pine Ridge Reservation in South Dakota, Terry is soft-spoken, bright, and a quick wit. They now live in Cambridge, Massachusetts, where Terry is pursuing a master's degree at Harvard and Olivia is a social worker.

Sherman and I meet at Penn Station and take the train to Princeton Junction. To our slightly bemused pleasure, our father is waiting for us. Normally it is our mother who meets trains. Dad sports a puffy down parka over a tweed jacket, bow tie, gray flannels, and loafers; he could pass for a tenured Princeton professor. True to his breeding, he grabs my duffel bag. It is filled with the gifts I have bought for everyone, for the first time with my own money. Sherman's duffel bag is stuffed with dirty clothes. During the twenty-minute drive home, we talk about his final exams and my job. Nothing about my father's behavior, aside from his meeting us at the train, seems out of the ordinary.

As we turn in to my parents' drive and approach the old farmhouse, slowing down for the ruts in the gravel road, I can almost smell the season's fragrances: the sweet, redolent spice of the cookies my mother has no doubt been baking all week, the piney Christmas tree, the smoke of the wood-burning stove. But I sense right away that something is amiss. There are no colorful lights on the spruce trees flanking the front door. Entering the kitchen, I notice piles of unopened mail on the counters. An undefined queasiness settles over and around me, as though all of the oxygen has left the house and I am breathing fundamentally altered air. There is no waft of seasonal aromas, no Ray Conniff Singers crooning their carols through the stereo speakers.

Sherman and I put our bags down and follow Dad into the Bird Room. It is Mom's masterpiece: an octagonal addition to the two-hundred-year-old house, with exposed wooden beams that meet at a central apex, lots of windows, and hand-painted bird wallpaper from France. Olivia, Terry, and Mom are all sitting at one end of the dining room table.

Olivia and Terry get up to greet us. My sister's embrace doesn't feel quite right. I glance over at Mom.

"Merry Christmas, dear," she says, without standing.

She never calls me "dear."

Our arrival has interrupted something. I look again at Mom, who is always beautifully put together. I recall how people used to say that my parents looked like Angie Dickinson and Burt Bacharach. Now, she is dressed in a bathrobe and slippers, even though it is five-thirty in the evening. Gray roots betray her blonded hair, and she is wearing a thick daub of makeup. I think back to my teen years. "If I can see it, it's too much," she used to say. Under the blush, I can see that my mother's skin is ashen.

What is going on here?

My eyes slowly stray to one corner of the Bird Room, where the Christmas tree stands, half-naked. The top portion of the tree is draped in a strand of colored lights. The remaining lights lie in a tangled mess on the floor. Without missing a beat, my father too cheerfully returns to the task of hanging the lights. Sherman, Olivia, and I exchange confused glances and guardedly join him in the ritual, adorning the Fraser fir with a boxload of ornaments from Christmases past. Sitting on a chair, Mom observes. We do the work in near silence—it *feels* like work.

Perhaps a half hour later, our mother excuses herself. "I'm just going upstairs to read a bit," she attempts to say casually, as though tonight is an average evening, not Christmas Eve. But her voice cracks, and she clears her throat. Dad follows right behind her.

Olivia, Terry, Sherman, and I are left staring at the doorway.

"What do you think is wrong?" I ask in a lowered voice.

"She's been upstairs practically all afternoon," Olivia says.

"She looks awful," Sherman says.

Perhaps because Terry is still new to the family, he keeps quiet.

"What are we going to do?" Olivia asks.

Later that night, I can't sleep. I lie in my bed on my right side, facing the empty twin bed where my sister used to sleep. Now she is downstairs on the pullout sofa with Terry. I remember the month before, when we were at Aunt Nan and Uncle Dave's home in Connecticut for Thanksgiving. Mom had been under the weather then too. Sherman, Mom, Dad, and I had driven out from the city together, with a stopover as usual at the Christian Science church in Pleasantville for its Thanksgiving service. Mom stood up to give a testimony, which was standard, but her words, come to think of it, were not.

"Sometimes," she said, grasping the pew in front of her, "healings are instantaneous. And other times, they are slower to come to fruition. I am so grateful for the healing power of Divine Science."

My gut tightens, and a feeling of panic grips me. I realize this illness may well have been going on for a while. I think back even further, to September, when I signed the lease on my first apartment, a one-bedroom in a five-story walk-up on the corner of Third Avenue and Twenty-ninth Street. I was so excited about my first place, and I knew how enthusiastically my mother would help me furnish it. When Olivia got her first apartment after college, Mom flew out to

Minneapolis to spend a weekend helping her get settled. I felt certain that Mom and I would buy everything: new linens, plates and pots and pans, flatware and candles, place mats and a doormat, a reading lamp, even a plant or two. She would find a few choice castoffs from Hopewell that would tie everything together, just like she had for Olivia. When I was in boarding school, we would make a shopping trip to the mall twice a year. She affectionately called them our Spoiled Brat Days, and they always included lunch and a movie. I figured Moving-In Weekend would be the enhanced version of our SBD.

But we never made a trip to Conran's or Macy's or even Woolworth's. She did find some mismatched towels and sheets from the linen closet in Hopewell and told me her best friend, Connie, was giving me an old sofa bed and a step stool from her basement. On Moving Day, my mother arrived at my new apartment with Harry and Debbie, the handyman and his wife who help my parents in Hopewell. They pulled up to my building in Harry's pickup. Harry and Debbie and I heaved the sofa up the three flights of stairs, and I wondered, halfway up, if it was even worth it. Mom waited in the double-parked truck until we were done with the lifting, and then came in briefly so I could show her the place. Looking back, I realize she probably climbed the stairs with effort and disguised the pain. At the time I had interpreted her behavior as only a puzzling sign of disinterest. I grew moody; she had done so much for Olivia . . .

Mom stayed just long enough to use the bathroom.

She must have been sick that day.

It is after midnight. The house feels eerily quiet, filled with illness and secrecy. I'm afraid to breathe, as though doing so might upset a precarious equilibrium, so with my head on my pillow, I close my eyes and take shallow, cautious breaths. My head is dizzy, swirling with questions and thoughts.

How long has she been sick?

She's not sick.

What are her symptoms?

Symptoms are error.

She's so pale. Frail.

She is not sick. She can't be sick. Jesus says, "Be ye therefore perfect, even as your Father which is in heaven is perfect."

What if she doesn't get better?

She is made in God's image and likeness. She is not material, but spiritual.

What should we do?

If it were serious, she'd be at Tenacre.

Be still and know that I am God.

O, God.

What if she goes to Tenacre?

I am startled by the voice in my head. It has been years since I've set foot in a church, except for the obligatory Thanksgiving and Easter services when I'm with my parents. I haven't read the Daily Lesson, or prayed since—when?—Claremont. I don't even know where my King James Bible and *Science and Health* are, maybe in an unpacked moving box. Four times a year, with a wink of encouragement, Dad gives me the new Christian Science quarterly. Later, I discreetly drop it into the garbage. Yet here I am reciting Mary Baker Eddy and her favorite Bible quotes.

I am twenty-three years old, and for as long as I can remember, our family has never faced anything like this, except that one time in Egypt. Curiously, it was also Christmas Eve.

I tap lightly on the wall behind my headboard. Three taps echo back. Sherman is awake. I get out of bed and tiptoe to his room. Together we head downstairs, pausing when the floorboards squeak.

"What are we going to do?" I ask.

Sherman and I sit in silence for several minutes. Then he pulls his guitar out of its case. Muting the sound by slightly pressing his fingers on the frets, he strums the same four chords, over and over again.

Christmas morning, Sherman somehow sleeps until almost eleven, and Mom and Dad stay upstairs even longer, which is alarming. Our parents are early birds, always. Olivia, Terry, and I stand in the kitchen for hours and drink too much coffee, waiting for Mom, Dad, and Sherman to emerge. Olivia and I speak in hushed voices while Terry listens.

"Maybe it's menopause?" I say. It is possible—but unlikely—that my sister at twenty-six knows more about menopause than I, who know nothing.

"I doubt it," Olivia says. "I don't think menopause makes you feel that ill for so long. I think you get—sort of, you know, fleeting hot flashes."

"Could it be the flu?" I offer, incredulous at my own hopefulness.

Olivia shakes her head but doesn't suggest any other possibilities.

We hear footsteps on the stairs. Our father pokes his head into the kitchen. I can tell he is exhausted. The dark circles around his eyes look like bruises. His smile is incongruous.

"Merry Christmas, everyone! You guys need anything? Toast?" he says, trying to be gracious. "English muffins?"

He sounds nervous, awkward, like he is accommodating first-time houseguests, not his own kids.

I look at Olivia and Terry, and we all shake our heads no. He retreats upstairs.

Olivia's eyebrows go up.

Eventually Sherman appears, looking for coffee and food, lured by the smell of the bacon in the oven. His tousled, sandy hair and days-old stubble belong to the heedless college kid he was until last night. He sits down at the kitchen table and stares into his coffee mug.

We make breakfast. As I am pouring the orange juice, I hear footsteps again on the stairs. Dad is helping Mom one deliberate step at a time, and there are muffled words of encouragement. Our parents appear with broad grins, but Mom's gaze is vague. She is wearing her Christmas sweater paired with a denim skirt, an odd choice—probably the first thing my father stumbled on in her closet. I can see her obvious makeup again.

With everyone assembled, Christmas morning starts around

noon. By the hearth in the living room, we open our stocking presents, which are sparse and not gift-wrapped, but we pretend not to notice. The tension is palpable. What is this charade? Do Mom and Dad really think we're convinced that everything is okay? And why are we going along with it?

We make our way into the Bird Room.

"Look at this!" Dad exclaims, eyeing the food with forced enthusiasm.

We all take seats.

"Here's to Terry and Liv," I say, looking for something to celebrate. I raise my orange juice glass, and everyone follows suit.

My toast feels fake.

Dad reaches out both of his hands, offering his left to me, his right to Olivia, the opening gesture of our meal's blessing. We all hold hands.

Heads are bowed. I look around without moving. This should be a happy occasion, the newly married couple spending their first Christmas with the bride's family. Olivia bites her lower lip, and her long hair falls in front of her, a curtain closing on her face. Terry's hair is pulled back in a ponytail, and he sits stiffly, his posture leaning him slightly toward his wife. Sherman is stone-faced. Mom's hands are limply offered in grace. Normally we all squeeze hard when we hold hands, sending hugs in the form of firm grips around the table. Not today.

Dad enunciates every syllable of the grace while the rest of us mumble.

I was looking forward to handing out my presents. In the past, Mom has always given me a modest Christmas fund to make my purchases, but this year I wanted to do it on my own, and generously, despite exhausting a whole week's pay. But there is no joy in it now.

This Christmas, my parents' gifts reek of pretending: expensive tennis racquets, down comforters, microwave ovens. Each time one of us opens a present, Mom's eyes well up. I am overcome with the feeling that we are being given these things to assure Mom that we have them. I start to cry, confused by my parents' disproportionate generosity and the underlying sadness.

Apparently, my mother's tears are tolerable; mine are not. My father glares at me from across the room, so I excuse myself to the bathroom, where I splash my face with water, trying to compose myself. As I open the door to leave the bathroom, I face my father in the narrow hallway. I reach for his embrace.

"What's the matter with *you*?" he whispers through gritted teeth.

I pull back.

"What's the matter with *me*?" I shoot back. "What's going on here?"

"Nothing!" my father hisses. "Nothing's going on here."

"What's wrong with Mom?" I persist.

My father looks at the floor and pauses.

"Your mother has a little problem she's working out," he says, too lightly.

"Thanks for telling us!" I reply.

"Your mother's situation is none of your business, young lady."

"Did you think we wouldn't notice?" My chin trembles slightly.

"In Science we don't draw attention to error," he says, speaking gently now. He puts his hand on my shoulder. "You know that."

"How long has she been...like this?" I ask.

"I'm not going to discuss this with you. But"—he pauses, deciding to give me something to hold on to—"it's recent. And already, she's made a lot of progress."

This little acknowledgment from my father offers some relief, some hope.

"The best thing you can do for your mother right now is to show your love and support."

We return to the Bird Room. I try to smile. Mom confesses that they have one more gift for each of us. Dad pulls three envelopes from his blazer pocket. In each is a check for four hundred dollars, twice as much as they have ever given us for Christmas.

JANUARY 5, 1986
NEW YORK CITY

On the first Sunday in January, just ten days after Christmas, I am sitting at a table for two at the Mad Hatter, a restaurant on the Upper East Side, waiting for my cousin Mary. She is a senior at Barnard, the youngest of my aunt Nan's six children. We have chosen the Upper East Side as a midway point, and the Mad Hatter for its bargain brunch. We have scheduled and canceled and rescheduled this brunch for months, ever since I started working in the city, and when the date came up again, and I considered whether to postpone once more, I decided not to. Now I question that decision. It would have been far easier to say I have a deadline at work than to sit across from Mary and pretend everything is fine.

Mary arrives wearing a knitted hat and a heavy wool coat, with a long bohemian scarf wrapped around her neck. She removes the hat and scarf and shakes out the glossy, dark head of hair so prevalent in Dad's family. We order the complimentary mimosas.

"How was your Christmas?" she asks.

"Good."

"And how's Condé Nast?"

"Good," I say again, but I am picturing Mom in her bathrobe on Christmas Eve.

We sit for a minute in silence, examining the menu. My heart is racing.

"Mary," I suddenly blurt, "Christmas wasn't good. Mom's not okay. She's sick."

I have betrayed my mother. I fidget with the stem of the champagne flute and glance away. Why did I do that? It was so easy to unburden myself, but, quickly, the ramifications of my hastiness are all too clear. If Mary tells her mother (and why wouldn't she?), Aunt Nan might call Dad.

"Listen, Mary," I say and pause, "don't say anything to your mom. Please."

Mary looks puzzled. "But if your mom is really sick . . ."

"Maybe she isn't," I try to counter.

"But what if she *is*? Is she? She won't go to a doctor?"

I shake my head. My cousin's family is Episcopalian. She knows that we are Christian Scientists, and that Christian Scientists don't go to doctors, don't smoke, don't drink. I take a sip of my mimosa.

"Christian Scientists don't discuss illness," I say. "They believe that, if they discuss it, they acknowledge it. And acknowledging illness gives it power. Mary, I'm not a Christian Scientist, but I guess I believe I should respect my mother's wishes."

I guess I believe I should.

The following week, my great-aunt dies. Lucia Chase was a prominent figure in the ballet world. My father calls me at work to tell me he's attending the funeral.

"I'd like you to come too," he says.

I have never gone to a funeral, and I'm not eager to go to one now. I didn't actually know Lucia Chase, so I'm not sure about the propriety of attending. I'd feel like an impostor. And Mary might be there with her parents. If Mom doesn't go to the funeral—and how can she?—her absence will be noticed by Aunt Nan. Mary may feel compelled to tell her about our brunch, about what I said.

"Come on, Loosh," my father says. "I'd like you to meet some of your Ewing relatives. And you never know who might be there."

I remain silent. I am confused about my father's motives, and angry. How can he go to a funeral, or be excited about who's who for that matter, with Mom so sick? And why does he care if I go? Does he just want me to go as a stand-in? The whole thing seems hypocritical. Christian Scientists strive to deny sin, disease, and death, and yet my father is going to attend a funeral *now*? Wouldn't the mere act of attending a funeral—acknowledging death in the face of Mom's situation—be tantamount to leaving a newborn in a snowdrift (to borrow my father's analogy)? How can going to a funeral support the healing process? I think now I'm afraid to go.

"Mom is coming too," he adds.

Mom must be doing better.

"Okay," I say, relieved. We hang up. I call Sherman and Olivia to update them.

I arrive at my parents' apartment, a pied-à-terre on Seventy-seventh Street, at 10:00 A.M., so we can head to the funeral together. The notion that Mom is feeling better is quickly dispelled: she looks terrible. Her dress—a fitted floral print with a black background—hangs on her. Her cheeks are nearly skeletal, and her face looks alarmingly ashen. Still, my mother seems happy to be back in the city, even if it's to attend a funeral. When she hugs me, I want so much for the embrace to feel good, but it doesn't. I can't help it; I pull back reflexively, shocked by the degree of her infirmity.

The service is held at a church only six blocks away, but my father hails a cab. Entering the church foyer, the three of us sign a guest book. Mom's handwriting is shaky. We are ushered to our seats in the fourth pew, left of the center aisle, in an area reserved for family. Mom sits on the aisle; Dad is next to her; I sit to his left.

I have not prepared myself for the reality of my first funeral. The church interior is beautiful, with Gothic-arched ceilings and rich wooden pews, but it feels dark, cold, and cavernous. The organ music and candlelight, fittingly somber, are, for me, macabre. All of these people have congregated for Lucia Chase's funeral, but I feel that I am face-to-face with my own mother's mortality. For the moment, among the throng of mourners, I realize that only my father, mother, and I know that Mom is sick. I wonder if that will change once the service is over. Surely someone will notice the difference in her appearance.

Four men who I assume are my relatives, wearing dark suits, roll the casket down the center aisle toward the church's apse and stop right beside our pew. The coffin holds my great-aunt's body, a body that will decay and decompose, the minister reminds us, "to nothing but ashes and dust." The coffin is shut, and it remains right there, two feet beyond my mother, who wears a dress three sizes too large for her frame. I see her clutch the side of the pew for support.

The minister speaks of my great-aunt's abiding devotion to her beloved cause, and of her profound sense of family. He talks of her "unspeakable sadness—the loss of her son at sea," and I can't contain my tears, not for this woman and her life's trials and extraordinary accomplishments but because the horror of my own mother's situation is no longer abstract or, as a Christian Scientist would say, "an opportunity for spiritual growth." My father ignores me. My mother doesn't notice, focused as she must be on making it through the service.

Aunt Nan and Mary are waiting for us in the foyer afterward. My mother excuses herself to find the bathroom, which is in the basement.

"Do you want me to come with you?" I whisper in her ear, gently rubbing her shoulder. I need to comfort her—and myself—and I want to stay close.

"No," she answers quietly and heads for the stairwell. She grips the handrail. Slowly she makes her way down.

I turn back toward the foyer. The only person I want to be with now is Mom—not my dad, not Aunt Nan, and not Mary, who I suddenly fear might ask me questions. And if she does, what will I do? To say anything at all will mean either a second betrayal of my mother or an outright lie. I'm not prepared to commit either. Still, won't Aunt Nan be alarmed by the sight of her sister-in-law? And, if Mary hasn't already said something to Aunt Nan, won't she have to now? I hover in a corner of the foyer.

Why is Mom taking such a long time in the bathroom? I wait for her to reappear, and when she doesn't, and the church is nearly empty, I beckon my father and frantically whisper. "Dad, shouldn't I check on Mom?"

"No, no," he answers, trying to sound nonchalant.

"But she's been downstairs for twenty minutes."

Dad glances at his watch. I watch him stroll back over to his sister and niece, to tell them to head to the reception, we'll follow shortly.

I doubt we will. I figure we'll get Mom back to the apartment as quickly as possible, and Dad will make excuses to his sister later. As the custodian prepares to close up the sanctuary, I resolve to head downstairs to find Mom, but then she appears. The urgency is gone from her face, replaced by an effortful smile. The immediate crisis is over; we go, as planned, to the reception.

We take a cab to my great-aunt's home, a few blocks away. During the short ride, my father tells me about the elegant dinners that he attended there, served by white-gloved help. Is he attempting to divert my attention from my mother? She winces, clearly in pain again. Turning toward the window, she lowers her head and closes her eyes for several seconds.

Why are we doing this? I want to scream. This is crazy.

At the reception, a butler stands at attention in the entry, taking coats.

"Could you keep these somewhere handy?" my father asks, discreetly. "We won't be staying long."

People are milling about in clusters, speaking softly, sipping the drinks they've taken from trays being passed by waiters. We spot Aunt Nan and Mary at one end of the dining room, where a table is laid with silver platters of finger food. We head in their direction.

I watch my mother steady herself with one hand on the dining room table as my father chats dutifully with cousins, putting in just enough time before he can leave. His smile is forced, I think, but he looks remarkably relaxed.

Look at my mother! We need a doctor! Nobody seems to notice anything. I want to shake my father.

I stand with Mary. She points discreetly at a woman I don't recognize and whispers, "I'm pretty sure that's Margot Fonteyn!" But my eyes are on my mother, who moves tentatively from my father's side to perch herself on a small chair beside a window. I leave Mary, and as I walk toward my mother, she stands up and returns to my father's side and whispers, "It's time to go."

The three of us exit quickly. We say good-bye to no one.

Outside, my mother announces, "I want to walk home."

"Are you sure, Jo?" my father asks. For the first time there is worry in his voice.

We walk two blocks, very slowly. Then, my mother doubles over.

"Heff, get a cab. I need a cab," she groans.

I hold her with one of my arms supporting her back, the other clutching her arm. Dad frantically tries to wave down a cab, but there are none in sight.

My mother moans. She is in agony.

"Mom?" I ask, utterly helpless. "Do you need to lie down?"

"Oh, Heff!" she cries.

A cab finally comes to a halt. My father holds my mother and tells me to open the cab door.

"Sit in front," he orders.

My mother continues to cry. I watch, stunned, as my father, with great effort, helps her into the car, one arm on her back, the other supporting the crooks of her knees while her legs dangle over his forearms.

"The hospital?" the cabbie asks.

Please say yes, Lenox Hill.

"No," my father says, "between Park and Madison. Number Sixty-one."

The emergency room is right there!

"Ohhh," my mother groans. The cabbie eyes my parents in his rearview mirror. I stare straight ahead. *Please, God. Help.* I am praying the most basic, desperate, intercessional prayer, not the kind I'd learned in Sunday school, about Divine Love and Infinite Mind.

Help.

My father hands me his wallet and his keys and starts to help Mom out of the car.

"I hope she'll be okay," the cabbie says to me.

In the lobby, I open the door easily, but upstairs at my parents' apartment, I can't get the dead bolt. Wrong key.

"Here, I'll get it," Dad says. "You take Mom."

I try to support my mother's weight as she struggles to remain standing. I'm afraid I might be holding her too tightly. With the door to the apartment finally open, Dad rushes Mom into the bathroom. I sit in the living room and wait.

On the coffee table I see a current copy of *The Christian Science Journal.* Somewhere in the back, in the New York section, I know I can find my father's name, Frank H. Ewing, followed by the initials C.S.B., the church's official designation for teacher. I have no idea what the initials stand for. At some point after we moved back from London, Dad was invited to go through something called Normal class, an honor that elevates a journal-listed Christian Science practitioner to the role of teacher, who is authorized to teach the course called Primary class, which trains the practitioners.

That, I realize, is the extent of my knowledge of Christian Science hierarchy.

On the front cover of the publication, I read the familiar words,

HEAL THE SICK • RAISE THE DEAD • CAST OUT DEMONS •
CLEANSE THE LEPERS

Do my parents actually *believe* Christian Science can do all this?

After several minutes, my father comes out to the living room.

"Mom's going to be fine," he says firmly.

"Dad, can't we take her to a doctor? The hospital is right down—"

"No, Lucia," he says without rancor. "Your mother doesn't want to resort to medicine. Believe me, if she did, I would be the first to take her. She wants to use Science."

I sit down and bury my face in my hands.

My father comes to my side and puts his arm over my shoulder. I stiffen.

"She's going to be okay. I think coming to the city was too much for her. But she was determined."

"I don't get this," I say, shaking my head.

"Lucia, you and I both need to affirm your mom's perfection; her dominion over mortal mind."

I move away from him.

"Fear needn't have any hold on you," he continues.

Shut up. Shut UP! I want to say. I am so angry—at him, at my inability to act. I am completely immobile, terrified, on the verge of tears, or rage. She could be dying! And we sit here doing *nothing*. I want to call an ambulance. I want to bring my mother to the hospital. I want to get Uncle Jack on the phone. But I can't even tell my father to shut up with this . . . this nonsense.

My father is oblivious. He goes on: "Mrs. Eddy states, 'Error theorizes that spirit is born of matter and returns to matter, and that man has a resurrection from dust.'" He quotes slowly, deliberately, "'Whereas Science unfolds the eternal verity, that man is the spiritual, eternal reflection of God.'"

There is a long silence. I can tell Dad thinks he's got me on track.

"And from *Miscellaneous Writings*," he continues, his eyes closed, chantlike, "'Divine Love is our hope, strength, and shield. We have nothing to fear when Love is at the helm of thought.'"

"I want to say good-bye to Mom," I say.

In fact, I don't really want to say good-bye; I don't want to leave her here, but I know there is nothing more I will do.

"I'll say good-bye for you." Dad tries to hug me.

Stunned by my own helplessness, I slowly walk to the subway station, two blocks east. Ahead of me stands Lenox Hill Hospital. It takes up the entire block on the south side of the street. Two ambulances are idling in front. Directly across the street, on the north side of the block, is the austere brick façade of Eighth Church of Christ, Scientist.

Yesterday, the space shuttle *Challenger* blew up.

The private crisis of Mom's health, which has consumed me for over a month, is now overlaid with the national, yet somehow personal, tragedy of the *Challenger*. I am numbed by the devastating news. I stop at the coffee shop on the street level of my dreary walk-up and take a seat at the counter to read. The front pages of all the papers show the already iconic photograph of a pure white cloud of smoke, with a long tail and the vaguely recognizable shuttle debris. Talk of the tragedy dominates the breakfast conversations around me, and I listen as the regulars—normally a reticent lot—speak mournfully of the schoolteacher astronaut, as if each had known her personally.

As I walk up Third Avenue toward midtown, everyone I see clutches a newspaper.

By nine o'clock, I have fielded three calls from Colette, the picture editor in Munich. At 9:05 the phone rings again.

"German *Vogue*," I say.

"Hi, Loosh." My father's voice is raspy and quivering. Instantly my chest squeezes, and my palms go clammy.

Oh, no. No. I sit down.

"Mom had a bad night," my father says. There is a muffled sound as he covers the mouthpiece. Is he crying? I realize I have never heard my father cry before.

"Dad?" I say.

"I'm taking her to Tenacre," he manages, choked up, before surrendering to full-out sobbing.

Oh, my God.

The relief that Mom is still with us is immediately replaced with dread. Tenacre. I've driven past the entrance numerous times on my way from Hopewell to Princeton, but I've never set foot on the wooded property. Mom was tight-lipped about her training there, except when she said cryptically, "There are a hundred ways to make a bed: with Love, Principle, Truth, Mind..." She never completed the training, and I never learned why, but it had something to do with her wanting to take art classes in the city.

I wonder if I can suggest again that Mom see a doctor.

I can't predict what the mention of a doctor might do right now. Maybe, maybe Dad wants an option? But he sounds resolved, and I know how irrational and defensive he becomes when he feels cornered; I know how his self-control can just snap. I remember my Eyeglasses Rebellion and, more recently, the acrimony I created by announcing my intention to get health insurance after college.

"That's just a slap in my face!" he had wailed. "A stab in the back!"

My father is still sobbing, and I am paralyzed with fear.

"Are you okay, Dad?" I don't know what else to say. Obviously he isn't okay.

"Yes, I'm fine," he says. He sighs loudly, collecting himself, and blows his nose.

"She'd like to see all of you...," my father says, choking up again.

"Can I talk to Mom?"

There is silence as he hands her the phone. I worry about what I should say. Mom speaks first.

"Hi, dear." Her voice is strained, like a squeak. I hardly recognize it.

"Hi, Mom."

"I'm going to be all right," she says, barely whispering. "Your daddy is taking me to Tenacre."

She always refers to him as Daddy, I guess because that's what she used to call her own father. Ironically, we, his children, have never called him that.

"I didn't want to go," she confesses, "but now I think it's best."

Does she not want to go to Tenacre in the same way that most people don't want to go to a hospital but do anyway when they have to? Or does it mean that she's thought about going somewhere other than Tenacre? A hospital?

"Are you sure, Mom?" I ask, wishing my question were more assertive, more pointed.

"Yes."

What I want to say is, *Mom, we have to get you to a doctor.* But I can't.

"I love you, Mom. Whatever you need to do, you know I'm behind you."

I'm not sure I mean it, but I want her to feel reassured.

"That's...very...nice."

Mom's demeanor is more remote than ever. Should I read something into it? Does she doubt my support? Or does her reply simply require the least effort?

"Can I bring you anything from the city?" I ask.

"No." My mother hesitates. "Are you going to tell Sherman?"

"Do you want me to?"

My question, or maybe the way I ask it, doesn't sound to me like a daughter talking to a mother. I feel like I am speaking with someone else, someone much older, less familiar, like a great-aunt.

"It's Sherman's concert tonight, isn't it?" she says. She is weeping now. "We so wanted to go. Don't tell him about Tenacre until after he's done singing. I don't want to spoil his big night."

Sherman's band, the Bureaucrats, is playing for the first time in public. He's the lead singer. *Concert*—a mother's euphemism—brings a smile to my face for one flickering moment before it is snuffed by the sound of her crying, which I just can't bear.

"I'll take notes," I say, "and tomorrow I'll give you the full review. I love you, Mom."

"I love you too, darling."

Dad is back on the phone.

I'm almost too afraid to ask my next question. "Are you going to tell Grandma?"

There is a long silence.

"I think so," he says, and I am relieved. "Your mother and I discussed it this morning. We'll probably call Grandma once she gets settled at Tenacre."

An enormous weight has been lifted from me. It was awful talking to Grandma on Christmas Day, pretending everything was fine. And I have hated dodging Mimi's calls: Mimi, my cousin, my best friend and confidante. We usually meet after work several days a week to exercise at the same health club. Now I have stopped going so that I won't see her. I can't tell Mimi that Mom is really sick. Mimi is Aunt Mary's daughter, and Aunt Mary is Mom's sister.

Tomorrow, it will all be out in the open. Everyone who needs to know will know. Mom's family: Aunt Mary, Aunt Kay, Uncle Jack, and Grandma; and Dad's family: Aunt Nan, Aunt Lucia, Ammie, and Dad's brothers. I only have to get through Sherman's gig tonight, where Mimi will be with her boyfriend, and then tomorrow I can tell her everything. Maybe then we'll get Mom to a doctor.

"Have you called Olivia?" I ask Dad.

"I'm going to call her now."

I stay at the office doing mindless paperwork until four. I am in no hurry to get to my apartment, even though the weather is chilly and damp, so I stroll the aisles of Duane Reade and buy a pack of Marlboro Lights and, strangely enough, a box of cookies: chocolate digestives, a teatime favorite at Claremont that I haven't come across in years.

The cookies are half-gone by the time I reach home. I call my sister in Cambridge for the third time today. I finish off the cookies and smoke three cigarettes while we talk.

Since Christmas, Olivia, Sherman, and I have spoken daily, sharing reports of what we think has been happening with Mom. We've based our sketchy conclusions on the brief conversations we've had with our parents every morning, during which Mom or Dad or both have reported that she is "making good progress." One of us has always initiated the phone call, never our parents, and we've sensed that our inquiries are little more than an intrusive nuisance to them. The truth is, I've never believed, not really, that Mom's health is improving, and after Lucia Chase's funeral, I knew she was getting worse.

But I kept clinging to the comfort that, as long as Mom wasn't at Tenacre, maybe everything would be okay. Maybe Christian Science was going to work.

But now, Mom's at Tenacre.

Olivia tells me that she can't get home until tomorrow, and that Terry isn't coming with her because Dad wants this first visit with Mom at Tenacre to be immediate family only.

"You okay with that?" I ask.

"Oh, it's pretty typical," Olivia says, sounding both nonchalant and bitter. "Terry has to study anyway. What time is Sherman's band playing tonight?"

"Ten-thirty."

"You going alone?" she asks.

"No, Mimi's coming with her boyfriend."

"Are you going to be all right?"

I'm not sure. I know it will be difficult: Sherman singing, looking for Mom and Dad in the crowd; Mimi, wondering why I've been so aloof lately, and why my parents aren't there, knowing this gig is something they wouldn't miss; and me, clapping, smiling, faking, thinking about Mom lying in a bed at Tenacre.

"God, Liv," I say, "Mimi's going to know. She probably senses something already."

"Maybe since Mom and Dad are talking to Grandma tomorrow anyway, you can tell her and ask her to keep quiet until then."

"I feel like that's betraying Mom."

I don't mention that I've already told our cousin Mary.

Tramps is a bar not far from Gramercy Park: dark, divey, the air heavy with the stench of stale beer and cigarette smoke. Mimi and her boyfriend are already there when I arrive. We find a table in the center of the room. The music is loud enough, fortunately, that conversation isn't an option. The Bureaucrats are really good, and I'm impressed by Sherman's stage presence. *Mom would love this.* Mimi and I swap surprised glances across the table, and she hollers over the din, "Where are your mom and dad?"

"It's Wednesday evening. They have church," I say without missing a beat.

At the end of each number, I throw a red and white tulip, from a bunch I bought at Mom's request, in the direction of the stage. At first, the stems landing near Sherman's feet embarrass him, and he tries to ignore them, but eventually he sticks one behind his ear and winks. At eleven-thirty, Mimi and her boyfriend leave. I sit at the table, alone.

Finally, it is over. Sherman flings himself into the chair next to mine and drains a mug of cold beer.

"You were great," I say, surprisingly self-conscious that the lead singer is sitting at my table.

Women are eyeing him. I wish I could put off the next words, but it is late and I am tired.

"Come here a second," I say, heading for the door.

Various buddies pound Sherman's shoulders, and pretty girls offer him kisses. As we leave the bar, its steamy warmth gives way to the sharp chill of the street.

"What's up?" Sherman asks. The empty street is not where the action is.

"Dad took Mom to Tenacre today."

Sherman turns away and leans against a streetlight. I can feel his distress. He rubs his eyes with his shirtsleeve.

"Come on, I'll get you a cab."

"Wait, Sherm. What are you going to do now? Do you want to stay at my apartment? Should we go up to Seventy-seventh Street?"

"Naw, I've got to go back to the frat," he says automatically.

"Please? Then we can head out to Hopewell tomorrow."

"Lucia, I can't. I'll meet you in the morning, and we'll ride the train out together. I have to turn in a paper."

"Sure," I say. I am pissed off, and scared to be alone, but I don't want to fight.

"I'll call you when I get to Fiji," he says, referring to his fraternity.

"Hi, Liv, it's me," I say. "I know it's late, but I can't sleep."

"That's okay. What's goin' on?"

"Sherman's a jerk," I say.

"Why?" she asks. "What happened?"

I tell her about the evening, about how Sherman blew me off.

"It's rotten what he did," Olivia says in a low voice, trying not to sound sleepy. I know Terry's head is on the pillow next to hers. My sister's empathy brings out what I am really feeling: unbearably alone. In all of New York, there is no one aside from Sherman with whom I can speak freely about Mom.

"I was hoping we'd go get a bite to eat," I sob, "or hang out at Seventy-seventh Street."

"Lucia, he's not doing this on purpose. He's still a kid," she says.

Twenty-one isn't a kid.

"He said he'd call me from the fraternity"—I glance over at my clock radio: 3:00 a.m.—"big surprise, he didn't."

Olivia chooses not to reply.

"It's late," I say. "I'm really sorry I woke you up."

"I'm glad you called," she says, and I know she means it. "Loosh," she adds tenderly, "Sherman means well. He doesn't know what to do either."

In the morning Sherman calls as I'm leaving for Penn Station to say that he is taking a later train. Dad meets me at Princeton Junction, with outstretched arms, puffy eyes, and a big, incongruous smile; he looks as though he hasn't slept in weeks. His salt-and-pepper hair is mussed, like he ran his fingers through it instead of a comb. He is wearing a red and blue bow tie, the knot so tight I know he struggled with it, a light blue oxford shirt, a tweed jacket, gray trousers, and a heavy, tan-colored down jacket. He hasn't shaved.

"How was the train ride?" he asks anxiously. "I see you got the bud vase."

I hand him a red Steuben gift bag.

"I saw it before the lady boxed it," I say. "It's beautiful."

My father manages another smile, but the crow's-feet around his eyes remain pinched long after the smile has vanished.

"How's Mom?" I ask fearfully as we exit the parking lot.

"I really think the *Challenger* tragedy put her into a tailspin. She watched the news updates over and over."

Tailspin is a timely word choice.

"Dad," I asked, "is it her belly?"

My father takes a deep breath, noticeably uncomfortable with the question. I figure I already know the answer, but I'm hoping to learn something new.

"Lucia, dear, you know we don't discuss symptoms in Christian Science. It doesn't support the healing process."

I close my eyes to fight off my frustration.

"I think you will be pleased with her room," my father says. "I think you'll be reassured by Tenacre. It's very clean. The staff is absolutely professional."

I don't know how to respond, but cynicism probably isn't the answer. Of course the place is clean! What else does a professional nursing staff do, if it doesn't assist doctors and dispense medicine? I can't be part of this conversation. My father is trying to convince me that all is going well. I'm not buying it.

We drive in silence through the center of Princeton, where preppy suburbanites are shopping and browsing, and college students with backpacks slung over their shoulders are strolling in groups. I feel a tinge of nostalgia for my life at Brown, when my biggest worry was the word count on a paper, or making a deadline. My father turns on the radio and finds a classical station. He has always preferred silence to any kind of sound in the car. The music is more for my benefit than his, and I appreciate the gesture. I remember our road trips to Florida and Montana when we were kids: the tedious stretches of time, sandwiched in the backseat of the car, where we had to sit in complete silence while our father did his metaphysical work, his head bobbing in deliberate, prayerful vehemence, no doubt affirming some mysterious patient's God-given dominion over error.

"How are you, Dad?" I ask, gently patting his shoulder. "Are you getting enough sleep? Do you need groceries at the house?"

"Oh, I'm fine, I'm fine," he says. "I've never needed much sleep. You know me . . . early to rise."

"Good," I reply, although I don't believe him.

I look at my watch. It is almost noon.

"Dad, have you called Grandma yet? Do you want me to talk to her first? I was thinking maybe if I—"

"Lucia," he says, hesitating. Immediately, I am filled with dread. *Tell me you called her.*

"Your mother and I have done a lot of thinking and praying about this, and your mother has decided that she would prefer Grandma not be told."

"What?" I hear my voice rising. "*What?* You said yesterday—"

I feel the rage coursing through my veins. I am suddenly nauseated. I want to punch a hole in the passenger window.

"I know what I said," my father tries to say calmly, "and yesterday, that's what we intended to do. But—"

"You *lied*!" I scream. "You *told* me you'd call Grandma as soon as Mom was settled at Tenacre! Those were *your* words!"

"I did not lie. Yesterday, that was the plan," my father says calmly. "But your mother discussed it with her practitioner and decided, after considerable prayer, against calling Grandma. You should know that I support your mother's decision one hundred percent. Try to understand, Lucia—"

"I don't understand," I counter. "This is wrong. This is lying. You are deceiving Mom's family. Mom is too sick for them *not* to know."

"I have to respect your mother's decision," he says firmly.

We turn off the Great Road onto a private drive. A sign announces:

TENACRE FOUNDATION
ESTABLISHED 1922

The wooded estate is pocketed with manicured lawns; a picturesque footbridge crosses a little stream. Winding paths connect the various buildings, which are well maintained but architecturally unremarkable. It looks like an upper-crust retirement community, or even a small liberal arts college, minus the students.

We pull into the visitors' parking lot. My father turns off the ignition.

"Yesterday your mother and I were very emotional. And we really did think it would be best to call your grandmother." My father rests his folded arms on the steering wheel and stares out to some fixed, imaginary point in front of him. "But to do so now would seriously undermine your mother's healing."

Your church is undermining her healing! I want to shout.

"My first concern has to be Mom. She has decided that she wants to work this out in Science. Believe me, Loosh, this has not been a hasty decision. Your mom has been a diligent, effective Christian Scientist for over twenty years. As a practitioner and teacher—you'll just have to trust me on this—I've seen cases far more serious than your mother's that have resulted in beautiful healings."

My father is trying to reason with me. But there is nothing reasonable about denying the existence of this illness (which, in accordance with Church teachings, is what they are trying to do), denying medical treatment, and deceiving Mom's family. "This is wrong," I repeat in a low voice.

"You may think we're being deceptive. But—as difficult as this may be for you—there are very good reasons for not calling your grandmother right now. We are working hard to protect Mom's healing from mental malpractice. That's in large part why we decided to come to Tenacre. Here, your mother is receiving expert care in a supportive environment. We simply can't have non-Scientists—especially those opposed to Christian Science—interfering. It could really hurt Mom..."

This idiocy is what's hurting Mom.

"...You know your grandmother would want to visit. And you can guess how your uncle Jack might react.

"Another thing," my father continues. "Mom is concerned for Grandma's health too. Naturally, she doesn't want to do anything to upset her, or put her under strain. As you know, Grandma is unaccustomed to the practices and concepts of Christian Science. She was an R.N. Your grandfather was a doctor. It would be very difficult for Grandma to accept that her daughter is not using medicine."

It's difficult for your three children, I want to say, but even stating this feels dangerous: how could Mom and Dad not view us as part of the problem? We may be accustomed to Christian Science, but we are *not* Christian Scientists.

"Grandma would want to hear a lot of descriptions," my father continues. "Symptoms. A diagnosis. That's totally opposed to Christian Science. You understand that, don't you?"

If we keep silent, and go along with their wishes for privacy, we could be—are—jeopardizing our mother's health. But if we betray our parents and take action, we risk being cut off from them completely.

"What about us?" I finally ask. "Have you considered the position you've put us in?"

"As I've said, your mother's health is my first concern. I'm not going to imperil Mom's health just because it's hard for you."

Her health is already in peril!

"It's not easy for any of us. But if we—your mother and I—were not Christian Scientists and your mother became sick and required hospitalization, that wouldn't be easy for you either. Believe me. In a different way, hospitals and doctors present their own difficulties. But I would hope and expect you to be supportive of that decision too."

"It's not that we don't want to be supportive," I say. "We do. It's that . . . she's not getting better. Anyone can see that!"

I shove my fists into my eyes. "She's getting worse!"

"No she's not! No-she-is-not!" my dad calls out emphatically, pounding the steering wheel, as though by doing so he is purging the possibility from his thoughts.

He is silent for a long time, and it occurs to me that he is praying.

"Do you want to show your support?" he says after a while. "Why don't you start reading the Lesson again." My father glances over at me, with tenderness in his eyes, awaiting my response, and I am incredulous.

The Lesson! He thinks that by reading Church-selected passages from the King James Bible, and correlative passages from *Science and Health,* I can help heal Mom! Does it follow that he thinks she's not getting better because I'm *not* reading it? I turn away from him and look out the window.

"Couldn't we at least call Ham?" I blurt out. The thought has come to me out of nowhere, but it seems like a good idea. Ham's a Christian Scientist. He knows Mom and Dad. We haven't seen him since he moved to Paris, but he'd know what to do.

"No, we can't call Ham!" my father snaps. He takes the key out of the ignition, gets out of the car, and slams the door.

I am bewildered at my father's reaction, and the mystery that lies beneath it. Dad and Ham must have had a falling-out.

My father walks briskly down a footpath. He turns and waits for me, and I can see the contours of his clenched hands outlined in the pockets of his gray trousers.

Mom's room is in South Hall Extension, a single-story building that we enter by walking down a footpath past the white clapboard administration house. Approaching the door, I feel my heart begin to race. I wonder what I will find. How will she look? Just inside the front door, on the wall, hang a portrait of Mary Baker Eddy and a sign:

PLEASE WAIT FOR AN ATTENDING NURSE TO ASSIST YOU

The place is very quiet and, I notice, spotless. The smell of Lysol is evident and curious: Lysol, which kills germs. *There's no such thing as germs,* I remember being taught in Sunday school. While my cousin Mimi planted bean seeds in dirt-filled Dixie cups at St. Martin's Episcopal Sunday school, we learned that the material world is unreal. I can't make sense of these contradictions. A woman dressed in a white nurse's uniform sits reading behind a desk. She stands up when she see us. Laid out before her are the Christian Science quarterly, a King James Version of the Bible, and *Science and Health with Key to the Scriptures.* In both volumes, selected passages have been marked in blue chalk. From these highlighted sections, and the movable wire page markers, I can tell that she is reading the weekly Bible Lesson, and that she is about halfway through it. The page markers are numbered, and on any given week there are approximately twenty-five designated passages in each book; her Bible is opened to the number 16 page marker.

My father introduces me, and the woman smiles warmly. I shake her hand and realize my palm is wet.

"Mrs. Ewing may be sleeping, but you can peek in and see," she says, pointing the way.

Dad leads, and I follow apprehensively. The first door on the left is slightly ajar. He raps on it lightly.

"Jo, honey?" he whispers. "You have a visitor!" He beckons me in.

Mom is lying on her back in a semi-reclined hospital bed. The room itself looks like a hospital room except there are no monitoring devices, no IV stands. She is wearing a flannel nightgown, and a crocheted blanket is folded over her legs. She looks tired, and pale. But she is awake and alert, so I feel relieved. I expected worse.

"Hi, Mom," I say, standing in the doorway.

"Come on in, dear," my mother says. That's all it takes for my eyes to fill.

"Come here and give me a kiss."

I set down the red gift bag, move to her bedside, and perch on the edge of the mattress. She hugs me, and I hold on, and smother my face close to hers in the pillow that is propping her up. I close my eyes. She pushes me away to look at me.

"Lucia, I'm really going to be okay. I know it. You have to trust me." She squeezes my arm for emphasis. "I've just had a little set-back. Okay?"

"Okay," I reply.

"Are you with me?"

I try to smile, and grab a tissue from her bedside table.

"Lucia's got a present for you," my father says.

"I'm only the messenger," I say, trying to sound up. "Dad bought it."

He hands Mom the red Steuben bag. She removes a white box and unties its red satin bow.

Inside is a crystal bud vase.

"It's exquisite. Thank you both."

Mom moves the Kleenex box; her hand trembles, and the tissue flutters. She sets the vase on her bedside table next to a glass of water. My father removes the cellophane wrap from a fresh red rose he picked up at the florist and places it in the vase, filling it with the water from my mother's drinking glass.

WEDNESDAY, APRIL 16, 1986
NEW YORK CITY
THE APPOINTMENT

"*I'll meet you* under the clock at Grand Central," I say to my brother.

It is a nasty New York day; the frigid wind and horizontal rain make it feel more like February than April. Inverted black umbrellas are strewn in the water-swollen gutters and discarded in the city garbage cans. Under my black raincoat, I am wearing a skirt and jacket, instead of my usual black leggings and top. It occurs to me that my boss might think I am using my lunch break for a job interview. I can't worry about that now—and yet I do. I haven't told her where I'm going because doing so might trigger questions I'd rather avoid. I see Sherman, on time. He is also dressed up—for a college student—in gray flannels, a wrinkled button-down shirt, and one of Dad's old trench coats.

The practitioner's office is on East Forty-second Street, across from Grand Central. So is Dad's. Sherman and I walk the short distance quickly, breaking into a light jog when the rain gets heavier. Once inside the lobby, we sit down on a bench. We are five minutes early; the extra time sets me on edge. We have made this appointment with our father's full knowledge, so we're not being sneaky, but still, I feel like a lawyer about to depose a hostile witness.

"What are we going to say?" Sherman asks.

I sigh. I don't have an answer.

I remember something I have in my handbag. I dig through the clutter—Filofax, receipts, lipstick, keys—to find a small pamphlet entitled "God's Law of Adjustment." The cover looks like an image of a galaxy: blue, black, speckled white. I found it on my mother's bedside table during my last visit to Hopewell. I'd seen the pamphlet before, but until last week I had never actually read it. I open up to a page where a paragraph has been underlined in pencil. In the margin, in my mother's handwriting, is the word *clarity*. In the text, the word *see* is circled.

"'When we in our helplessness reach the point where we see we are unable of ourselves to do anything, and then call upon God to aid us; when we are ready to show our willingness to abandon our own plans, our own opinions, our own sense of what ought to be done under the circumstances, and have no fear as to the consequences—then God's law will take possession of and govern the whole situation.'

"Can you believe that?" I say.

"Read it again," Sherman says. I hand him the pamphlet so he can read it himself.

"Doesn't that sound...extreme?" I ask. "Like brainwashing?"

"Let's ask her about it," Sherman says. "But careful, Loosh. Or you'll put her on the defensive as soon as you open your mouth."

Helen Childs, C.S.B.

We know from the initials on the door that she is not only a Christian Science practitioner but also a teacher, like Dad. I wonder if my father has ever had meetings like the one we are about to have.

Sherman knocks on the door, and we wait. A woman appears; she has silver-white hair, and there is a noticeable smell of hair spray. She is wearing a light blue wool dress and matching jacket, and a long strand of pearls. She has the pronounced crow's-feet and the sparkly eyes of an optimist.

"Come in," she says, motioning us through a waiting area. I set my umbrella down on the floor beside an end table, where I see the current issue of *The Christian Science Monitor,* a *Christian Science Journal,* and a stack of *Sentinel*s. On the wall hangs a portrait of Mary Baker Eddy.

Sherman and I take seats in the two armchairs that face Mrs. Childs's desk. She closes the door.

On her desk are the two volumes: a King James Version of the Bible and a copy of *Science and Health.*

"Now," Mrs. Childs says, sitting down behind the desk, folding her arms in front of her. Her eyes may be twinkling, but she is not smiling.

I look to Sherman, and he looks back at me. He is not going to do the talking, not at first anyway. I shift in my chair, but I can't find a comfortable position. Leaning back, I feel small and vulnerable, but sitting up straight with my hands folded in my lap feels awkward too. I settle on crossed legs and squared shoulders. Again, my hands turn clammy, clutching my bag.

"Well," I begin, "thank you for meeting with us. We wanted to talk to you about our mom."

Mrs. Childs says nothing.

"She's been at Tenacre for a while now," I say.

There is a lengthy silence.

"She's been sick for a long time," Sherman says.

Nothing.

"Our mom has been at Tenacre for seventy-eight days," I say, impatiently now, and immediately regret it. Christian Scientists deny (or try to deny) commemorations of the passage of time. Pointing out the running count of days—like it's tally-marked on a cell wall—isn't going to endear me to her.

"Not all healings are instantaneous," Mrs. Childs finally says. "Sometimes the demonstration is slower to unfold. But your mother's understanding of the Truth is deepening every day. What your mother needs right now is your unwavering support."

"She knows we're behind her," I say defensively.

"We're concerned," Sherman says, "that her family doesn't know."

Mrs. Childs looks at me, and then at Sherman. I'm thinking maybe she agrees it's time to let them know. This is a good sign.

"Why does this concern you?" she asks.

I'm not sure I have heard her correctly.

I am speechless. Mom's health is deteriorating. We are deceiving her family. And Mrs. Childs asks why this concerns us?

"Mom comes from a medical family," Sherman finally says. "She and Dad converted. Her father was a doctor. Her mother was a nurse. Her brother is a plastic surgeon. We understand Mom's desire to keep quiet about her problem, to protect the healing process from mental malpractice. But it's been. . . ."

"I understand your position, and, unfortunately," Mrs. Childs says, taking a deep breath, "it is one that arises when the patient is not surrounded by the love and support of family members who are Scientists. I will tell you this: I have three children; only one is a Christian Scientist. If I were working out a problem, I would probably share it with my daughter, because I know there would be harmonious, prayerful support. But my other two are not at all sympathetic. I would not tell them."

"Mrs. Childs," Sherman asks, "what if—hypothetically—your condition worsened? Don't you think your other children would want to know? Don't you think they have a right to know, being family and all?"

"No, absolutely not. That would not be in accordance with my wishes. With my religious needs."

"Well, what about your Christian Scientist daughter? What if she felt uncomfortable with the ongoing secrecy," Sherman presses, "even if she shared your religious views?"

"She would understand that it's not a matter of secrecy, but of loving protection. Now," Mrs. Childs says, leaning forward, talking just louder than a whisper, "I happen to know that it upsets your mother a great deal that none of you are reading the Bible Lesson or attending church. These are two seemingly small but very significant ways you can demonstrate your love and support. By doing so, you might better understand why your prayerful encouragement is so important. And you may be surprised by the results. I have no doubt that you will gain a clearer vision of the efficacy of Science."

I'm done with polite.

"Mrs. Childs, I'm not a Christian Scientist. I'm not going to pretend to you that I am," I say. "But I'm sorry. I won't listen to you insinuate that Mom's condition has anything to do with my beliefs being different from hers."

My heart is pounding. There is an intense, charged silence while this woman and I stare each other down.

I look away. What I have just told her places me squarely in the camp of the enemy, the nonbeliever, and puts the increasingly tenuous connection between Mom and me in jeopardy.

Unbelievably, I hear a small voice in my head saying, *What harm would it do? Read the Lesson. Go to church.*

I haven't read the Lesson since I was sixteen.

I picture myself sitting in the common room at Claremont with the rest of the fourth- and fifth-form boarders, some of us, myself included, engaged in bona fide reading of the weekly Christian Science Lesson; others sneaking peeks at folded articles ripped out of teen magazines, or making entries in diaries, or writing letters.

A much louder voice is saying, *No! This is all wrong!*

"I guess I don't understand the point of all this," I confess, shaking my head. "What's *wrong* with trying medicine? Maybe Mom's condition requires a minor operation, or some . . . pills."

"I see," Mrs. Childs says. "Let me try to explain." Her voice is too sweet. "Mrs. Eddy teaches us that every illness is mentally conceived. By treating the material manifestation of a problem, you are really only dealing with the symptom, not the root cause. If your mother goes to a doctor—and we'll assume for now that the treatment of this . . . foreign growth . . . is seemingly effective—she will still have to overcome the *real* problem."

A chill runs through me. What does she know about Mom's condition, what has she witnessed, that has led her to this conclusion? And what root cause could be any more serious than a *foreign growth*? What the hell is she talking about?

"Our mother isn't even fifty!" I blurt out. "If she were to go to the doctor and be treated with medicine, she could have another thirty, forty years to deal with the—with the *spiritual* problem."

"I said before, let's assume that your mother can be effectively treated by medicine," Mrs. Childs says, perfectly composed.

"Yes?" I prod.

"But can either of you—Lucia? Sherman?—think of a single case of cancer which has really been *cured* by medicine?"

Jesus Christ.

I feel like I've been punched in the gut.

"A lot of people are treated by radiation and chemotherapy. And surgery," I say, eventually. I look to Sherman, who nods in agreement, but he is ashen.

"But can you name a single case in which the cancer was *cured*?" she asks me again. "Can you?" She looks to Sherman.

His lip quivers, and I am about to cry. I pull a Kleenex from my bag and wipe the outer corner of each eye. This is unbelievable.

"There, there," the practitioner says.

I wonder how anyone can say anything as trite as "There, there" at a time like this. I refuse to yield to tears.

"We all have to know that your mother is going to get her healing. That Divine Love will triumph over error."

That ends the appointment.

Sherman and I leave the building in silence and cross the street. The rain is still coming down hard. We descend into the subway at Grand Central and are about to say good-bye when Sherman says, "Ronald Reagan, for one."

Of course, thousands of people recover from cancer every year, but in the practitioner's office, we could not come up with one.

MAY 3, 1986
TEA AT THE PLAZA

I wake up with a startle, aroused by sirens on Third Avenue. My heart is pounding, and my whole being is in a state of panic, as though I have just had a nightmare. But my mind is blank.

I glance at the clock radio on my bedside table: 7:45 A.M.

I fall back onto my pillow and close my eyes. I am dreading today. I'm down to my last clean clothes, so I'll be spending half the morning at the Laundromat. My apartment's a mess. I have bills to pay and errands to run. But these duties are mindless; I can handle them. It is this afternoon that worries me. I'm supposed to go to the Plaza for tea with Mimi, Diana, Diana's roommate Cindy, and Diana's grandmother, whom we all call Nana Edna. It is an obligation I cannot duck.

Back in September, I got a call from Mimi at work. She asked if I was sitting down and, in a low, trembling voice, told me that Diana's younger sister Juliet, who had just started her freshman year at Smith College, had been killed in a car accident.

I hadn't known Juliet well. She'd been in my cousin Teddy's class at Blake. I had met her once at Diana's apartment in Greenwich Village when she was visiting for a few days. Every December, when the Nelsons' Christmas card arrived in the mail, Juliet's image was one your eyes went to first, and lingered on. She was lovely.

I had called Mom right after Mimi and I hung up. When I shared the news, Mom was so shaken that she couldn't talk. I remembered needing some comfort, or reassurance—but what reassurance could anyone give to news like this?—and thought Mom would try to provide it, or at least we would remain together, in silence, on the phone. After Mom said good-bye and abruptly hung up, I stared at the bulletin board on the wall behind my desk and wondered what I should do next.

Mom did not fly back for the funeral. At the time, that didn't seem odd—and maybe it wasn't. Mom was not particularly close to Diana's parents. They weren't *unfriendly;* the family friendship had just sort of skipped a generation. If Mom and Dad had still been living in Minnesota, Mom would have gone to the service with Grandma and Aunt Mary and Aunt Kay.

Mom must have already been sick when Juliet died. Maybe that's why she was so short with me on the phone.

I haven't seen Mom in almost a month. When I ask if I can come out to visit, she says it's not a good time, not helpful to the healing process. I call her at Tenacre every morning. Dad always gives me the same meaningless update: Mom is making good progress. The few mornings when I have actually spoken with Mom, she has sounded tired and weak, her voice raspy. "How's work?" she always asks. She tries to sound happy and curious, but she doesn't stay on the phone for very long, and she isn't really present. I could probably tell her I got fired and she'd reply, "That's great, dear..."

Last week, however, she and Dad called *me* at work. After Mom asked me the perfunctory "How's work?," I learned the real reason for the call.

"I know there is a tea for Edna next Saturday," she said. Her voice cracked. "Lucia dear, I would come if I could. I just can't right now. Please tell Edna how sorry I am."

Edna is like an aunt to Mom.

"Mom, what will I say?" I ask, but she has already handed the phone back to Dad.

"You can tell her we're doing some work on the house," Dad suggests, like they've got it all figured out, "that we have a meeting with the contractor."

"Dad," I start, but there's nothing to say. Obviously, Mom can't come to the tea. But also obviously, their alibi is lame. Edna will feel—*should* feel—hurt.

And this puts me in a terrible bind.

If I go to the Plaza, I will have to pretend to Edna, Diana, and Mimi that everything is fine with me, and with Mom. But Mom's absence will make no sense to any of them.

Worse still, I just don't know how I will be able to sit at a table with Mimi, and continue this horrible charade, when what I need to do more than anything is tell her about Mom.

The phone rings. I get out of bed and walk to the living room to answer it.

"Hey there."

It is Stephanie, one of my roommates from Brown. She's from West Virginia, and her *hey*—with a diphthong—sometimes comes out closer to two syllables than one.

"Did I wake you up?" she asks, but before I can even answer, she goes on. "So, we're all set for tonight."

Tonight? I close my eyes and stifle a groan.

"Stephanie, I just can't," I say.

"Awe, c'mon. It'll do you good. Besides, you can't *not* come. You're the guest of honor."

Tomorrow is my twenty-fourth birthday, and Stephanie has arranged a small dinner.

"There will only be six of us," she says. "You can't just sit at home."

Mimi's going to be there. I am thinking I should stay home. "You *can't*," she says.

At ten after four, I walk through the revolving doors at the front entrance to the Plaza Hotel. The smell of the Stargazer lilies in the grand floral arrangement in the lobby is nearly overpowering, but the flowers are stunning. I check my appearance in a large gilded mirror; the reflection betrays nothing; I look fine. In the Palm Court, the opulent tearoom in the indoor courtyard, a musician in a floor-length skirt strums her harp while a line of well-heeled ladies waits on one side of the velvet rope. The tuxedoed maître d' is busy at work. When he returns from seating one group, I ask him if the Nelson party has arrived, and he pivots with flourish and says, "Follow me." Inwardly, I am a mess.

Everyone is at the table. Diana is seated on one side of Edna, and Mimi is on the other. Cindy is next to Diana. The empty seat between Cindy and Mimi, facing Nana Edna, is for me.

It has been a few years since I've seen Nana, and she looks older, weary. She is wearing a pantsuit in her signature color, lavender. Her face has aged, and her thick-lensed bifocals sit unevenly on the bridge of her nose. But her silver hair is beautifully coiffed, and her lips are a frosted pink. I am struck, today, by how much Diana looks like Juliet: same hair, same pretty face. Does Diana see it every time she looks in the mirror? It saddens me to think of how Juliet's death has taken its toll on Nana Edna, on Diana, on their whole family. My mind goes straight to the thought of Mom lying in a bed at Tenacre, and then it goes to Grandma. The sadness builds to anguish. My stomach knots up. I chase the thought away.

I kiss Mimi's cheek as I brush past her, and smile. She smiles back primly. I wonder if she is angry with me that I've been so remote. Last month, I did nothing for her birthday other than call her. It could be I'm reading something into her manner that isn't there. Maybe the Palm Court's formality and splendor, which should be a treat, make everything feel stiff and artificial to me.

"Lucia," Nana says, tenderly, standing to her feet.

"Don't get up," I say, approaching her.

"Oh, don't be silly," she says. She gives me a huge, warm hug, and then another.

"That's from your grandma. Now," she says, pulling back, "let me get a good look at you."

We stand there, face-to-face, hands clutching each other's elbows, and smile. I want to say how sorry I am about Juliet, but I'm afraid that maybe I shouldn't bring her up. I look at Diana, who is beaming at Nana's strength and poise. Diana's eyes are filled with tears.

"It's so good to see you, Nana," I say, and I realize my eyes are welling up too.

"It's wonderful to see you," she says.

Afternoon tea is a familiar and favorite ritual for all of us. For me, tea brings thoughts of Mom, and memories of Fortnum & Mason, and Claremont School.

The waiter takes our orders. Everyone requests Earl Grey, except for me. Mom's and my preferred tea, Assam, is one of the offerings.

Our conversation is pleasant. Edna wants to hear all about our jobs. I try to make a joke about how Mimi should really be working at *Vogue* and I at Marine Midland Bank, given Mimi's fashion sense and my lack thereof. But the joke is awkward and falls flat. I decide I'm better off keeping quiet. Nevertheless, Nana seems delighted to be here with Diana and her friends—all modern-day Manhattan versions of that quintessential Minnesota working girl, Mary Richards (Mary Tyler Moore)—and happy that we are close, as though our lives here together have fulfilled a dream of hers.

There is a lull while we take turns selecting finger sandwiches from the elegant three-tiered tray. The silence hovers over the table and feels like it may grow uncomfortable. I take a salmon and watercress, and a cucumber and cream cheese, and pass the tray to Cindy.

"I wish Juliet were here," Nana says, her voice quivering.

Diana sets down her sandwich and holds one of Nana's hands.

Mimi takes the other. Our gazes all fall downward. Eventually, we look up, as if a silent prayer is over.

"It's too bad Joanne couldn't come," Edna adds, sweetly.

"She so wanted to," I say, too quickly. Mimi and Diana both look at me, and I wonder, again, if I am being overly sensitive. "She couldn't make it. They're having work done at the house. The contractor's being a pain. They're meeting with him as we speak," I blather, ". . . that is, if he shows up."

"What are they having done?" Mimi asks.

I stare blankly.

"Oh, who knows?" I say, rolling my eyes. My stomach turns.

When we are finished, we exit, say our good-byes, and wait for the doorman to put Nana Edna, Diana, and Cindy in a cab. In parting, Nana hugs me again and hands me a small present.

"This is from your grandmother. It's for tomorrow. Happy birthday, dear."

I feel like I might start to cry. I am relieved when the taxi drives off.

"You heading home?" Mimi asks.

"I have to stop at the office first," I say, pointing my thumb over my shoulder, roughly in the direction of midtown.

"Oh?"

"We have a shoot on Monday," I lie. I'm afraid Mimi may ask if I want to hang out. I simply can't do it.

"Okay. Well, I'll see you tonight then," she says.

Back at my apartment building, I stop in the lobby to get the mail. There is one envelope in my mailbox, a card. The handwriting is my father's. I open it. It is a Hallmark birthday card, with a check folded in half, made out in my name, for five hundred dollars. I walk up the three flights of stairs, staring at the card. Dad has written "Dear Lucia" at the top, and "love, Dad and" at the bottom. Next to the word *and,* in wobbly handwriting, are three letters: Mom.

SATURDAY, MAY 24, 1986
MEMORIAL DAY WEEKEND
HOPEWELL, NEW JERSEY

I've taken a half share in a summerhouse on the Jersey shore, although I'm not sure why. It was a foolishly optimistic decision on my part. I was supposed to go down to Spring Lake for the opening weekend, but instead I am in Hopewell: Mom came home from Tenacre on Thursday, and Dad has said I may visit. I don't know what it means. Could it be she's been discharged, like a patient from a hospital after being successfully treated? I'm doubtful. But she must be doing better on some level.

When I arrive Saturday evening, she is already in bed, even though the sun has yet to go down.

"You'll see her in the morning," my father says, sensing my disappointment. It is his fifty-fourth birthday, but neither he nor I mention it.

Sunday morning, Mom and Dad don't go to church. I wake up and find her—after looking first in my parents' bedroom and then the kitchen—supine on the gliding sofa in the screened porch behind the house. I am surprised to see that her hair looks lovely, brownish gray now but done up—like she has paid a visit to a salon. Maybe she has? Her lips are a pretty shade of rose, and she has the healthy glow of a suntan. But she is in a bathrobe, with a blanket folded in half over her waist and legs, even though the temperature is in the high eighties. Her hands rest in her lap on top of the blanket. The two rings, a diamond solitaire and a simple platinum band, which I've never seen her without, are missing, and the reason is clear. Her fingers are skeletal.

The image is startling. And heartbreaking. I had bought into my own fantasy that she was doing better. My mother—or someone—has gone to considerable effort to make her *appear* well. But it is a mask.

"Hi, darling," she says, moving her eyes but not her head to greet me.

"Hi, Mom," I say.

I bend over to kiss her. Her forehead radiates warmth on my lips.

"Would you be a dear and bring me some hot tea?" she asks.

I go back to the kitchen, thankful that I've been handed a few moments to compose myself. What was I thinking? That everything would be normal? That Mom's "little problem" was in fact, miraculously, just that, and nothing more? While the kettle is heating, I try to call Olivia in Cambridge. No answer. I have no idea how to reach Sherman. He's somewhere in the city rehearsing with his band. After the holiday weekend, he'll be moving back home to live with Mom and Dad for the summer. He has taken a job with a landscaper in Princeton.

I return to the porch several minutes later with a tea tray. Mom eases herself up to a semi-sitting position, and I watch her reach for the teapot. Her arm is alien thin. She pours the tea, then the milk from the small pitcher. Her hand is unsteady. Very cautiously, she lifts the teacup to her lips, then replaces it on the saucer. It is uncomfortable for both of us to witness this: the teacup rattles nervously as she sets it down; the saucer catches the murky spillover. I stare silently, wondering whether or not I should have helped her. She deflates into the pile of pillows supporting her.

"It must be oppressive in the city," my mother says. Even the three syllables of *op-press-ive* seem too much for her. "Why don't you take a swim in the pool?"

For the remainder of the day, Mom, Dad, and I inhabit our separate orbits at home: Mom in the screened porch and later her bed, Dad in his office, and I on an air mattress in the pool. Hopewell is not—nor has it ever really been—home for me, and this weekend I feel even more like an intruder. I don't think they really want me here. My presence feels tactical, part of an effort to placate me; a necessary, if temporary, evil.

In the evening I drive into Princeton to grab dinner.

At Hoagie Haven, a popular joint at the other end of town, I wait in line to order a cheesesteak. Back on the street, I sit on a bench and eat, watching the students come and go. For some of them, their college years are almost over; commencement is less than two weeks away. I feel sorry for them, which strikes me as odd given the situation I face at home.

I'm transported back to Brown and the public speaking course I took my senior year. One of the assignments was a speech to a hostile audience. For me, any speech, even to the most hospitable of audiences, was terrifying. I couldn't come up with a decent subject, but the day before I was to give my speech I heard on the radio that Dr. David Sweet, the president of nearby Rhode Island College, had died of a heart attack. A known Christian Scientist, he was fifty-one. I had my topic.

Standing before the class, I took a deep breath. I felt like I was about to divulge some deep-seated family secret. (And I was, since I'd never really spoken about my religious background with anyone at Brown.) I looked down at my notes, and then up, and said something to the effect of "I was raised as a Christian Scientist, but while I am not one myself, I do support a person's right to choose prayer over medicine for one's health care needs." I pointed out—taking care to make eye contact—that people using traditional forms of health care had heart attacks too. I was strangely dispassionate, I didn't feel emotionally connected to the subject at all. And once I got going, I wasn't nervous.

"But what about the children who die of treatable causes?" a classmate asked.

"Believe me," I said, "my family has had years of good health and many healings. And there are numerous documented cases in *The Christian Science Journal*. I am a testament to its efficacy. Furthermore, choosing prayer over medicine is a right protected by the Constitution."

I was poised and calm. *Testament to its efficacy*... My parents and the Mother Church would have been proud.

"Well then," another student pressed, raising her hand, "why aren't you a Christian Scientist?"

I don't remember my response.

When I was twelve, I could have joined the Mother Church but didn't. To my parents' credit, I was never coerced into joining, nor was I cajoled. The most they did was bring up the subject occasionally, and casually, in conversation. And when I said it wasn't for me, they'd remark how one day, surely, I'd come back to the fold.

Sherman never joined either, but Olivia did, as soon as she could, at the age of twelve, probably out of a desire to please our parents. I don't know why I never felt that need. For years now, Dad has made Olivia's required annual gift to remain in good standing (minimum one dollar, but who knows the actual amount?). She has never officially renounced her faith, and while she and I haven't discussed it much, I know she's not—nor has she ever been—a believer.

The question for me evolved from "Why aren't you a Christian Scientist?" to "Why is anyone?" Some time after my speech I learned the true cause of death for Dr. Sweet. He'd been sick for several days, refused medical treatment, and had a diabetic seizure, followed by cardiac arrest.

Monday morning I wake up to the sound of the vacuum cleaner. My stomach is badly sunburned from the day before, and the skin of my midriff is emblazoned with the imprint of wrinkled bedsheets. A cold, wet washcloth brings the only relief. Obviously, I won't find any Solarcaine in the medicine cabinet: only toothpaste, soaps, shaving stuff. When I head downstairs, I come face-to-face with our cleaning lady, Carmen, who tells me, through a combination of fractured English and gestures, that Mom and Dad are over at Connie Reeder's and I should give them a call. Connie, Mom's best Christian Science friend, is so close to my mother that, when her kids left home and she wanted a smaller house, she moved from Princeton to Hopewell to be closer by. Carmen pauses and says "you mommy," and her hand goes to her mouth, and she takes a step back and shakes her head slightly. She makes no effort to hide the worry in her beseeching eyes. I have no idea what to say to her, so I say nothing. She is not a Christian Scientist; she is from somewhere in South America, and I assume she is Catholic. What must be going through her head?

"Hi, Dad," I say when he answers the phone. "Why are you at Connie's? I thought she went to the shore."

"She did. We're just here while Carmen cleans. Did you sleep well?"

"Yeah." I know this is not his real concern.

"I'll be home in a bit. We're just finishing the Lesson."

That's the end of the conversation.

In the next room, Carmen is folding laundry. I am sprawled out on the living room sofa, reading the paper and watching *Donahue*. Mom's practitioner would say this is a perfect time to open the books.

I won't do it. I refuse to make this tiny gesture, and yet I am puzzled. Why am I taking *this* stand but not a meaningful one, the only one that even matters? What is stopping me from picking up the phone and calling Uncle Jack?

I have seen Mom for all of twelve minutes so far this weekend. I wonder if today will be any different from yesterday.

A little while later, Dad walks in.

"You think Mom might be hungry?" I ask.

"Why don't you call her and ask?" he says before disappearing into his study.

I pick up the phone and dial Connie's number again. Mom answers it after the first ring. Her voice is very low, not much more than a whisper.

"Hi, Mom," I say. "Would you like me to bring you something to eat? A sandwich maybe?"

"Thanks, sweetheart, but no," she says, and I feel rejected, even foolish. I *knew* that answer before I called. "Maybe later," she adds before saying good-bye and quickly hanging up.

Not thirty seconds later, the phone rings.

"On second thought," my mother says, "I'd love a PBB."

When I was a kid, Mom's and my favorite sandwich was peanut butter and banana on toast. The very mention of it used to make my dad grimace in disgust, and nobody else in the family liked it much either. But, oh, what comfort: the warm, gooey peanut butter, all melty from the heat of the toast, and the cool, slippery sliced bananas. This was our common craving, a mother-daughter thing.

I decide not to toast the bread. By the time I reach Connie's, it will be hard and dried out, and there's nothing worse than a cold, dried-out PBB. But the Skippy is in the fridge, not in the pantry, where it should be, and nearly unspreadable—further proof that someone other than Mom has been at the helm in her kitchen. The peanut butter steadfastly clings to the soft bread, pulling it apart. Nervously, I try to put the mangled sandwich together. Oh well, it will taste good, even if it looks awful. I also pack up a slice of the rhubarb pie that someone—I wonder who—has made.

Mom is lying on one of the twin beds in Connie's guest room, covered with the bedspread. She doesn't hear me when I come in. She's wearing earphones and holding a Walkman.

"What are you listening to?" I ask.

She looks up and removes the earphones.

"Oh, hi. A lecture. Just marvelous," she says.

I unwrap the sandwiches and hand her a quarter of one. When I was a kid, she always cut my sandwiches up into quarters. Now I've done the same for her, thinking it will make eating easier, but somehow having done so feels inappropriate, jarring. I wonder if she feels it too. She takes a hardcover book from the bedside table, hands it to me, and asks me to read to her. It is *On the Road with Charles Kuralt.* I sit on the other twin bed facing her.

I guess Charles Kuralt is a welcome break for her from Christian Science lectures on tape. I start reading aloud a passage about some of the men who helped build the Golden Gate Bridge. After several minutes, I pause to take a sip of water.

Mom is staring at me. "I don't get it," she says.

What is there to get?

I am taken aback, unnerved, ill at ease. I set the book down and grab a quarter of a sandwich. I want her to think I'm only breaking to eat, but the truth is, I don't want to read Charles Kuralt. I'm scared. What is going on here?

But then I think—maybe I want to think—she must be tired of doing nothing but reading the Bible and *Science and Health,* and listening to lectures, and lying here or wherever, day in, day out. Even as a diversion from her routine, maybe the building of the Golden Gate Bridge just doesn't hold her attention at the moment. I switch gears.

"Bill Cosby was on *Donahue* this morning," I say. "Did you watch?"

"No."

"I almost called you to tell you to turn it on," I say, nibbling, making the sandwich last, "but I figured you and Dad were reading the Lesson."

For a moment, neither of us speaks.

"Cosby," Mom says. She looks at me, confused. "It's crazy, I know," she says, "but my mind is running a blank."

Running a blank on *Cosby*? A show she watches every week?

"Oh, you know, *The Cosby Show*?" I say, as casually as I can.

My mother's face registers nothing. I try to change the subject again, because the silence is so awkward, but just below the surface I am barely keeping my composure.

"It will be nice having Sherman home this summer, won't it?" I say. I am nearly in tears, and my voice is shaky, but she doesn't notice.

"Oh, it will be wonderful," my mother says. "Cosby . . . I just . . . can't . . . place it."

I want to shake my mother.

"It's on Thursday nights," I say, fighting back tears, "before *Cheers. The Cosby Show.*"

"Does Cosby have a family?"

I cannot bring myself to answer this question. "Would you like anything else? Some pie?"

"No, but you could take this to the kitchen," she says, handing me an empty glass.

I go to the kitchen, somewhat relieved that I have been granted permission to flee that room for the moment. I tear off a piece of paper towel to use as a tissue. My tears burn. I try to take deep, even breaths, but I can't. I am sobbing, choking. I need to call Olivia and Sherman immediately, and I need them to be there to pick up the phone.

I should call for an ambulance. I should call Uncle Jack.

I rest my arms on the edge of the sink, and my head in my arms, and wait. For what? Incredibly, I am listening for the "still small voice" my Sunday school teachers always talked about, or for some inner compass to point me in the right direction. But nothing, nothing at all, is clear, except that I have to go back into that room. My head hurts.

I rinse the few plates in the sink, load them in the dishwasher, keep breathing deeply, and head back to the guest room. I take a seat on the other twin bed again.

"Did I tell you who's going to cut my hair?" I ask. Mom shakes her head. Absurdly, I find myself telling my mother about a recent fashion shoot at German *Vogue,* how the hairstylist, one of the most sought after in New York, showed up two and a half hours late.

"Rados was furious, so she said—"

"Now, who's Rados?" Mom asks, blankly.

You've met her, damn it! We've had long conversations about her.

"Oh, you remember," I say lightly, my voice cracking, "my boss?"

I am terrified, but I clear my throat and push on.

"So he's cutting my hair for free," I say, pretending to examine my fingernails. "He usually charges, like, a hundred and fifty dollars."

My mother is smiling at me, pleased at my good fortune.

"Mom," I say, "I have to leave soon."

I have to call Olivia and Sherman.

"Do you have a date tonight?" she asks.

I'm caught off guard; I do, in fact, have a date. And because I do, I feel ashamed. If we were a normal family, I would be staying right here to care for Mom. But this situation is not normal, not even close, so I am returning to the city, to carry on the pretense of a regular life, with a job and the occasional date.

"What's he like?" she asks. It has been so long since she has asked me anything like this. But instead of feeling good, or even nostalgic for this type of exchange, I feel distracted. I can't even pull up an image in my head.

"He's got dark brown hair and green eyes," I say.

"Green eyes?" she asks and winks, but I'm not even sure that he does.

We both smile, and I am aware that, for Mom, this chat must feel good, significant, as it allows her to be something she hasn't been for months: my mother.

"Does he have brothers and sisters?"

"Brothers. Four, I think—"

"Five boys and no girls?"

I nod.

"And his parents? Are they both alive?"

I have to look away. I am disarmed by the question. Asking about siblings is one thing. Asking if his parents are both alive is something else altogether.

"Uh," I manage, "uh . . . yeah. I think they are."

I face her again, and it is my mother who looks away.

"Mom?"

"Yes?"

She has turned toward me again and is looking straight into my eyes. I have to ask the question.

"Look, Mom, are you sure you don't want to go see a doc——"

"No, Lucia. No." She is shaking her head vehemently. "I just know this will be met. It *will* happen.

"You know, Connie and Susie are such good Scientists...," Mom says wistfully. "Having grown up in the Church, their understanding is just, well, more pure. You may not see it this way now, but, Lucia, you are so blessed with this upbringing."

I bite my lip.

I want to tell my mom that her illness isn't the result of some sort of failing or shortcoming on her part. But I don't. I say nothing.

"I am working very closely with Mrs. Childs. She is an excellent practitioner. I know I'm making progress. But I need you to be behind me."

I remember what Mrs. Childs said to Sherman and me about her three children, and keeping the ones who are not Christian Scientists at a distance. I take a deep breath and tell my mother what she wants to hear me say.

"Mom, whatever you need to do, I support you. I love you."

I hug her, squeezing maybe too hard. I don't want to let go.

Once I'm in the car, I want a cigarette. I search my purse but can't find the box of Marlboro Lights. Am I really craving nicotine? Is that why I'm shaking? Or do I just want to fill my father's Honda with smoke, commit the ultimate Christian Science fuck you?

I speed back to my parents' house. Driving fast feels strangely exhilarating. I wouldn't mind if I crashed. I blast the stereo to drown out everything.

Turning in to my parents' driveway, I slow down to twenty, which is still way too fast for the rutted gravel road. The woods are so dense and green I can't see the house through them, but then, suddenly, here I am. Why the hell did I race back? At the bend, I coast to a halt, put the car in park, and rest my head on the steering wheel. My eyes well up again, and I feel I may completely lose it, but then I look up and see that my dad is walking toward the car. I lower the volume on the stereo and roll down the window.

"So you brought my car back in one piece?" he says, clearly trying to be funny.

I'm in no mood. I turn off the ignition, get out, and walk past him.

"I'm going to pack up my stuff. Any time it's convenient to take me to the Junction, I'm ready."

My father says nothing.

A hundred and seventeen days ago Mom went to Tenacre. Yeah, she's out. So what? It's not like the doctors have said, "Okay, you're all better. You can go home now."

Her birthday is in five days. She will be fifty.

JUNE 7, 1986

I take the train out from Penn Station and pick up Mom's car, which Sherman has left for me at Princeton Junction. I wish he were here, but he's gone to the city overnight. I don't blame him for needing to get away. The last time I left Hopewell, I thought about never coming back.

Turning in to the driveway, I see Mom and Dad approaching me in Dad's car. We pull up side by side and both roll down our windows.

"Hi," we say in unison. "Hi, Mom," I add. She looks, I think, about the same, but she is wearing a pink cable-knit sweater, and her face is, maybe, a bit fuller. In spite of the confused mental state I found her in nearly two weeks ago, and the complete lack of evidence of physical improvement, I still cling to the hope—or the fantasy—that Christian Science can work.

"We're going into town for some ice cream," Dad says.

"All right," I say. "Can I drop my bags first?"

I expect to hear him say, "Great!" and mean it, or at least acquiesce to my wish to join them.

Instead, he looks at Mom, and she looks at him, and then she glances down at her hands, and Dad turns back to me and says, "Gee, Loosh," wincing. "I think, I think we're going to go just the two of us. We won't be long. Can we bring you something?"

I roll up my window and feel hurt, shut out. It's probably a ruse anyway. She won't touch the ice cream.

But then I think: maybe she *does* want some ice cream. Maybe she really doesn't have the energy for the three of us. Wanting to go out for ice cream could still be a good sign. I'm aware of my need to see just about anything as an indication that she might be getting better.

I bring my weekend bag up to my room and set it on the far twin bed, the one that used to be Olivia's. The room is cozy enough, with pretty Laura Ashley bed linens and curtains. I first stayed here in August of '78, after Claremont and before I went off to Emma Willard. My parents have lived here for eight years now, but I've never slept here enough to think of this room as anything more than a guest room. I lie down on the bed and close my eyes.

About half an hour later, I hear the churning of car wheels on gravel. A car door opens and closes. Then another does. I approach the window, where I see my father helping my mother walk. She's fifty now, but she looks as old as Grandma. Dad's right arm is around her waist, and his left hand is holding her left arm at the elbow. They are moving very slowly but urgently. He struggles with the screen door, and they step into the kitchen together.

My mother moans.

"We're almost there. Do you want to rest?" my father asks.

"The bathroom . . . ," she says.

I tiptoe toward the hallway. I feel like a spy.

"Oh, uh," my mother says, changing her mind, "no. Upstairs."

I hear the shuffle of footsteps. I return to my room and quietly close the door, hoping it won't squeak.

I am ready for bed, even though it's only nine-thirty. I've brushed my teeth in the bathroom down the hall. Washing up has given me something to do while Dad helps Mom settle in for the night. There is a whispered conversation, but I can't make out what they're saying. Dad closes the door to the master bedroom and quickly heads down the hall to his study, pulling the door shut behind him.

I walk from my bedroom, past my father's study, to my parents' bedroom. I'm pretty certain he has heard me, but I don't feel like talking to him. It might lead to a confrontation, and I feel as though my status here is already in jeopardy, like my parents see me more and more as part of the problem. If I'm not careful, there may come a time—soon—when I'll be asked to leave, or I won't be invited back.

I knock lightly on the door.

"Mom?" I say. "Can I come in?"

"Sure, dear."

The bedside light is on, and Mom is propped up with pillows. Her Bible and *Science and Health* aren't open to the Lesson, and she is not wearing the Walkman earphones. She is staring aimlessly into space, or maybe she is praying. Even though it is a muggy summer evening, she is wearing a flannel nightgown, and the air-conditioning is turned off.

"How are you?" I ask.

"I'm fine."

"Here, come sit with me," Mom says, turning toward me and patting the down comforter.

I'm pleasantly caught off guard. I climb in next to her and pull a section of the comforter over me. It's good to feel welcome.

"Did you see what your daddy gave me for my birthday?"

"No," I say, surprised, grateful, glad.

There's no such thing as birthdays, I was told as a kid. It was the most depressing of all the Christian Science truths, because we were usually reminded of this a week or two before a birthday.

"Birth and death connote beginning and end," our parents would say, "and in Science we know there is no beginning, no end." Not going to doctors was no big deal, but no birthdays? Of course, every year we did celebrate our birthdays, and our parties were every bit as good as anyone else's. Maybe Mom and Dad loved the tease of it all. Or, possibly, Dad felt strongly about it and Mom was torn, and as each birthday drew near, Mom won? In truth, the uncertainty made birthdays that much better, knowing we were getting something we shouldn't.

Mom and Dad, on the other hand, didn't celebrate their own birthdays. I can't remember a single party for either one of them when we were growing up. They never went out for special birthday dinners. At most, we got to bake and decorate a cake, and light candles, but that was for our sake, not theirs.

My mother pulls her left hand out from under the covers and extends her fingers elegantly toward me. In place of her wedding band, I see a beautiful new ring, with rubies and pearls arranged in a circular pattern. She is beaming. I think, *Well done, Dad.*

I take my mother's hand and hold it in mine. We sit there quietly, and the silence feels, somehow, nearly perfect. A few moments later, I look up at her face again. She has tears in her eyes.

"Lucia," she says, "maybe one day you'll get to have it."

My mother has said this with such tenderness, but all of a sudden I'm so fucking angry I might explode. *What, am I supposed to thank you? How can you do this to me? I couldn't care less about a stupid goddamned ring. You are abandoning me!*

I need to excuse myself.

I lie in bed, waiting for sleep, trying to do it without my Halcion—not out of deference to Mom and Dad while I'm at their house but because I'm pretty sure these pills are intended for occasional insomnia, which I am long past.

"Maybe one day you'll get to have it."

She thinks she's dying, yet she refuses to change course. And here I sit doing nothing.

God, please make Aunt Mary or Aunt Kay or somebody call here. Make someone act on a hunch and fly out here and get Mom to a doctor.

I don't even believe in God.

Tomorrow, Mom will stay in her room and Dad will bring her a tray with tea and sandwiches that she won't touch. Or maybe she'll make it down the stairs, with his help, and out to the screened porch in back, where she'll lie on the gliding sofa. I'll watch the Sunday morning news shows in the next room and hang out by the pool with *The New York Times,* maybe go for a jog. And then I'll head back to the city.

Worse yet is this: Dad is scheduled to conduct his two-week Primary class, a closely guarded annual event central to the work of a Christian Science teacher and the Church's training of practitioners, in the city next month. Normally, Mom and Dad stay in their apartment for the duration.

Sherman and Olivia and I are worried that Dad will send Mom back to Tenacre. If he does, I just know she will never come out. But what are his options? He can't leave her. He can hire a Christian Science nurse who makes house calls, but that still leaves Mom alone for much of each day.

He should postpone his class. Maybe we can convince him. We have discussed this possibility over the last few weeks, but we have not broached the subject with Dad. Everything about his practice is strictly off-limits to us.

What little I know about Primary class I have pieced together from Mom and Dad's cryptic, sporadic comments, and from what Mary Baker Eddy outlines in the Church Manual: Christian Scientists may apply to specific teachers to take the two-week course, which is centered on the teachings of one particular chapter in *Science and Health* entitled "Recapitulation." Each class is made up of no more than thirty pupils and is taught only once a year. The teacher can determine whether membership in the Mother Church is a prerequisite. In addition to the annual Primary class, a teacher holds a one-day meeting of his association of all students who have ever taken his class. At that, he gives an address, which he spends weeks preparing. My father's Primary class is held in July, his association, in August.

We will have to say something soon.

But I can't confront Dad face-to-face. So Sunday evening, after returning to my apartment, I light myself a cigarette and pick up the phone to call my father on his business line, which rings only in his study. He answers right away.

"Hi, Dad. I just got home. Do you have a minute?" I ask.

"Sure," he says. "What is it?" In those four words I can hear, instantly, that he is on the defensive. I sit down and nervously flick the ashes from my cigarette.

"I'm worried about what will happen to Mom if you teach your class next month."

There is silence from the other end of the phone.

"Lucia," he says, in a low, even voice. "This is not your concern."

"Well, actually, it is." I have said this too quickly, so I attempt to be conciliatory. "I'm not trying to stir up trouble. Really, I'm not. I just think maybe it would be best for Mom if you postponed your class."

"How dare you tell me what I should and shouldn't do!" my dad yells.

I pull the phone back from my ear and remember his rage when I told him I wanted to see an eye doctor. I'm afraid that Mom will hear his end of the conversation, even though I was careful to call him on his office phone to avoid this possibility.

"Young lady," my father goes on scornfully, "why should I listen to this...this...impudence? Don't you think I've given the matter some thought?"

I am thankful, at least, that I had the foresight to wait until I was safely in New York before taking on this conversation.

My father pauses, and then his voice softens. "Your mother happens to be making good progress."

How many times have I heard this now?

"If she goes back to Tenacre, she'll continue to make progress. She'll be under the best of care there. In fact, they're probably better equipped to care for her than *I* am anyway. And for your information," he adds almost parenthetically, but I can hear the bitterness returning, "I've already discussed the matter with her practitioner, and she has given her full support."

"Dad," I say, trying to sound reasonable, "Mom will be alone there for two whole weeks! How do you know she'll be okay? What if she takes a turn for the worse while you're gone?"

"I'll be checking in with her regularly, and I'll be home over the weekend. Maybe even midweek. It's only an hour away. I have every confidence in Tenacre."

When I think of my own confidence in Tenacre, my reaction comes out as a grunt, which doesn't go unnoticed.

"That's just the kind of negativity we *don't* need around here!" my father snaps.

"Dad," I say as gently as I can, wondering how—if—I will ever get through to him, "Dad, I'm sorry. Mom is not getting better. She just isn't."

"Yes she is!" My father's voice is pleading now. He truly believes she is improving or will improve, and he is incredulous, and indignant, that I don't share his conviction. "And if she could count on even a little support from you kids, she'd probably be better already!"

"So this is *our* fault?" My voice cracks.

"Your attitude is exactly what your mother and I have to guard against," my father says. I am so angry I want to hang up.

"...you haven't once gone to church since she's been sick. I bet you haven't once read the Lesson."

I hold the phone away from my ear again until he is finished.

"I won't be emotionally blackmailed," I say calmly, rubbing out my cigarette.

"Emotional blackmail," my father says with an audible sneer. "This isn't blackmail. I'm talking about love. If you *really* loved your mother—"

I close my eyes.

"—if you *really* cared—"

"Dad," I say, "this is wrong. You are abandoning Mom when she needs you most. And if anything happens to her while you're away teaching your class, I swear I'll never forgive you. Never."

My father hangs up the telephone, and it occurs to me, before I have even finished speaking, that it is he—and Mom—who feels abandoned: by Olivia, Sherman, and me. A few minutes later he calls back, and we have the same conversation all over again, and again he hangs up on me. It is not a new pattern. I recall other fights, and they always proceed the same way. I yell, or he yells; I yell back. Eventually, he slams down the phone, and minutes later the phone rings again and he's back. There is a soft, whispered "I'm...sorry... Lucia...but...," and then the whole thing starts all over.

On this particular night, we more or less call it a draw. Or more accurately, I concede, exhausted. Conversations and fights never end in our family without the mutual reassurance of "I love you," but this time, I don't say it after my father does.

The next morning, Monday, Sherman calls me at work. I had expected he would call me Sunday night after I had it out with Dad, since he was at the house. But at midnight I stopped waiting for the phone to ring. I learned in the morning that he had been afraid Dad would catch him if he called.

What must it be like for Sherman living in Hopewell this summer?

He tells me that he and Mom were sitting in the living room, watching *Murder, She Wrote,* when I called. They heard the whole thing, or Dad's end of it. At one point, Mom turned to Sherman and said, "That was Lucia, wasn't it? She doesn't think I'm getting better, does she?"

I feel sick to my stomach.

Tuesday morning, June 17, Mom is rushed back to Tenacre. As Dad explains to me on the phone, "She has taken a turn for the worse."

In the evenings, when I come home to find a blinking red light on my answering machine, I get a sick feeling in the pit of my stomach. It used to be that a blinking red light meant the possibility of plans for the evening: dinner with friends, a party at Area or Limelight, an occasional date. Now, it feels like a bad omen.

One night I see the blinking red light before I'm even inside my apartment, still struggling with the key that always gets stuck in the dead-bolt lock. I walk across the room and stoop down to my answering machine. I hit the Play button.

"Hi, Lucia. It's Aunt Nan."

The pit in my gut expands and fills with angst.

"I'll try to call you again this evening. Or, if you like, you can call me in Greenwich. Bye."

Aunt Nan and I are not that close. She has never called me. I know her mostly from Thanksgivings in Greenwich, which are always big gatherings. I wonder if Mary has told her about our brunch back in January.

What should I do? If I call Aunt Nan, I will have to lie to her in order to honor Mom's wishes. If I call Dad, and tell him that I think Aunt Nan suspects something, he may discover that I betrayed Mom's trust months ago.

Panicky, I call Olivia in Cambridge.

"What if she knows?" I ask. "What if she asks me point-blank?"

"Maybe she should know," Olivia says. I find her response less than helpful.

"But what should I do?"

"Maybe you should tell her," Olivia says. "Maybe you need to do it for yourself."

Thanks, Liv.

"Look," she says, "if Aunt Nan suspects anything at all, she's probably going to call Dad, not you. And if she does ask you, maybe you should be straight with her, because it means that she already knows."

"Well then, why don't *you* tell her!"

I want to slam the phone down, or throw it against the wall—like Dad might do. It is so easy for Olivia to be analytical and dispassionate: she didn't get the phone call. Or maybe—probably—it isn't. She and Sherman are grasping at the same hopeless options I am. In our daily conversations about the "progress" reports we're given, there is little discussion of how we are being affected.

It's possible, I guess, that Aunt Nan or Uncle Dave would know what to do, would act. But there's no reason to believe that telling Aunt Nan will get Mom to a doctor. It's just as likely—if not more likely—that Mom and Dad will retreat further into their faith, further from us, and we'll find ourselves at a worse place than we are right now. Mom could take another bad turn and point the accusing finger at me. She could shut me out for good.

I can't call Aunt Nan.

Half an hour later, the phone rings four or five times while I debate picking it up; in the end, I do. It is Aunt Nan.

"Oh, hi!" I say. My heart is pounding fiercely. "I just got your message. How are you?"

"Fine, thank you," she says.

There is a long silence.

"How are your parents?" she asks.

A wave of anxiety sweeps over me.

"All right. They've been doing some work on the house."

"Oh?"

"So they haven't come into the city much."

I shove aside a pile of clean laundry and sit down on the sofa to light a cigarette.

"Were you home for your mom's fiftieth?" Aunt Nan asks.

"Yes," I lie. "We had a small party, just Dad, Sherman, Mom, and me. There was a cake. A few presents," I say. "You know they don't make a big deal of birthdays."

"Uh-huh," she says. There is another pause.

I think of my mother's ruby-and-pearl ring, and my chest tightens.

"I sent a card to your mom," Aunt Nan says, "and then I called her and left a message. I said that I'd love to take her out for lunch sometime in the city. When she called me back, she said she wouldn't be coming in for a while."

"I guess she's been busy," I say.

I can't keep doing this.

"Well, I just thought I'd touch base with you." My aunt's voice is strained. "If you ever feel like coming to Vermont, give us a call."

"Thanks, I will."

I rub out the ember of my cigarette.

"Aunt Nan?"

"Yes?"

"Mom is . . ."

I close my eyes. *Just say it.*

"Mom's not okay. She's sick. Very sick. She's been sick since . . . since before Christmas."

I tell her about Tenacre, about the day after the space shuttle blew up, how she was a *guest* there until a month ago, and how she's gone back there again.

I feel a huge burden lift.

"I knew something wasn't right. That's why I called." Aunt Nan's voice is higher now. "I love your mother a great deal."

My aunt is crying. She asks me about the symptoms, and I offer what little I know.

"She isn't eating much," I tell her. "She's very thin. It seems to be abdominal."

"Is she continent?"

"I . . . don't think so," I say reluctantly.

I hate telling her this. I shut my eyes and try to forget the opened package of Depends that I found hidden behind the toilet paper in the master bathroom cabinet in Hopewell. I can no longer hold back my own tears.

"Is she bedridden?"

"She can walk a little. But not up or down stairs without help from Dad. She's extremely pale. And weak. When I was at home with her, right after her birthday, we had lunch in the screened porch behind the house, Mom, Dad, and I. It was horrible. She was lying on the glider, picking at food from a plate I had set next to her on a little coffee table. Every time she took a bite, she said how great it tasted, how she was so hungry. But it was just an act. She hardly ate a thing."

I can't stop talking.

"Aunt Nan, she was lying down because she *couldn't* sit up, but she wanted me to think she was just enjoying the glider. And then she got really negative."

"What do you mean?" Aunt Nan says.

"She told me to push the table closer so she could reach it. It was only about two inches away from her, but I moved it closer. And she got really impatient and said, '*No, Lucia,*' like she was really fed up with me, '*push it right here.* Right here!' So I did. I was trying to do exactly what she wanted, and Dad just watched and pretended it was totally normal. Her hand trembled when she lifted the fork. I asked if I could help her eat, and she just got annoyed, you know, like *never mind,* and pushed the plate away. Aunt Nan?"

"Yes?"

"Mary and I had brunch in January, and—"

"I know, Lucia. That's why I called. Mary was home last weekend, and I told her I thought your mother was angry with me, because she'd been so short with me on the phone on her birthday. All of a sudden, Mary burst into tears. Then she said she couldn't talk about it. But I pushed. I forced it."

We are silent for a moment.

"Your parents have put you in a very difficult position. I wish I could tell you what to do," she says.

"Aunt Nan, I'm scared."

I am terrified, and overcome with regret.

"Lucia, I—" Aunt Nan hesitates. "I'd really like to speak to your father. Would it be all right with you if I called him?"

"Yes," I say.

The relief I feel at having told one of my father's siblings is immediately supplanted by the sheer terror of wondering if I'll ever see my mother again.

Within a few days of my conversation with Aunt Nan, Mimi calls me at work to remind me about a party on Thursday night.

"How's your family?" she asks.

"Good."

"How's Aunt Jo's health?"

Did she really say that?

"Fine," I say. My reply comes out as more of a question, and I wonder if I sound like I'm on the defensive.

"Because I haven't seen her in so long."

What do I do? How should I answer?

I give her my canned response, about my parents working on the house and being busy. I keep the conversation brief, and I hang up as soon as I can.

I leave a message on Dad's answering machine that I need to speak with him right away.

Mimi's inquiry could be a good thing, I reason. If I tell Dad that Mimi suspects something—that maybe she's already spoken with Aunt Mary—perhaps he will realize it is long past time to tell Mom's family.

Dad calls me late in the afternoon, just as I am leaving the office. I tell him about my conversation with Mimi.

"I think she knows, Dad."

"Oh, I don't think so." He sounds distant, unfazed.

"I'm supposed to see her on Thursday night," I say. "She's going to ask me about Mom again, I just know it."

"Oh, I really don't think she will. You may be overreacting. And as far as your aunt Mary is concerned," he goes on, suddenly more focused, "I doubt she's a bit concerned. She didn't even send your mother a card for her fiftieth birthday."

This comment irritates me. In another situation, I could imagine him testifying at a Wednesday night service, in a pious I'm-so-grateful-for-Christian-Science voice, "We've been so beautifully protected, her sister even forgot Jo's fiftieth birthday!"—as if Aunt Mary *not* sending a card is evidence of prayers being answered.

It never occurs to him that Aunt Mary might not have wished her happy birthday specifically out of respect for Mom's religious views.

But I wonder if Aunt Mary, like Aunt Nan, tried to call Mom on her birthday and got a bad feeling. Maybe that's why Mimi called me.

"You're putting me in a very difficult position with Mimi," I say. "You're asking me to lie."

The tension is building. It feels like we're headed for another fight.

"Look, if Mom comes up again, have Mimi call me," he says. This sounds to me, remarkably, like a tiny opening. "Although," he adds, "I don't know what I'll say to her."

THURSDAY, JUNE 26

I am sitting in Mimi's studio apartment in Greenwich Village, smoking a cigarette and sipping a glass of wine at her small café table. I am watching *The Cosby Show*—*The Cosby Show*, as if nothing's wrong!—while Mimi stands in her bathroom with the door open, applying her makeup.

"So, what have you been up to?" she asks. "You're never around."

"Work," I say.

"Been out at all?"

"Not really."

"Everything okay?"

"Yeah," I say, shrugging my shoulders.

I take a long drag on the cigarette. I can tell Mimi is eyeing me in the mirror.

"Are you sure?"

"Yeah," I say, trying not to sound defensive. "Yeah, why?"

There is a long silence before Mimi turns to look at me.

What am I to do? I cannot look her—my cousin, my best friend, my mom's sister's daughter—in the eye and lie any longer.

"Everything's not okay," I blurt out.

Mimi waits.

"Mom's sick."

Mimi pulls up a chair and puts her arms around me. I rest my head on my folded arms and begin to cry.

I confess everything to Mimi, just as I did to Aunt Nan a few days earlier.

Mimi tells me she will respect Mom's wishes and keep her illness a secret. I don't know whether I feel better or worse.

A few days later, Aunt Nan calls to say that she spoke with Dad, and he told her that Mom was "working out a problem" and that she was staying at Tenacre. When Aunt Nan asked if she could visit Mom, or at least talk to her, Dad said no: If Mom knew that Aunt Nan—or anyone else—had knowledge of her situation, she would be very upset. "Already I'm betraying Jo's wishes by admitting anything at all," he said to his sister. "I'm not going to risk upsetting her. Nor am I going to undermine her efforts to rely on Christian Science."

JULY 4, 1986

Olivia, Terry, Sherm, and I are all in Hopewell. Olivia and Terry are en route to Arizona, where Terry will be starting law school in the fall. Their U-Haul sits unhitched in our parents' driveway. It is a somber gathering. Olivia is worried about being so much farther away from Mom.

To "celebrate" the Independence Day holiday, we all go to Tenacre to sit with Mom and Dad and watch the televised festivities for the centennial of the Statue of Liberty. We eat Nilla wafers, drink ginger ale, and watch the fireworks display on a television suspended from the ceiling. It feels like we are in a nursing home with a centenarian, not with our mother, who is only fifty. After the fireworks are over, we turn off the TV and call Grandma in Minnesota to wish her a happy Fourth, Mom expending all of her energy to sound chipper. The occasion is anything but happy. We all play our parts in the charade, and then we leave, angry.

A few days later, I am back at work, and my French office mate, Ann-Isabel, asks if I want to skip out early and catch a movie.

On the street, we squint as we dig into our handbags for sunglasses. The air in midtown is lighter and cooler than the day before, when the midsummer city stench of urine, garbage, and street-vendor food blinded and choked. Today, Manhattan feels like the island it is. We can smell the ocean.

"How are things at home?" Ann-Isabel asks. Whenever she approaches the sensitive subject, her tone softens and her musical French voice creeps higher.

I sigh and shrug. I don't really want to talk about it.

"Did you talk to your mother today?"

"Yeah, she sounds the same."

Ann-Isabel means well by her concern. Her own mother died when she was a teenager and over the last several months, Ann-Isabel has shared her story. Together, we have drawn comparisons— unintentionally but unavoidably—which I have come to resent. *Just because your mother died doesn't mean mine is going to.* My relationship with Ann-Isabel has always been the nicest part of my job, but lately it has felt like more of a burden.

"How's your father?" she asks.

"I don't know," I say. "He never tells us anything."

Ann-Isabel and I walk a few blocks in silence.

"He's planning on teaching his class in a few weeks," I say.

"What kind of class?"

I don't have the energy to explain the intricacies of Christian Science. I wish I hadn't brought it up. "It's just a thing he does every year. A course that Christian Scientists take."

"You know, your dad has to go on with his life," Ann-Isabel says. However well intended, her words sound to me like a comment for a widower's daughter.

"You never know how long something like this will go on," she adds. "Your father can't just drop everything."

We go to see *Ferris Bueller's Day Off.* Matthew Broderick is lying in bed in his suburban Chicago bedroom. He is planning the perfect day of hooky from school when I feel a rush of adrenaline, and my heart starts racing. Nothing has happened in the movie to provoke that kind of reaction. There have been no screams. No blood. No car chases, not yet. I'm thinking it is claustrophobia, but I've never been phobic. I try to ignore the heart palpitations and the anxious feeling that is coursing through my body. Gripping the armrests of my chair as inconspicuously as I can, I try to breathe evenly and wonder if my distress is noticeable to Ann-Isabel. Eventually, the anxiety subsides. But while Ann-Isabel and the other patrons in the theater laugh, I grow restless. At the end of the film, Ann-Isabel stays to catch the last half of another movie. I head home.

Somewhere on the five-block stretch between the theater and my apartment, I start feeling panicky again, but this time it doesn't go away. It feels like an overcharged bout of stage fright: butterflies in my stomach, tingling in my fingertips, between my shoulder blades, behind my eyes. Could I be having a heart attack? I feel as if the buildings on either side of Third Avenue are getting taller and closer. The traffic is a bombardment of noise and motion, total confusion. My apartment is only a few blocks away. If I keep walking, one step after another, I'll get there.

At last I am at the front door of my apartment building. Three flights of stairs, and I'll be home.

By the time I reach the door to my apartment and fumble with the keys, I realize that this is the last place I want to be. I don't want to face the mess: the trash I need to take out; the clean clothes I need to fold; the answering machine, which might, at any moment, convey terrible news.

The phone is ringing. Right after I pick it up, I think, What am I doing? I don't want to speak to anyone.

Maybe it's a wrong number.

I cover the mouthpiece with my hand because I realize I am panting.

"Loosh?"

It is Stephanie, my Brown roommate. She knows about Mom. I told her back in January, when Mom went to Tenacre; I figured my secret was safe with her. Since then, we haven't talked much. I suspect that my situation at home is impossible for her to comprehend, since she is the daughter of a doctor.

"Lucia? Are you okay?"

"Yes," I say. "Well, maybe not... I can't feel my fingers. Or my hands," I say, perplexed. They are completely numb.

"Lucia, I want you to listen to me," Stephanie says. "Take a deep breath."

I try to, but I am shuddering.

"I'll be there in fifteen minutes."

"Okay," I say.

"Go unlock your door so I can get in."

"Yes," I say, like I'm some kind of robot.

Stephanie's voice is reassuring, but again, as soon as I replace the phone on its hook, I panic. I am hot. I feel disgustingly drunk— even though I've drunk nothing—and so foggy that I may puke. I make my way into the bathroom. My head throbs with the congestion of crying. I sit on the edge of the bathtub, elbows on my knees. A wave of nausea washes over me, so I sink to the floor and wrap the bath mat around my shoulders. The mat warms my bare arms. The floor's cold tiles soothe my face.

"Lucia?" Stephanie calls from the entry.

"I'm in here," I yell back, getting up from the floor. I head to the front door. The nausea and tingling have passed. I turn around and notice a large black garbage bag overflowing with newspapers, junk mail, and coffee grounds. A withered ficus plant stands in one corner of the room.

"Hi, Steph," I say. "I'm okay. How do you like my blotchies?" I ask, trying to make light of my swollen eyes. I am uncomfortable having her see me like this.

Stephanie sits on the club chair in the living room and starts pulling things from a grocery bag.

"I brought some salad and a couple of beers," she says. "Want some?" She gestures with the clear plastic container from the deli.

"I'm not really hungry."

She pulls out her pack of Marlboro Lights and offers me one. I take two and walk over to the gas stove to light one for each of us.

"Now. Tell me what happened," Stephanie says. I hand her back a lit cigarette.

"I don't know," I say, shaking my head. "Ann-Isabel and I left work early to see a movie. I was feeling a little shaky anyway, I guess, and when the lights came up, and I started walking home—something just...hit me. I started freaking out."

I return to the kitchen to get us an ashtray.

"Maybe it was seeing a movie where everything works out in the end," I say.

"How's your mom?"

"Shitty. The same, I guess. Maybe worse."

"I thought she was back at home," Stephanie says.

"She was. But three weeks ago Dad and I had a huge fight about the whole thing. Mom overheard it, and two days later she was back at Tenacre. They've been talking about *progress* for months—since Christmas—but, Stephanie, it's all bullshit. It's really bad. She's never going to get better."

I pull smoke deep into my lungs. I'm beginning to feel shaky again—the nicotine probably doesn't help—but while the smoke remains in my lungs, I stay in control. Exhaling brings on a storm of tears, and heat, and shaking.

"Oh, God. I can't do this anymore. I just can't."

Stephanie comes over to the couch and rubs my back.

"Is there somebody we can call?" Stephanie asks.

"It won't change anything."

"How about Mimi? Does she know?"

"She knows. She's going to honor Mom's privacy, which is what I asked her to do. So is my aunt Nan."

I decide I will call Dad and tell him that I intend to call Aunt Lucia, but I don't want to go behind his back. Aunt Lucia used to teach a course on counseling at Yale Divinity School; maybe she'll know what to do.

I tell Stephanie my dad's phone number, and she dials it for me. The phone is back in my hand and ringing. Dad answers. I am crying again.

"Lucia?"

I don't say anything. I'm so angry, I want him to hear me. All of this is his fault. His, and his goddamned church's.

"Loosh?" His voice is gentle, and it makes me cry harder. He sounds fatherly.

"What's wrong, Loosh?"

What's wrong?

"Dad, I really can't do this anymore. I need help."

"What kind of help are you thinking of?" he asks in a tone I can't interpret. Does he think I'm calling him for help? Christian Science help?

"I don't know," I say. "Maybe if I talk to someone—"

"Well, who do you have in mind?" The softness of his voice is laced with something.

"I don't know." I pause. "Maybe Aunt Lucia."

The suggestion is like a lit match to kerosene.

"Aunt Lucia? You don't even know Aunt Lucia!"

This is essentially true, and my father pointing it out makes me feel stupid. I have never had a single meaningful conversation with his sister. She is a person I see only at Thanksgiving. But I think: If there is anyone in the family who might be able to deal with this, it is she. And maybe Aunt Lucia, together with Aunt Nan, will do something.

"Well, maybe I don't know her very well," I say, "but I feel close to her."

"Close to her? First of all, young lady"—my father's voice gets louder. I hold the phone away from my ear and look over at Stephanie, who is watching me—"your aunt Lucia is in Alaska with Aunt Nan and Uncle Dave. You can't even reach her."

"Aunt Nan gave me their itinerary," I let slip and wonder if my father will question why his sister has done such a thing. But he is already listing the reasons why Aunt Lucia won't speak to me.

"She's on vacation. She doesn't know the first thing about Christian Science. She doesn't want to hear your sniveling..."

I shake my head.

"Put Olivia on the phone," I say.

Moments later, "What's goin' on?"

Now the three of us are on the phone. Thank God my sister is in Hopewell. She and Terry don't leave for Tucson for another few days. I feel homesick. I want Mom. I want things to be the way they were before she got sick. I start to sob again.

"Olivia, I need help. I can't do this anymore. I think maybe I should call Aunt Lucia."

"I've never heard anything so ridiculous in my life!" Dad interjects. "Honestly, you kids have no regard for what we're trying to do! What we're up against! You're just going to stab us in the back, aren't you? I can't believe it! And now you're going to turn my family against us." He pauses. "That's real gratitude!"

I roll my eyes in exasperation and look over at Stephanie. She can hear nothing of the conversation.

I repeat, "I think I need help, Dad."

"Help? Help? What *kind* of help? A psychiatrist? You need someone to listen while you complain about your problems? I'll tell you something, young lady, if you—if you— You've not once read the Lesson! You've not once gone to church! Your mother happens to be up against some pretty tough odds, and do you think she feels like she's had any support from you kids? If you just tried, in a *meaningful* way, maybe your mother wouldn't be—"

There is a pause, and then he slams down the phone.

Moments later, the phone rings.

"For your information," he continues to rant, "three weeks ago your mother overheard you telling me how I should be handling this, and the next day she plummeted. She was making good progress—she was—until you—"

"Dad, that's not fair," I say.

"—until you threatened me. You said I'd be abandoning her if I taught my class! You said that if Mom died while I was away, you'd never speak to me again! Isn't that right? Isn't that what you said? And your mother overheard you, and two days later I had to take her back to Tenacre."

"Not fair," I repeat.

"Don't speak to me about fair!"

"Dad, you're irrational. I won't talk to you when you're like this. Mom didn't overhear me," I say. "We were talking on the phone. If she heard anything, she heard you yelling."

"I'm telling you," my father continues, "I had to take her back to Tenacre. And it wasn't easy. Sherm knows. He was here. It's the hardest thing I've ever had to do."

My father is sobbing now.

"Mom was never getting better," I say firmly. "I was home that weekend. I know—"

"See what I mean? See what I mean?" my father says again in a fury. "You don't know *how* to be supportive!"

Again he slams down the phone. This time, he doesn't call back.

By now, I'm long past needing to call my aunt. After all, telling Mimi and Aunt Nan in June didn't lead to anything. Stephanie and I eat the salad she brought. I see a ziplock bag of marijuana on the coffee table—a "sleeping aid" from Sherm—and think about rolling a joint. But I'm already tired. Stephanie listens as I recount in no particular order the various incidents that got me to tonight: Mom's return to Tenacre; the pressure of the secret of her illness, which in truth I haven't really kept; the confessions to Aunt Nan and Mimi that led nowhere but made me feel at once both relieved and even more desperate; the phone call to Grandma on the Fourth of July.

We sit in silence for a while. It is after midnight when Stephanie leaves.

I brush my teeth, take a Halcion and a sip of water straight from the faucet, turn out the lights, and go to bed.

The next morning, Ebit, a friend from Emma Willard, calls me at work. I have avoided her, and all my friends, since Mom became sick. I decide to tell her about Mom.

"Do you need to talk to someone?" she asks after I am done. Her father is a Presbyterian minister, and so are two of her brothers. The way Ebit asks me, very gently, makes me feel not only that, yes, I do need to speak with someone, but that doing so is really okay. She gives me the name and telephone number of Rick Spalding, an associate minister at Central Presbyterian Church, on Park Avenue at Sixty-fourth Street, who had once been a student minister under her father. His church is on the same city block as Third Church of Christ, Scientist, one of the grandest branch churches in Manhattan.

I am self-conscious about calling a complete stranger—and am more pessimistic than ever that anyone can help—but I dial the number during my lunch break from a pay phone on the street corner. I feel as if I am calling a help hotline.

I don't know where to start, so I just plow my way through. He says nothing while I'm talking. The more I say, the more I wonder why I am even bothering.

"I'm really glad you called, Lucia," Rick Spalding says. "I'm so sorry for what you're going through. There are no easy answers here..."

I should have known he couldn't help.

"...but this is something I've learned. When someone is drowning, he—or she—will grab on to the closest thing in reach."

"Uh-huh." My throat aches with tightness.

"And they will hold on for dear life, Lucia, even if that thing doesn't float."

I stare blankly at the bulletin board in front of my desk at German *Vogue,* thinking about my father, twenty blocks uptown, bestowing his spiritual understanding of the Science of Christianity on his beloved students. Meanwhile, Mom lies in a bed at Tenacre, alone. As in: without her husband, without us, without the rest of her family. Sherman is still in Hopewell, agonizingly nearby; Mom has asked him not to visit while Dad is away. I try to picture my mother listening to recordings of Christian Science lectures on her Walkman, or reading the Lesson, because the alternative image is unbearable. Is she calling out in pain? Is she confused, like she was at Connie's?

If she is too weak to sit up, to hold her King James Bible and *Science and Health,* does a nurse sit beside her and read aloud? Is that how a Christian Science nurse cares for patients, when she isn't making beds or pouring Ensure into paper cups?

The first three mornings of my father's class, I call my mother at Tenacre right after I get to the office. Each time, a nurse answers the phone.

"Mrs. Ewing's room."

"This is Joanne's daughter. May I speak with her?"

The nurse puts Mom on the phone. *Is she holding the phone to Mom's ear?* Mom talks to me for less than a minute.

On the fourth day, I call again, this time late in the morning. As before, the nurse puts Mom on. She sounds like I woke her up.

"Hi, dear," she whispers, weakly clearing her throat.

"Mom? How are you?"

"I'm doing just fine."

"Mom, can I . . . help you?"

"No, sweetheart. I have everything I need right here."

"Can I come see you? I could come out right now."

"Lucia dear, please don't ask me again. I am making good progress, you have to trust me."

I squeeze my eyes tightly shut, and shake my head. "Please, Mom?"

"No. I need to be alone."

After a long, hopeless silence, with renewed strength my mother utters more words than she has managed in weeks: "Lucia, I'd rather you not call me right now. Please don't be upset. I am striving to keep my thoughts elevated, and . . . and . . . I can't have any . . . distractions. You understand, don't you? Please understand."

My mother says good-bye. I hold the phone, wondering what to do next.

I don't understand at all.

I can't work. I can't go see Mom. I should call Uncle Jack. But I can't. I cannot do it.

I tell my boss that I have to take a few days off, and I leave work quickly.

I walk back to my apartment, pack a bag, and take the train out to the Spring Lake beach house. It is midweek, so the house is unoccupied.

The sky is cloudless, the beach is beautiful, and everything is numbingly surreal. When I call Sherm to ask if he'd like to come down for a night, to my surprise and relief, he says yes. We sit on the beach and stare at the ocean, the only two people in sight who are not elated by the perfect day. We talk for hours, mostly about

Mom; but we *do* nothing. In the evening, we call Olivia to touch base, but there is nothing to report, from either end.

She shouldn't be in Tucson; we shouldn't be at the Jersey shore. We should all be with Mom.

After we hang up, Sherm rolls a joint, which we smoke. I retreat to my room and bury my head in my pillow.

After two weeks, Dad finishes teaching his Primary class and returns to Hopewell. Sherm is back at the house too, but Dad now spends every night at Tenacre. He stays in Mom's room round the clock, returning to Hopewell only to shower in the early morning. Every few days, he asks Sherm to get up at dawn to play an hour of tennis with him. It feels to Sherm that *playing* anything is odd, but my brother obliges because he is trying to be helpful, and this is the only way he is permitted.

Now whenever I call Mom, she is unavailable to talk. Dad whispers that she is "resting comfortably" or that she has had "some discomfort overnight but is sleeping now."

I ask if I can come see her.

"Gee, honey," he says, ill at ease. "I don't know. Mom insists that she doesn't want any visitors right now. I'm sorry."

JULY 28, 1986

Two days before Sherm's twenty-second birthday, Dad calls me at the office.

"Lucia, dear," he says. His voice is shaking.

My heart stops. Fifty, twenty-seven, twenty-four, twenty-two. We are too young for this.

"I have wrestled with this decision," Dad says, choking up. He is fighting back tears. "I know I am going against your mother's wishes. I hope I'm doing the right thing."

I'm overcome with relief, and surprise, and shock.

"Dad, can we take Mom to a doctor?" I say.

"No! That's not what she wants! But I think . . . maybe we should tell Aunt Mary. I think she needs to know," he says.

Dad tells me he has written Aunt Mary a letter, explaining Mom's situation and her wish for privacy. He hopes that Aunt Mary, being "a woman of faith," will honor Mom's wish. He is sending it today by overnight mail.

"Honestly, I don't know how I managed to put pen to paper," he says, "but the words just came."

I stifle a groan. In the midst of this unequivocal failure of his beloved Christian Science, he is testifying to me—between the lines of our conversation—about its efficacy.

"I think someone in Mom's family needs to know," he says.

The next morning, unable to sleep, I look at my clock radio. It is four-forty-five—an hour earlier in Minnesota. Sometime in the next several hours Aunt Mary will hear the doorbell ring and see the FedEx man standing at her front door.

Yesterday I called Mimi to tell her about the letter. Mimi told me her mom was visiting friends at a cabin in Wisconsin. She tracked her down and told her to drive home because Uncle Heff was sending her an important letter.

I try to imagine what he wrote:

Dear Mary,

This is the hardest letter I have ever had to write. By the time you get it, I fear the worst may have happened, which is why I am writing to you now.

First, you should understand that Joanne loves you all— you, Kay, your mother, and Jack—very much, and that she has not made any of the decisions which I am about to relate to you with the intention of hurting you. But you need to under-

stand that her love of God and Christian Science is far greater than any human love.

Joanne does not know that I am writing this letter; in a sense, I am betraying her, but I feel it is time to come to you. Arriving at this decision has been extremely difficult.

For some time now, Joanne has been facing a serious health situation. (Christian Science does not dwell on symptoms, or time lines, so I hope you will respect my wish not to do so here.) Since last winter, she has been working to demonstrate her God-given perfection, and she has grown tremendously in her understanding of Christian Science. But recently she has taken a turn for the worse, even while remaining determined to rely solely on prayer for her healing.

Because you are a woman of faith, I hope you will respect Joanne's wishes for privacy.

Will Aunt Mary intervene? Is that why Dad is writing to her now? Or has he chosen to write to Aunt Mary, instead of Uncle Jack or Aunt Kay, because she won't?

Aunt Mary receives Dad's letter. Out of respect for her sister's faith, she does nothing.

THURSDAY, AUGUST 7, 1986

I have just arrived at work. I'm about to sit down to read the daily stack of telexes from Munich when the phone rings.

"German *Vogue*," I say.

"Hi, Loosh."

It is my father. He clears his throat.

I plant my elbow on the desk and prop the phone between my head and my hand. I close my eyes.

"Hi, Dad."

"I think you should come..." My father takes a deep breath. "I think you should come home."

"Are you with Mom? Are you at Tenacre?"

"Yes. She's right here."

I wait for my father to tell me more about Mom's condition, or put her on the phone, but instead he starts talking about the family. At first, I'm confused. What he is saying should be obvious to me, but it is not.

"Aunt Nan and Aunt Lucia are on their way here—I mean, not here, on their way to the house. And...Olivia is flying back...from Tucson. And I think—I think, honey, I think—" He cannot finish his thought.

I close my eyes and shake my head, suddenly aware that what I am hearing is his surrender. I force myself to listen, pressing the phone hard against my ear.

"...Lucia, dear, I—I don't think Mom's going to make it."

You asshole! You fucking asshole! I want to scream down the phone. But I remain silent. I say nothing, and the mounting rage feels like it will consume me.

Drowning out the voice in my head are my father's choking sobs. In them, I hear not only his anguish, which is real, and raw, and heartbreaking, but mine.

I take the E train to Penn Station and catch New Jersey Transit to Princeton Junction. I skip going back to my apartment to pack a bag first. I can't think beyond today, or even beyond buying a ticket and boarding the correct train.

The train jolts forward, pulls, tugs, bumps, and navigates the darkness of the tunnels beneath Penn Station and the Hudson River. Emerging from blackness into the stark, industrial daylight of New Jersey, I turn off my Walkman and close my eyes.

Shouldn't Dad have called Aunt Mary first? She's had his letter for over a week now, and she, like the rest of us, has kept this secret. But now, my father's actions feel inconsistent with his and Mom's faith; they feel more like a tactical retreat. He is circling the wagons, and leaving Mom's family out. That's nothing new, except that he has pulled his own sisters into the circle.

Mom is going to die without ever having seen a doctor, without giving medicine a chance. She is going to die, and we will be left to try to make sense of it with no answers at all, only questions: Was it cancer? Could she have lived if she'd seen a doctor? Should we—should I—have been more forceful? Oh, my God, how on earth could we have let this happen?

Back in January, two days after the space shuttle blew up, I rode this train to Princeton Junction. Thinking then that Mom was close to death, I was resigned that her refusal of medical help was the only path she'd take.

Now, six months later, as I stare out the train window again, watching the freight hoists and chemical plants of northern New Jersey pass by and wondering again if my mother is dead, or still dying, I am filled with dread: I fear the reactions of Grandma, my aunts, my uncle. I *hate* my father. But even now I pity him: he's my *father.* This polarity unsettles me. He was supposed to love and honor Mom in sickness and in health. But he won't—can't—even acknowledge her sickness. Christian Science forbids it. On some level, I believe I've had no choice but to respect my parents' unswerving adherence to faith. But on another level, I know absolutely that I don't.

When my father decided to go away for two weeks to teach his class, he abandoned Mom to save face in front of a group of people who had come to learn from him the practice of Christian Science healing. This wasn't love.

But I also recall one of the last times I was allowed to visit Mom. The first thing I noticed as I entered her room was the crystal bud vase on her bedside table, holding a fresh rose. It was always a fresh rose. That afternoon, Mom and I played backgammon. She was propped up in bed and looked, I thought, not so bad. She was able to roll the dice and move her pieces. But the dice dropped onto the board without much vigor. She beat me handily and smiled. It felt so good to be doing something—anything—with her.

Too soon my father gave me his cue—raised eyebrows—that it was time for me to go. I was angry and upset. I didn't want to go after only fifteen minutes, but I acquiesced. I kissed my mother on the forehead and left the room. As I passed through the reception area, a nurse came up to me and touched my arm. I bristled. I didn't want to hear anything she would likely choose to tell me. Dressed in her white uniform, she looked every bit the part of a caring, capable, credentialed health care professional. A fraud, I thought to myself.

"You know, Lucia," the petite, pretty woman whispered to me in a gentle voice. Just moments before I had wanted to stay by my mother's side, now I was desperate to get out of there. "Late at night I watch your father and mother dancing, just the two of them, down the hall in the common room. They hold each other and sway. Very slowly. And oh, so tenderly. Usually it's to Frank Sinatra. Sometimes, Tony Bennett. . . . I don't suppose they know I'm watching," she continued, "and maybe I shouldn't. But it's just about the sweetest thing you ever saw."

The image is a painful one for me, and confusing. It is hard not to see it as love.

The train pulls into New Brunswick station. Oddly, while I wrestle with intensely vacillating and conflicting emotions toward my father, toward my mother I feel almost nothing. Where is *she* in all of this? Several months back I read in a magazine about the five stages of grief. I try to remember them now: denial, anger— Then what, bargaining? Next, depression, and finally, acceptance? I don't think any of these even apply to me. Or maybe they all do. I've been grieving my mother's death for months already.

Out the window, industrial monochrome has given way to greens and blues. The clouds are clearing, or maybe that was smog ten miles back. I realize that what I am feeling now, above all else, is a sense of anticipation that the shroud of secrecy is about to be lifted. This is dimly comforting. Any sense of relief feels altogether wrong.

Once again, Dad spent the night in Mom's room at Tenacre. It is seven o'clock in the morning now, and we have not heard from him. If this particular Friday were even a few months earlier, I might be feeling a hint of optimism because we weren't awakened in the middle of the night with a phone call. But sitting silently in Mom's kitchen, staring at the steam on the surface of my coffee, I feel only regret. The presence of Dad's sisters, Aunt Lucia and Aunt Nan, confirms for us that the end is near.

I wonder what, exactly, my aunts are thinking and feeling, if they harbor doubts about the choices they've made, as much as my siblings and I are surely questioning ours. Have they been torn between preserving Mom's privacy, respecting her faith, and wanting to take action? Waiting here like this would be harder without them, but we do not discuss our conflicted feelings. We are eating because it is something to do after a sleepless night of waiting. I wonder what Aunt Nan and Aunt Lucia really think of their brother. Of us. Are they judging our lack of action? Do they share our helplessness?

The telephone rings. I look at the clock: 7:20 A.M. Aunt Nan answers it immediately. The rest of us stare at the floor, listening. *It's over,* I think.

"That was your father," Aunt Nan says. "He wants you to go to Tenacre for a family conference, immediately."

"Careful, Loosh," Sherm says as I take the road's curves too quickly. He is sitting beside me in the passenger seat of our mom's

Honda Accord. Olivia sits in back. These are the only words spoken during the fifteen-minute drive from our parents' house in Hopewell to Princeton.

Last weekend, Sherm and I made this same trip for what our parents euphemistically called a visit but was in effect nothing more than a confirmation of our mother's further decline. For ten minutes we sat in her room silently while she slept. She opened her eyes and smiled her recognition. Then Dad said we should leave, and we complied.

Another day several months back, I had come out from the city for the weekend. Cynthia Jones, one of my parents' earliest Christian Science friends from their years in Chicago, was staying at the house, to lend her support by cooking for Dad and praying with Mom. A large woman with puffy jowls, she asked me to drive her to Tenacre so she could spend the morning with Mom. I dropped her off at the entrance and watched as she took heavy, labored steps toward the door. Mom was no more than fifteen yards away, on the other side of one wall, and I was forbidden to see her yet Mrs. Jones could. Her Christian Science status gave her clearance. I hated her for that. I thought, if there is any truth to the notion of mental malpractice, Mrs. Jones is definitely headed for trouble.

Two hours later, I returned to Tenacre to pick her up. As she got into the car, I couldn't look at her. I wouldn't make pointless conversation. In response to the angry silence, Mrs. Jones put her hand on my forearm and said, "Lucia, you have to remember that God is your real Father-Mother."

Fuck you.

I slow down to make the left-hand turn onto the Great Road. Up ahead, we see the large wooden sign marking the entrance.

We park in the visitors' lot and walk toward South Hall Extension, the building where we last saw our mother.

A well-dressed woman in her sixties appears on the footpath. "Hello," she says, clearly expecting us. "Why don't you follow me to the administration building? Your dad is waiting there in a conference room."

It's over.

My brother, sister, and I exchange silent glances. I hold my breath.

We follow a few paces behind the woman, and Sherman whispers to me that she is the chief administrator and has spent the last couple of nights in the room with Mom. I wonder how he knows this and I don't. Sherman, Olivia, and I have each been used and manipulated by the secrecy. I grit my teeth.

This woman, a perfect stranger to me, has sat beside my dying mother, maybe even holding her hand, yet we, her own children, have been denied any right to see her. Now, on August 8, when it seems there is nothing left to do but hear an administrator tell us that Mom has passed on—as if it is something beautiful—my brother and sister and I are relevant. The most normal thing for me to feel would be utter, gut-wrenching despair, but all I harbor is bitterness. I wonder why they couldn't just tell us by phone. It's probably a legal thing.

The administrator holds the door for us and directs us through the reception area to a room with a large round conference table. Dad is there, wearing the clothes he probably slept in. Sitting on the edge of his chair, his shoulders slumped, he looks both anxious and defeated. His eyes are swollen. He has been crying. We take a seat.

"Mom isn't doing very well," Dad says.

She's alive?

Incongruously, the administrator pushes a large canister of M&M's toward my father.

"Joanne has had another restless night," she says. "She is very confused. She is asking to go to Minneapolis. She wants to be with her mother."

Going to Minneapolis doesn't sound at all confused. Minneapolis means Mom's family, and Mom's family means medical care. It is the first reasonable thing I've heard from anyone in nearly seven months.

"I don't know, kids," my father says, "she hasn't been lucid for a few days. She's saying she wants to see her daddy, and she is very upset with me."

My mother's father has been dead for twenty years. Dad shakes his head in disbelief. "Mom thinks I'm forcing her to be here against her will."

My father looks down at his hands, and his shoulders begin to shake. Sherman, Olivia, and I watch, like bystanders, as he sobs. Not one of us moves to comfort him.

"We have to determine what it is that Joanne wants," the administrator says. We turn our attention to her. "Because, as you know, this has been her decision all along. If she would rather be in a hospital, it is our responsibility to get her there."

I am stunned. Olivia, Sherman, and I quickly decide that Olivia should talk to Mom.

She leaves the conference room immediately. We sit in silence and wait. I try to picture the two of them talking. Is Mom ready? Is she wavering? Will Olivia be forceful enough? Suddenly, I find I am almost giddy, soaking up the unexpected fantasy of possibility. Maybe we *can* save Mom. Maybe she will consent to medical treatment. I nervously dig my thumbnails into the nail beds of my fingers until my fingertips ache. Olivia reappears five minutes later. Her face is ashen.

"She's talking about flying along the ground back to her daddy— like she's on a magic carpet or something. But I think she'll go to the hospital. Talk to her, Loosh," Olivia says, turning to me. "I don't know. I don't know. She . . . it's . . . it's bad."

PLEASE WAIT FOR AN ATTENDING NURSE TO ASSIST YOU

I ignore the sign in the reception area and walk directly into my mother's room. The curtains are closed, and no lights are on; it's stifling, and the air smells acrid. I am terrified. In the bed I see a ghostly white, jerking body gasping for breath. This can't be my mother. I wonder if perhaps I have entered the wrong room. Then on the nightstand, I see the Steuben bud vase. It holds a fresh red rose. The back of my neck is like ice and damp. I kiss my mother's forehead.

This is my mother. She is fifty years old.

"Hi, Mom," I whisper. My mother's eyes stare into mine.

"Now look what you've done," she says. "Why have you... kept... me here?"

I can't believe what I am hearing.

"I want to go home. I want to see Mother and Daddy." My mom begins to cry like a child.

"Mom, we can't take you to Minneapolis, but we can get you to a hospital."

"That's non...sense," my mother says. "There's...the, you know, the...river."

I notice a white film around her lips. I cannot make sense of what she is saying without staring at her mouth. Yet it is almost impossible for me to look at her.

"Mom, listen to me," I say, clutching her hand. It is radiating heat. Suddenly, I have become the mother, and she the child. "Grandma is old. She's not capable of taking care of you, but—"

"Then take me to Abbott Northwestern," she says. "Daddy will help me."

Abbott Northwestern is a hospital in Minneapolis.

"Mom, we can't take you there, but we *can* get you to Princeton Medical Center."

"No! No! No!" my mother wails. "No hospital. I want Daddy to take care of me."

"Mom, nobody—not even your daddy—would transfer you to Abbott Northwestern right now. But if we can take you to the hospital here, then you can go to Minneapolis when you're feeling better. Okay? Mom?"

"Okay," she says, breaking into a full sob. I try to hug her, but she turns away.

Olivia walks into the room. "Liv," I whisper. "Call an ambulance."

My mother's breathing is fitful. I watch her eyes roll back into their sockets. Am I watching her die? Her mouth is agape, her tongue extends and tightens. Her lips somehow disappear.

"I love you, Mom."

Then something occurs to me: If my mother is about to die, maybe there is something she needs to say.

"Mom?" I say softly.

She gazes around the room with big, searching eyes.

"Is there anything you want to tell me?" I ask.

She looks directly into my eyes.

"Later, Lucia. Not now." She sounds only annoyed.

Oh, God. I have asked my mother for her last words and she has brushed me away. In these final moments at Tenacre, while waiting for the ambulance to arrive, the fear that I am watching my mother die before my eyes, leave me forever, is eclipsed by another fear: that her final, enduring thought of me will be *Shame on you.*

EMERGENCY ROOM
THE MEDICAL CENTER AT PRINCETON

We arrive at the hospital ahead of the ambulance and wait in the admitting area of the emergency room. My father sits alone and stares at the gray linoleum floor. Olivia wanders from one corner to another. Sherm and I just stand. Isn't an ambulance supposed to beat the traffic? What could be delaying it? If the worst has happened, will they still bring Mom here?

John Florence arrives shortly after we do. He is our family's stockbroker, someone my father considers a friend, probably the only friend he has nearby who is not a Christian Scientist. He has been summoned today not for financial advice but because Dad vaguely remembers him mentioning once his involvement with the hospital's capital campaign. An ex-Marine and former college football player, Mr. Florence greets each of us warmly. His hug feels accepting and protective, but I wonder what is going through his head. Has he ever sensed, from his frequent conversations with my father over the months, that something's not right at the Ewings'?

We hear the wail of an ambulance siren. Suddenly, there is a great deal of commotion as a pair of emergency medical technicians hastily pushes a gurney past us, disappearing through swinging double doors and behind a partitioning screen. Dad, Olivia, Sherm, and I quickly follow them. Is it Mom? I'm not certain. People are moving back and forth behind the curtain.

"I need to speak with a member of Joanne Ewing's family. I need a medical history," a nurse says urgently, sticking her head out around the curtain.

My father is totally bewildered. He approaches the curtained area cautiously and turns around, beckoning with his eyes for one of us to accompany him, which I do. There, on the other side of the curtain, my mother lies on an examining table. She is surrounded by a platoon of doctors, nurses, and young interns. There's not enough room for everyone.

"Full name?"

"Joanne Johnson Ewing," I say.

"Age?"

"Fifty."

"Address?"

"Box 431, Hopewell, New Jersey."

"Occupation?"

"Housewife."

"Spouse's occupation?"

"Christian Science practitioner."

It seems to take forever for the nurse to write down the three words. I wonder if those words remind this nurse of others who may have made the eight-minute trip from Tenacre to the hospital and arrived like . . . this.

"Medical insurance?" The nurse looks up.

I shake my head no.

"Doctor's name?"

I shake my head again.

"The last time she was seen by a doctor," I tell the nurse, "was when my brother was born, twenty-two years ago. We were all C-sections."

"She had her appendix out as a child," my father offers feebly.

"What have her symptoms been?" the nurse asks.

Silence. My father shakes his head almost imperceptibly, as though trying to make sense of a foreign language. I watch him struggle to answer the barrage of questions and wonder what he is feeling.

Does he feel responsible for the condition my mother is now in? Because I do.

"When was the last time she ate?"

I turn to my father.

"She's been eating regularly," he says, "until yesterday. She hasn't had much of an appetite. But she's been drinking milk shakes."

Not exactly milk shakes, I think, nutritional supplements. But I don't correct him.

"Has she been in a lot of pain?" the nurse continues.

"I don't know if you'd call it pain, really," my father says, his eyes wincing. "She's experienced some . . . discomfort."

Discomfort! I cringe when I think of how many times I have heard this euphemism over the last seven months.

"Is there blood in her stool?"

"I wouldn't know," my father says.

I look into my father's eyes. I want to know if this is true. I know it is possible, in theory, for Mom to have blood in her stool and him not to know, but it seems likelier that he would know, does know, did know.

"Has she passed any blood going to the bathroom?" the nurse tries again.

"I don't know"—my father sighs—"maybe."

Maybe? I am seething.

"How long has she been in this condition?" the nurse asks.

I wonder myself. And I wonder how my father will answer. There must have been early symptoms. She must have been sick since well before last Thanksgiving.

"Well," my father says, "quite a while now."

"How long is a while?" a doctor presses, barely masking his impatience. I realize the rest of the medical team is looking at me. I wonder if it's because they want an interpreter, or because they think I have the answers.

More silence. It is as though my father cannot process the question.

"How long has she been sick?" the doctor continues. "When did she first show signs of illness?"

My father breathes in deeply.

"It started sometime last year. But she was getting better this spring. She was really beginning to show improvement. She would sit in the garden. Or in the screened porch..."

"Dad," I say firmly, "she wasn't getting better. She was just *home*. She was never getting better."

"That's just not true!" my father shouts. His fists clench, and then he lowers his voice. "She *was* getting better."

The medical team looks startled by our angry exchange.

My father's eyes meet mine and stay there.

Suddenly, his eyes fill with tears, which he wipes away with his shirtsleeve. He looks completely defeated. He turns toward Mom, and immediately I picture the Steuben bud vase that stood on her bedside table in the room at Tenacre, those single roses that my father always brought her. Never once did I see a rose in it that had even begun to wilt. It is an image I cling to.

"She went to Tenacre the day after the space shuttle blew up," I say, turning to the doctors and nurses. "She's been there ever since. Except for two weeks earlier this summer."

I look down at my mother, who is more alert than she was an hour ago at Tenacre. There, while we waited for the ambulance, she lay in her bed in a fetal position, shivering beneath several blankets, her eyes rolling back in their sockets. Here, she lies nearly motion-less on the examining table, as her eyes search those of the doctors. She looks like a terrified child, small and vulnerable, hesitating slightly before handing the nurse her wrist to take her pulse.

I hold my mother's hand and try to comfort her. "They're going to help you, Mom. I'll be right here."

It feels odd—unfamiliar, good, unsettling—to be saying these reassuring words. I feel like an actor on a movie set, reciting memo-rized lines, and I wonder if I believe them. Will my words be true? Yes, I will be right here. But can the doctors help her?

A nurse pulls back the white sheet to expose everything that has been happening to my mother's body over the last several months; everything I have not insisted on seeing; everything the practitio-ner, the "nurses," my father, and my mother have kept denying. I am startled by the small voice that creeps into my own head.

There is no life, truth, intelligence, nor substance in matter...

For months I have watched my mother's face and arms wither to little more than skin-covered bones. At Tenacre, she was always covered up to her neck with sheets and blankets. Now, I see her nearly naked body on the table. I am shocked. Her legs are swollen to three times their normal size. Her feet look like water balloons ready to burst, her toes like fat dumplings, clammy white. How did everyone at Tenacre witness this for months and continue to claim that she was getting better?

How did I witness her deterioration for months and do nothing? Even when I knew she wasn't getting better?

I know the doctors and nurses are asking themselves the same questions.

Dr. Sierocki will be Mom's doctor. He greets us, "Joanne's fam-ily," in an adjoining conference room. His eye contact with each of us moves in advance of his handshake, and I feel like we are being surveyed. Like a prisoner who has just seen daylight for the first time in months, I feel overexposed. We are an odd bunch. I glance at my father. He could still pass for a Princeton professor, every bit the WASP in his scuffed Gucci loafers and golf shirt, but he is weary, his posture bowed. Olivia is wearing a beaded cotton dress, her long dark hair falling forward like blinders. Sherm is unshaven, in a T-shirt and faded jeans, but he has incongruously thrown on a blue blazer. I'm in a white linen jacket, a white tank top, and black linen pants; I could pass for a caterer.

The doctor sits before us with his arms folded. Sometimes he calls his new patient Mrs. Ewing, other times Mother, or, glancing down at his notes, he pauses (is he looking for her name?) and calls her Joanne.

He peers over his reading glasses at us. "Mother's hemoglobin count is very low. She arrived in a premorbid state. Let me give you some figures: twelve is a normal hemoglobin count," he says, again looking down at his clipboard. "Joanne's is hovering around three."

Premorbid. My body sinks into itself.

"She needs a blood transfusion. And we've put her on hyperalimentation," he says, clicking his ballpoint pen, "which is essentially megadoses of calories. Mother is in a state of advanced malnutrition."

Dr. Sierocki looks up again, but I can't face him. I look at my fingers instead. My hands are folded, as if in prayer, and I am digging into the quick of my fingernails again.

"We'd like to get her strength back. As you know"—the doctor looks at Dad, then me—"we inserted a main-line catheter into her chest cavity. This will aid in administering the intravenous feeding, the medications, and the transfusions."

The doctor has a clipped, precisely articulated voice; he speaks as though he is dictating to a secretary. He stops talking, and we sit in silence for a moment.

"Do you know what the nature of the underlying illness is?" I ask awkwardly. Giving voice to this question that has haunted me for so long makes my voice quiver.

"It's too early to say. Mother is very, very sick. Until she stabilizes, we will not be able to proceed with diagnostic tests. It appears she has some sort of blockage or tumor in the abdominal region, but until we can do a biopsy, we won't know if it's malignant."

Tumor. Blockage. Biopsy. Malignant.

Again, I hear an unwelcome voice.

Therefore man is not material; he is spiritual.

It shocks me that these words are still with me. I thought I had exorcised them years ago.

"The whole region of her lower abdomen is infected," the doctor continues. "We've started her on antibiotics. But there is also a sizable fistula..."

He takes a deep breath and looks down at his notes again. "Until we can do something about that..."

His voice trails off momentarily. He hesitates. It seems he is unclear whether to proceed or stop.

He unfolds his hands and stands up.

Then he adds, "It's quite possible she won't make it through the night."

We sit nervously in the Intensive Care Unit family lounge, waiting for Mom to be brought up from the ER. There is some debate over who should be contacted, and who will make those phone calls. We decide that Olivia will call Aunt Mary, and I will call Uncle Jack. Aunt Kay is somewhere in Wyoming on vacation; we will have to find her, probably through Aunt Mary. Sherm will call the house in Hopewell and tell Aunt Nan and Aunt Lucia. We—Olivia, Sherm, and I—want to call Ham too—he has been living somewhere in Paris—but when we mention this to Dad, he is adamant and becomes visibly distressed.

"We're *not* calling Ham," he says through clenched teeth and gets up from the table. We drop it.

To have gone from being bound in silence to making phone calls feels revolutionary, historic, as though Olivia, Sherman, and I have staged a coup, although we know we have done no such thing, any more than the crew of a ship can take credit for the shifting wind. Dad stands alone in the middle of the lounge, dazed, hands in his pockets, staring vacantly at a television suspended from the ceiling. He can't possibly know he is tuned in to the ABC afternoon lineup: *All My Children, One Life to Live, General Hospital.*

I press my forehead against the cool aluminum interior of the telephone booth in the opposite corner of the lounge and wait for the pounding in my chest to quiet. When it doesn't, I dial Uncle Jack's work number anyway. Suddenly, I'm at a party at Aunt Mary's house a few years back, where I encounter my uncle standing in a hallway. Cocktail in hand, he wraps his right arm over my shoulder, leaning toward me to bestow some avuncular advice. (He is, after all, my godfather.) At six foot seven, he towers over me. It feels like he is leaning on me and I may fail as a prop. The drink, gimbaled in his hand, hovers over my velvet dress sleeve and threatens to spill.

"Lucia," he says, with his raspy voice, which always sounds like he has a secret to share, "do you know the key to a woman's success?" He pivots so that we face each other, his arm-drape transformed into a loose half-embrace. His eyes are ice blue, and his complexion is tanned. I have a horrible feeling that he is going to try to sell me a pair of breast implants.

"No?" I hear myself ask uneasily, as if it were yesterday.

"Lose a few pounds," he answers, holding up one finger. "Not too many. Three, maybe four," he says, "and learn to play a *great* game of tennis."

That was the last time we'd spoken.

A receptionist with a thick Minnesota accent answers his phone and puts me through without delay.

"Hi, Uncle Jack, this is Lucia."

"Hi, Lucia," he says. He doesn't sound surprised to hear my voice.

"I'm calling from Princeton Medical Center," I say, nervously running a pencil along the booth's smooth, perforated metal. It makes a clicking sound and breaks the lead, so I stop.

Silence.

"We rushed Mom here about an hour ago. We— She's—"

I take a deep breath. My uncle waits. I would prefer to flee, to hang up, but I can't. I push through the feeling of dread.

"She's in critical condition. They're moving her to ICU. She's been sick for a long time—since Christmas." My words barrel out of my mouth. "We came home for the holidays and realized something was wrong, but Mom and Dad didn't want to talk about it . . . maybe they thought we wouldn't notice."

Not a sound from the other end. I continue.

"Uncle Jack, she wanted to use Christian Science. She wouldn't go to a doctor. And they wouldn't let us call you. Dad was going to call you back in January, when she went to Tenacre—a nursing home for Christian Scientists in Princeton. But then they—she— they didn't want anyone to know. They were keeping it a secret— Church doctrine. But she got sicker and sicker, and we wanted to call you—Olivia and Sherm and I—but we didn't want to—we felt we couldn't—betray her wishes. They're saying . . . the doctors are saying, she may not make it through the night."

More silence.

"I'm sorry. I'm so sorry, Uncle Jack."

The more I speak, filling the emptiness, the more frightened I feel. What am I going to hear?

Then, in a calm voice my uncle simply says, "Lucia, thank you for calling me." I sense he is pausing long enough to . . . what? Light a cigarette? Jot something down? Is he at a loss for words? Or is he choosing them extra carefully? Has he been caught unaware? Or did Aunt Mary already tell him about Dad's letter?

"What your mother needs right now, is for you—you and your brother and sister—to be strong," he finally says with conviction.

He doesn't include my father in this piece of advice, but the omission seems fair to me, generous, even. I know that my father and Uncle Jack's relationship has been acrimonious at times, and he might very well have responded by going on the attack; that he hasn't—that maybe he has chosen not to, or has restrained himself with me—is an act of kindness. Instead, he offers advice that, for me, is a salve. I am overcome. My eyes brim.

"Thank you," I say. "Uncle Jack?"

"Yes?"

"Can you help us?" I know this request comes much too late, and may elicit his anger, but I also know there is nobody else in our family with his medical background, so I need to ask him. "Can you help us with the doctors? We are in over our heads."

He asks for the name of the attending physician. I tell him: Dr. Sierocki.

I return to the round table and sit with Olivia and Sherm for what feels, again, like too long. Dad and Mr. Florence are talking quietly at the other side of the waiting room. Where is she? What is taking them so long to bring her to the ICU? Should one of us go check on her? (Are we allowed to?) Each time the elevator doors open, we stand up and move closer to get a better look. And each time we see somebody other than our mother. Once, it is a team of bespectacled med students in white coats, all holding clipboards. Another time, an orderly pushes an old man in his wheelchair, while the old man tugs at a rolling stand from which several IV bags dangle. In his free hand he holds an extinguished, half-smoked cigar. I notice that neither he nor any of the other patients coming off the elevator look all that sick to me.

Eventually, Sherm and I position ourselves at the elevator. Each time we hear the rumble of the car moving up and down the shaft behind the closed doors, our nerves shift to high alert. Suddenly, the doors open again, and two orderlies struggle to pull and push a hospital bed and two IV posts strung with countless tubes and clear pouches through to the lobby. The mattress is propped up facing the back of the elevator, making it impossible to see the patient.

The hospital bed rotates to reveal an old woman convulsing in a semifetal position. The only sounds I hear are moaning and gasping and wheezing. For a terrifying moment I think, Is this Mom? But then I see that the woman has only clumps of matted hair between patches of baldness, and the sheet covering her torso has been cast aside, revealing a left breast, shriveled, folded, and scarred. I turn away and seek assurance in my brother's eyes. I feel ashamed, frightened, relieved, nauseated, bereft, and guilty, all at once. The bed disappears around the corner, through the double doors leading to the Intensive Care Unit, and my brother and I are left in our aftershock to process what we have just witnessed.

Is this what we can now expect? Is this what we have brought our mother to the hospital for? Maybe she should have stayed at Tenacre?

The elevator bell sounds twice, and Sherman and I, acting on impulse, escape through the closing doors into the privacy of the car, leaving Olivia, Dad, and Mr. Florence. I lean against the back wall, and my knees buckle under me as I slide to the floor. I look up at Sherm, who is still standing, his back to me, shoulders shaking. I stand up, move over to him, and each of us leans our head on the other's shoulder.

"Lucia, do you think Mom's going to die?"

I am caught off guard by the question, but it brings into focus the difference between how my brother and I see things. For Sherm, this is a new possibility, while I have been expecting our mother's death for months. Now that she has been admitted to the hospital, I don't know what to think.

The elevator starts moving. When it stops, the doors open again and a man and twin carrot-topped boys, who look to be about four years old, get in. The father looks tired but happy; his kids look dazed. Maternity ward, no doubt. The father pushes the button for the first floor. When the doors open to the lobby, one of the boys cautiously reaches for his father's hand, while the other one rushes out. I know how they both feel. I want the comfort of an older, wiser protector. I also want to get out of here as fast as possible. Sherm and I remain in the elevator, grateful when the doors close again before anyone else can join us. I push 5.

When we return, Dad is sitting at the table, mindlessly folding the edges of a newspaper and scratching scribbles with his thumbnail. Olivia stands at the pay phone, talking to Terry.

"Where did you two go?" Dad asks. He seems relieved that we have returned. Mr. Florence has left.

Sherm sits down on the windowsill, facing the elevator and the table, and I head over to stand near Olivia. The elevator doors open once more, and this time in the bed that emerges we see our mother. She is propped upright, snugly tucked under crisply pressed white sheets, which are clean except for a maroon blotch near her chest, where the main-line catheter was inserted. We gather close and offer smiles and "Hi, Moms," then back away as the orderlies push her down the corridor.

I pucker my lips and blow a kiss. My mother's head rests on its side, and she follows me with her eyes, but there is no real sign of recognition.

It is late at night, and I am back at the house, as are Sherm, Aunt Nan, Aunt Lucia, and Dad. Dad was going to spend the night with Mom in the ICU, but Olivia urged him to get some rest at home while she took a night shift. This plan—*a plan!*—feels for me so inconceivably normal.

I have escaped to my mother's Nook. Concealed behind double doors at the end of the upstairs hallway, the space is filled entirely by a berth-size water bed set to a soothingly warm temperature and piled high with pillows. The wobbly effort of climbing into this hideaway somehow improves my spirits. I lie still while the bed's waves ebb. I close my eyes.

I am in shock over the day's turn of events. This morning, benumbed, Sherm, Olivia, and I sat downstairs in the kitchen with our father's two sisters, sipping coffee, waiting for word that Mom had died at Tenacre. Now, near midnight, she is lying in the Intensive Care Unit at Princeton Medical Center. Along the life–death spectrum—if there is such a thing—I believe our mother's condition has inched ever so slightly in the direction of life, even if her doctor—*her doctor*—the very words in their combined form are like a jolt; I shake my head, stunned—told us that she arrived in the emergency room in a premorbid state; that she might not make it through the night.

But now that a team of doctors and real nurses are caring for her, I feel, for the first time, hopeful. In the ICU she is clinging to life, and that should sound bleak, but to my ears it sounds positive. Given this new tack we are on, it feels like there's a real, if outside, chance that Mom will survive. Her departure from Tenacre is nothing short of a miracle: leaving Christian Science for real science, rejecting the denial of illness for the possibility of diagnosis and treatment. I feel—viscerally—that another miracle can happen.

Down the hall, Aunt Nan and Aunt Lucia are asleep in my room. In the master bedroom, Dad snores loudly. Sherm is downstairs in the living room, sharing the couch with Felix and Oscar, my parents' Doberman-shepherds.

My eyelids quiver. I am restless, in part because of the dreadful hospital coffee. In the next few days Aunt Mary, Aunt Kay, Uncle Jack, and Grandma will no doubt be arriving. So will Terry. Between now and then, there will be much to do: talking to doctors, trying to learn about Mom's illness and the options for treating it. But for now all we can do is wait for her to regain her strength.

I can't sleep, so I slip into my shoes and head downstairs.

The television is tuned to a rerun of *Taxi*. The dogs are curled up near my brother's feet.

"Sherm, you awake?" I whisper. My brother sits up with a start. I feel bad that I have awakened him with nothing to report.

"Sorry. Go back to sleep."

"What's up?" he asks, rolling onto his side to face me.

"No news, if that's what you mean. I'm going back to the hospital."

"Do you want me to come?" he asks.

"Nah. I'll take over for Olivia. Maybe she'll come home for a few hours."

"What time is it?"

"After one."

I drive Mom's car, park in the deserted hospital garage, and, after informing the night receptionist that my mother is a patient here, I head up to the ICU.

I find Olivia asleep on one end of the L-shaped couch in the lounge. I'm not sure how visiting hours work at hospitals, especially in the ICU. Can I just walk up to Mom's bed? I don't want to disturb Olivia to ask her, so I sit down in a lounge chair and gaze up at the television. *The French Connection* is on.

I feel myself dozing off when someone taps me on the shoulder. A nurse stands in front of me.

"Would you like a blanket and a pillow?" she whispers. She has frosted hair, and a lovely smile that reminds me of Mom's. That she is caring for me too, and not just her patients, makes my eyes well up.

"No, thanks. Uh . . . can I go see her?" I ask. "My mom? I mean, is it okay?"

"Sure."

She smiles again and beckons me with a nod of her head. When the nurse turns her back, I use the shoulder of my sleeve to wipe my eyes.

I stand at the curtain that separates my mother's bed from the next one over and peek in to see if she is awake. She sees me right away. I love that I am face-to-face with her, and there is nobody else here. Just Mom and me. Her cheeks look rosy, flushed, and she is calm. A real change from Tenacre.

"Are you tired?" I ask. I hold my mother's hand, and it feels so good.

"I'm sleepy, but I can't sleep," she says, smiling at me when I squeeze her hand. She sounds groggy, tranquil.

"Me too."

We sit there for several minutes in silence.

I realize that she should at least try to sleep.

"Mom, you need rest," I say, reluctantly. I would rather stay like this, holding hands.

"I know," she murmurs. "This is fascinating."

"'Scuse me?" I ask. "Did you say something, Mom?"

Reaching under the bedsheet with her left hand, Mom pulls out a black satin eye mask and holds it up proudly, as though she has pulled a rabbit from a top hat.

"Have you ever seen one of these?" she asks, clumsily securing it over her face. "All the pretty colors change . . ."

"What?"

"It's very interesting. The patterns change . . ."

"No, Mom. That's an eye mask, to block out light."

"Oh."

My mother readjusts the mask on her face, and her hands retreat beneath the sheets. I can't know if she feels defeated, ashamed, or at ease behind the mask. I am relieved that she can't see my face, read my fear. She is quiet again, and soon she drifts back to sleep.

I sit beside Mom and fend off sleep for another hour. Being here, I feel like a good daughter. At three, Olivia taps me on the shoulder.

"When 'dju get here?" she whispers, pulling up a chair. She is wrapped in a hospital blanket, wearing a pair of hospital socks.

"About one-thirty. You were asleep, so I didn't wake you up."

My sister looks away, and I can't tell if she is too tired for conversation or if perhaps she's miffed that I've stolen her spot. Now that Tenacre is behind us, we can vie for our mother's attention unfettered by the Christian Science gatekeepers.

We sit together in silence and watch our mother sleep.

At four-thirty, I surrender. I'm exhausted. My sister will get credit for the first overnight shift. But maybe Mom will remember that I was here too. It is comforting to feel that now I *can* be a good daughter. I am tempted to remain in the ICU, but there really is no point in both Olivia and me staying up all night. We could have weeks of this ahead of us, months even. I get an uneasy feeling when I consider the days to come, but the fact that we got Mom here, that maybe it's not too late, brings tears to my eyes. I wipe them away and take a deep breath.

When I return home, Sherm is still crashed out on the couch with the dogs, our aunts are asleep in my bedroom, and Dad is breathing quietly, no longer snoring, behind the master bedroom door. I crawl back into the Nook before anyone stirs.

SATURDAY, AUGUST 9
INTENSIVE CARE UNIT

Sherm and I arrive at the ICU later in the morning to find Dad at Mom's bedside, holding a full IV bag in each hand while a nurse disconnects the empty ones. My anger toward the situation, the Church, my parents—especially my father—which has been careening toward a point of no return, seems to be losing its power. A Christian Science practitioner in an ICU is the proverbial fish out of water. That he is even trying to adapt is remarkable.

I see, at my father's feet, the white canvas PBS tote that holds his Bible and *Science and Health,* and the Christian Science quarterly. The tentative tenderness I am feeling is suddenly supplanted once again by an onslaught of anger, resentment, and irritability, which I manage to hold at bay with one question: How does he reconcile all of this?

After less than twenty-four hours, the change in Mom's appearance is dramatic. She is alert, lying calmly in a bed, hooked up to various pieces of equipment that hum and beep and click rhythmically, one slowly spitting out a stream of paper. Her cheeks are rosy, not gray. Her lips are full again, whereas yesterday they seemed withered. Her breathing is steady, no longer fitful. Today she looks closer to her true age; sick, but stronger. There is a dark purple bruise on her chest where the doctor inserted the catheter, but if she looks this much better after one day, I reason, there is no telling what medicine will be able to do. I catch Sherm's eye, and we both smile in silence. However foreign it feels to be here, it feels right.

"Hi, you two," Mom says. She no longer seems confused.

"Hi, Mom," Sherm and I say in unison from the foot of the bed before drawing closer. Now we stand opposite our father and the nurse, who look like they are engaged in a game of cat's cradle with the tubing. I kiss the top of my mother's head.

"How do you feel?" Sherm asks, holding her right hand, the one free from needles and tubes.

"Fine," my mother says in a high-pitched whisper, like the ethereal voice of E. B. White's spider-heroine, Charlotte, in *Charlotte's Web*.

I look at Sherm.

Always the embodiment of propriety, Mom chats politely with the nurse, mustering short bursts of energy to make abbreviated introductions.

"This is my second daughter, Lucia. A writer. And my son, Sherm, my baby." Mom grins. "He's in a rock band. Lead singer. A senior. At Columbia."

The nurse smiles warmly, and I feel relieved. Since our arrival at the medical center, I've worried that the nurses and doctors will view and treat us with suspicion, but so far I haven't felt this. The nurse, a woman about my age, could not be kinder. I am embarrassed and surprised at my mother's description of me, and I worry that the nurse may ask what I have written and I'll have to confess: nothing. In my publishing job, I am little more than a gofer. I look again at Sherm, who clearly shares my self-consciousness. At least he can say he is in a band.

I wonder if Mom is aware that it is August, that Columbia's graduation came and went two months ago, without Sherman in it. I remember the Sunday night in May when he called me, sobbing and desperate, just ten hours before final exams were to start. He hadn't been able to study for months and didn't know what he should do: sit for the finals and fail, or go talk to a dean. He withdrew two weeks before commencement. All I've had to manage, in addition to *this,* is my desk job at Condé Nast.

In contrast to my mother's, my father's appearance is unchanged. He is wearing a light blue collared shirt, a bow tie, and summer-weight gray slacks; the whites of his eyes are still bloodshot. Maybe he's been crying again.

The nurse is having some trouble with the valve on the IV, so she flicks the tubing with her middle finger and squeezes the bag. The solution seems to drip too quickly, or it halts completely. She doesn't get flustered, but the valve doesn't cooperate. I wonder what it feels like for my mother to have liquid dripping into her veins; if it feels cold, weird, or like nothing at all. I read somewhere once about a rogue air bubble that almost killed a patient. I resist the urge to ask the nurse about that possibility.

I notice she is wearing an inverted timepiece, a nurse's watch pinned to the front of her white uniform. My father gave my mother a similar one years ago, when she decided to pursue a career in Christian Science nursing. She was so proud of that watch. Today it sits in her jewelry box on her dresser.

All of a sudden, I feel as though I am viewing this scene through the objective eyes of a reporter. How is it that this patient—who was raised by a doctor and a nurse—made the mutinous decision twenty-odd years ago to turn away from her upbringing and conventional medicine? I could ask myself the same question about my father's motivations, but his father never carried a black doctor's bag or wrote prescriptions or made house calls in the middle of the night. His mother never took a patient's pulse.

It dawns on me that for my whole life up until now—even though I've known, intellectually, that my parents converted to Christian

Science—my perception of their faith has been of something constant, immutable. But the truth is that both of my parents rejected the faiths of their upbringings to embrace, fervently and ultimately fanatically, a religion of their choosing.

The nurse jots an entry on Mom's record. "I'll be back in a bit," she says, patting my mother's leg.

"Your father and I are going to read the Lesson," Mom announces after she leaves.

My body tenses. Sherm and I are being given our exit cue, just like at Tenacre. I remember a day in late April when I was home for the weekend; I had just visited Mom for all of twelve minutes at Tenacre. My father and I were standing in the kitchen when I had cautiously suggested to Dad that we could take Mom to the hospital and *still* use Christian Science; the discussion quickly escalated to an all-out fight.

"No we can't!" my father had exploded, his face reddening. The weight of his body tipped forward onto the balls of his feet, and his fists were clenched at his sides. It was as though an invisible cord, attached to an imaginary point on the floor behind him, was restraining him. I had the panicky feeling, that hollowness in the bones one gets at the sight of a fierce dog behind a fence. The dog jumps, growls, and bares his teeth, ready to attack: will that fence hold? "Christian Science and medicine don't mix," my father had said in a more controlled tone. He'd breathed deeply, measuredly, in through his nose, and continued: "And until you accept that, young lady"—his voice had grown nasty and threatening—"you won't be doing anything to help your mother. . . . You may even be hurting her!"

Now, in the midst of IV bags and monitoring equipment in the ICU, Mom and Dad are going to read the Lesson. I want to scream. Then I notice my father's reading glasses on her bedside table. For the last couple of years, I've seen him seated behind his desk at home, in his little study, peering over tortoiseshell frames that make him look so professorial, authoritative. At first I was taken aback at the sight, remembering my Eyeglasses Rebellion, but over time, I got used to it. Only now is the hypocrisy so glaring.

Suddenly my head hurts, and I feel claustrophobic. I need air.

"We'll see you a bit later," I try to say cheerfully to Mom, to cover my anger. I know that upsetting her won't help anything. "Keep it up, Mom. Already, you're looking so much better," I add, the phrase like an arrow aimed at my father and at Christian Science. I turn on my heel.

Sherm and I leave the ICU with his arm over my shoulder. We separate; he goes to the cafeteria for a Coke, and I head outside.

I find an empty bench along the circular driveway of the hospital's main entrance. The air is thick with humidity. Lighting a cigarette, I inhale the smoke defiantly: the daughter of a Christian Science practitioner, outside a hospital where my mother lies dying, most likely of cancer. I rest my elbows on my knees and fix my gaze on the curb to avoid eye contact with anybody.

The presence of my father's Bible and *Science and Health* in the ICU is an affront to me. And yet—I am trying hard to be less judgmental in light of my mother's improvement—what harm is there now, really, in reading the Lesson? So it's hypocritical. So what? Maybe my father is going through the motions of reading the Lesson with Mom to comfort both of them, the way a new retiree keeps putting on his suit. Is that really so bad?

I want my mother to surrender unequivocally to the new reality of the hospital, falling backward into the embracing arms of medicine. But can she do this if she is still reading the Lesson, relying, even in part, on the Church doctrine that has gotten her into this crisis? Psychologically speaking, is it better to deny the reality of illness while treating it medically, or to accept it?

And might I be placing too much stock in the power of medicine? I think of the ravaged breast cancer patient we saw coming out of the elevator yesterday and know there are no assurances.

I can't answer any of these questions.

It occurs to me that we haven't heard back from Uncle Jack.

Almost twenty-four hours have passed since I gave him the doctor's name. We haven't talked to Grandma either, because Uncle Jack was going to break the news to her. Maybe my uncle wants to hold off telling Grandma about Mom until he has spoken with Dr. Sierocki. Maybe he hasn't gotten through to him yet. Or perhaps he and Aunt Mary won't tell Grandma until Aunt Kay returns from Wyoming. The silence disturbs me, nevertheless, given the urgency of Mom's situation. I wonder if there aren't other reasons, reasonable ones, for the reticence—outrage, a feeling of betrayal by Mom, by Dad, by Liv and Sherm and me. Maybe he *has* talked with the doctor and that is precisely why we haven't heard back. I decide to call Uncle Jack again at his office.

I throw the rubbed-out cigarette into the trash and head back upstairs.

"Doctor's office," the friendly woman's voice from the day before answers the phone.

"Hello, this is Lucia. Is my uncle in?"

"One moment, please," she says. I hear her cover the mouthpiece. The possibly paranoid notion that Uncle Jack is right there only intensifies my suspicion that he is avoiding me, us. Moments later, she speaks again.

"The doctor is in surgery."

"Will you tell him I called? He can call me at the ICU lobby pay phone." I give her the number.

My father is sitting next to Sherm at the round table in the waiting room, watching the overhead television, which seems odd: It normally takes forty-five minutes to read the Lesson aloud, but they have stopped after fifteen at most.

"How was Mom when you left her?" I ask. I wonder *why* he left her.

"Oh, gee, I don't know," he says, searching for words. That she is "making good progress" would still sound hollow now, even if for the first time since Christmas it might actually be true. If the doctors had performed an overnight miracle—if Mom had been completely healed—it might be difficult for Dad to accept. Might he be torn, I wonder, between wanting her to get better and not wanting medicine to succeed where Christian Science has failed?

It is inconceivable, yet the thought crosses my mind.

"She's dozing in and out," Dad says. There is a wobble in his voice. He starts to cry, and then to shake, a head-to-toe, fevered shiver. I try to comfort him, gently rubbing his back, but I am not drawn into his anguish. I have my own, and it is a complicated mess of scorn and duty and despair. I feel separate, disconnected. Here is a man who is my father, and here is a daughter's hand, mine, comforting him.

He immediately freezes, straightens, and wipes his eyes with his palm. "I'm okay, I'm all right," he says, drawing in a quick breath. "I'm okay."

I know that, according to Christian Science, it isn't the religion that has failed. It is my mother who has, and probably my father. I remember a particular passage from *Science and Health* that I memorized years ago at Claremont:

Science reveals the possibility of achieving all good, and sets mortals at work to discover what God has already done; but distrust of one's ability to gain the goodness desired and to bring out better and higher results, often hampers the trial of one's wings and ensures failure at the outset.

Mortals must change their ideals in order to improve their models. A sick body is evolved from sick thoughts. Sickness, disease, and death proceed from fear.

According to Mary Baker Eddy, my mother has given in to fear. She has failed to correct her thinking, and that is why she is sick.

There will be consequences for going into the hospital, I am certain. My mother's practitioner, Mrs. Childs, will no longer "treat" her (not to punish Mom's decision, Christian Scientists will say, but because medicine and Christian Science are incompatible). And there will be implicit retribution: Not only will Mrs. Childs stop praying for Mom (even if Dad continues to do so) but she will also never visit Mom here. I doubt that any of my parents' Christian Science friends will come to the hospital. And what, I wonder, will happen if she ever gets out? Will she be excommunicated? Since she still wants to read the Lesson, she probably isn't thinking about leaving the Church.

Soon, the shunning will be felt. I didn't have to grow up Episcopalian or Lutheran to know that church communities typically rally around their members with flowers, hospital visits, and Prayers of the People at times of personal or family crisis, none of which will be forthcoming. There is a fresh pan of lasagna in our refrigerator at home, but it came from Mrs. Florence—the stockbroker's wife—along with homemade chocolate chip cookies and a fruit salad. What kind of a church turns away from one of its members at her darkest hour? I think of my Dad too. Will his "practice" suffer? (I can no longer use that term without quotes.) Will he be shut out? An expanding sadness for both of my parents outweighs—for now—the anger.

Dad, Sherm, and I return to the ICU and gather around Mom. The nurse draws the curtain back and sticks her head in.

"Lucia? There's a doctor on the phone for you at the nurses' station."

I stand up and excuse myself. It does not occur to me to pull the curtain shut. I walk around to the far side of the circular nurses' station and pick up the phone.

"Hello?"

"Lucia, this is Uncle Jack."

"Hi," I say, startled.

"Your aunt Mary and I are here with Grandma, and we've told her about Joanne. She would like to say a word."

My heart is racing. I was not expecting it to be Uncle Jack. There is a pause, followed by some murmuring I can't discern.

"Hi, Lucia...dear." My grandmother's vocal tremor, far worse than I've ever heard it, alters her speech significantly. I would not have recognized her voice.

"Hi, Grandma."

She is sobbing. Then there is the sound of a struggle. Maybe Aunt Mary and Uncle Jack are trying to take the phone from her, or maybe she is so upset that her hands are fumbling. I have never heard my grandmother cry before. It is unbearable. Mom is her *daughter,* I think to myself. I press the phone's earpiece against my forehead and close my eyes. I recall how Grandma used to make everything better for me when I was a wronged, wailing kid: how she'd take a seat on the glider in our screened porch and pat her thigh with her veined and bejeweled hand; how I'd come rest my head in her lap. I remember how her long fingernails lightly traced the path of my spine and ribs, calming me.

I clench my teeth to keep from crying and return the phone to my ear.

"Tell your mother—tell my Joanne—I love her . . . very much."

"I will, Grandma—"

I look up again and realize my mother's eyes are focused on me, and not on the two interns who are drawing blood from her arm. I try to smile, to mask the despair I'm feeling.

"And tell . . . your father . . . I will . . . *never* . . . forgive him."

If my grandmother had hit me squarely across the jaw, I'd have felt less stunned. I quickly turn my back so my mother can't see my face. I have to lean against the bulkhead of the nurses' station to steady my shaking legs.

There is a scuffling sound through the phone, and then it goes dead. Hearing the click, I feel both abandoned and scrutinized. I wonder if the nurses can tell I've been cut off. I turn around and try to replace the phone in its cradle as gently as possible, but both of my hands are also shaking. I have to get out of the ICU. I head for the elevator.

In the hallway I see one of the interns who has been caring for my mother. He approaches me. I wonder if my distress is obvious.

"Hello," I say, expecting him to reply and keep going. But he stops and turns to face me. He looks me straight in the eye. "I have one question: How could you let something like this happen to your own mother?" he asks.

Not waiting for a response, he turns and walks away.

I try to get my bearings, but I can't remember where I am headed. I feel dizzy. I hold my breath to contain the sob. I spot a bathroom and duck into it.

For several minutes, I weep as quietly as I can, holding my sides. Then I splash my face with cold water to keep my eyes from swelling. It is useless. My face is puffy and mottled. I take a brown paper towel and moisten it, holding it over my eyes. I have to stop crying. I take some deep breaths to calm the shuddering heaves of my gasps. In the mirror I see a face soaked with tears and running snot. I take another brown paper towel and blow.

I return to my mother's bed with dread.

"You've been crying," Mom says.

"It's nothing."

"Who was on the telephone?" she asks. "Tell me. Was it the doctor?"

My mother is trying to be brave, I can tell. She bites her lower lip. She expects me to say yes: yes, it was the doctor and the news is bad.

"No, Mom. It wasn't the doctor. I promise."

"Then who was it? Please tell me, Lucia."

"It's not important, Mom. Really." I hold one of her hands in both of mine. I wish I were invisible. I know she is studying my face.

"Tell me," she says softly, tilting her head like she might have when I was much younger, to coax the details of a playground incident from me. I swallow hard.

It was your asshole brother, I want to say.

"No, Mom," I manage, shaking my head. "People are upset that you're sick," I say, referring to her family in the most general of terms, hoping to avoid alarming her. "They're naturally concerned. We all are. And for some, this news has come as a terrible shock."

"Who was on the telephone?" Mom squeezes my hand and speaks with resolve.

"It was Grandma," I say. "She wanted me to tell you she loves you very much."

Mom stares at me briefly, and looks away, and I feel myself coming undone.

I realize I am no help to my mother in the state I'm in, which I am utterly unable to change, so I excuse myself to "run an errand," and I head out to the car.

On my way back to Hopewell, I pass Aunt Lucia and Aunt Nan heading to the hospital.

Olivia's car is in the driveway when I get home. From the kitchen I can hear the shower running in the bathroom off the den. I open the fridge and find it fully stocked, thanks to my aunts. For months Dad has been living on little more than Grape-Nuts and half-and-half. Now, in addition to Mrs. Florence's lasagna and fruit salad, there are cold cuts, apples, eggs, bread, some frozen Stouffer's entrées; even Häagen-Dazs in the freezer.

I grab a Diet Coke and walk to the screened porch, Oscar and Felix following at my heels. I stretch out on the glider, and my left foot, moored to the floor, sets it in motion. The dogs lie obediently nearby, Felix with his front paws crossed, which always makes me smile. I close my eyes and listen for sounds: frogs and birds, the hum of an air conditioner in an upstairs window, the dogs panting. I try to take a deep breath, but I am still in the grip of my earlier conversations, with Uncle Jack and Grandma on the phone and the intern in the hallway of the ICU. Now I hold my breath. Hold it, hold it.

Olivia appears.

"Hi," she says with a tone of foreboding. "We need to talk."

I exhale. I haven't seen my sister since early this morning in the

ICU; she has no idea what I've just been through, and I am not inclined, at the moment, to fill her in. Nor am I in the mood to hear whatever she feels the need to tell me. Olivia opens the screen door, comes in, and sits down across from me.

"Mom was saying some pretty awful stuff last night," she says. I stare at the ceiling fan above me to avoid my sister's eyes.

"I think Mom was saying that Dad forced her to stay at Tenacre."

"That's bullshit," I say reflexively. I won't listen to this. I can't.

"Lucia, would I lie? Would I make this up?"

Maybe, I want to say, not because I think she would but because it is easier to think that than to consider the alternative: that Dad kept Mom at Tenacre—a prisoner—against her will.

"About a half hour after you left, Mom woke up. It was probably four-thirty in the morning. She said, 'I wanted to come here a long time ago, but someone wouldn't let me.' I couldn't believe it. I just froze, Loosh. I felt—oh, my God—I felt ill. But then, I needed to know *who* she meant. So I said, 'Who wouldn't let you?' And she wouldn't answer. So I said, 'Was it someone at Tenacre?' And she was silent. 'Was it your practitioner? Mrs. . . . Childs?' I asked. She shook her head. I wanted to say 'Was it Dad?' but I couldn't. 'Who was it, Mom?' I asked. And then she said, '*He* knows.'"

I sit up and meet my sister's eyes.

"Liv, she could have left Tenacre," I argue, my impatience seeping through as bitterness, aimed at her, the messenger. This cannot be true.

Mom had choices.

"She could have said something to me," I say. "Or to you. Or Sherman. I asked her to go to a doctor. She wouldn't. Liv, she wouldn't even discuss it.

We sit for a few moments in silence.

"But what if it's true?" Olivia asks tentatively.

"It's not. Maybe you heard wrong."

"Fuck you," my sister says. "I know what I heard."

"I talked with Mom last night too," I say, "and again this morning. She sure didn't say anything like that to me. And then she asked Sherman and me to leave so she could read the Lesson with Dad! Would she have done that if she'd been forced to stay at Tenacre against her will?"

I know I shouldn't walk out on Olivia, but I am angry. Angry at her—even though none of this is her fault—angry at Dad, Mom, that asshole intern; Uncle Jack; angry at this whole fucked-up mess. What's more, I cannot believe that right now I am defending my father, who I'm already angry at, against this charge. I go upstairs to change into shorts and a T-shirt; I pull on my running shoes, grab my Walkman, and head down the driveway at an uncharacteristically fast clip. The humidity might kill me, and I'm exhausted from lack of sleep the night before, but I need to get out of there.

I have to think. I don't want to believe what my sister has told me. But as my pace slows in the oppressive heat, my feet heavy on the pavement, I ask myself, What if? What if Olivia heard right?

She must have heard wrong.

Mom cannot stand to face the consequences of the choice she's made. So she's taking it out on Dad, making him the scapegoat...

But what if it is true: that Dad kept Mom from seeking medical attention?

I realize it is conceivable—maybe even likely?—that my mother, after months of unrelenting pain, and the creeping progression of unknown but undeniable disease, wavered in her conviction, and suggested to Dad that she go to a doctor.

I can picture my father, hear him, feel the explosiveness of his reaction.

"If you give in to mortal mind, Jo...Don't do it! Just *don't*! You must claim your dominion over this erroneous belief! There *is* no substance in matter!"

Could the mere declaration of disappointment by my father have kept my mother from asserting herself?

"Oh, Jo. Jo—please. Honey, please..."

I don't know. I don't want to know.

I stop running.

I can't bear this. I can't.

I look up at the dizzying vastness of the sky and try to catch my breath. *Oh, God.* I sit down on the shoulder of the road, rest my elbows on my knees, and stuff the palms of my hands into my eyes.

MONDAY, AUGUST 11

2 A.M.

I am back in the ICU taking a night shift with Mom. She stirs.

"I wonder what's wrong with me," she says.

"I'm sure the doctors will have some answers soon," I reply.

"Lucia, dear, will you do something for me?"

"Sure, what?"

"Will you call your daddy? Ask him to pray that I sleep tonight."

"I'll call him right away." I move to the edge of her mattress and half-sit on it. "Have you been praying too?"

She nods. This, and the fact that she has asked for Dad to pray for her, is paradoxically reassuring to me. Olivia must have heard wrong.

I kiss her on the forehead. She feels warm.

"Mom, I love you. I'm glad you're here."

"I love you too, dear. I love you too."

I walk out to the pay phone in the lounge. My father answers before the second ring.

"Hey, Dad," I say. "Mom's awake. She asked me to call you. She wants you to pray for her. That she sleeps."

"Oh, good. Yes, right away," he says, sounding relieved. "I'll get started right way."

Does he notice, as I do, that she isn't asking him to pray for a healing, only for some rest? Does he feel like the police detective reassigned to desk duty? When I hang up the phone, one of the interns (not the mean one) is waiting for me with a blanket and a pillow.

"Here," he says, with a kind smile. "Your mom's asleep. Want these for the couch?"

4:20 A.M.

I go check on Mom, and she stirs again. She smiles at me, and then she turns away, to rest on her right side, her back to me. I move my chair closer.

"I should have come here a long time ago," she says just above a whisper, but the words are unmistakable.

My stomach knots up. Even after my talk with Olivia, I am not prepared for this.

"I wanted to," Mom says. She rolls onto her back again, so that she is looking straight ahead at the curtain separating us from the nurses' station. "I wanted to come sooner, and your father knows it."

She closes her eyes and goes back to sleep.

Head in my hands, I am left with this. I don't know what to do.

I feel someone gently pressing my forearm, trying to rouse me. It is my father.

"Loosh, why don't you head home," he whispers. "Get in a real bed."

Somehow, I was sound asleep on the couch. I look at the clock on the wall. It is 6:15 A.M. My father is freshly showered and shaved, dressed, carrying a Diet Coke in one hand and the PBS tote bag with his *Science and Health* and Bible in the other.

I think about what my mother told me in the early hours of the morning, how she had wanted to go to the hospital when she was at Tenacre. And Dad knew it.

I am too scared, too confused to confront him right now, because if I do, then what? I try to sort out the possible consequences, but none of them are good. Maybe because I'm so tired, I can't even really process them. In chess, I'm not one who can see two or three moves ahead.

If I ask Dad, and he admits it's true, then what? Is this a police matter? And a police matter *now*? If I ask Dad and he denies it, then what? What is the truth? What is my moral responsibility?

And why is Mom saying these things while still reading the Lesson with Dad? Why is she asking him to pray for her at all?

I watch as he heads through the swinging double doors into the ICU. I stand, fold the blanket, place it under the hospital-issue pillow, and leave.

Mimi is here. She rode the train out this morning, and Sherman picked her up at Princeton Junction while I was sleeping. I haven't seen her in weeks; we've talked on the phone only briefly and sporadically, but ever since late June, when I finally told her about Mom, she has honored Mom's wishes, better than I. Maybe because of this she knows what Sherman, Olivia, and I have been going through. I'm hoping—perhaps unrealistically—that she will be able to help us in dealing with her mom, Aunt Kay, Grandma, and Uncle Jack. If she is angry with me for putting her in this untenable position—or with Dad, or any of us—she hasn't let on. The fact that I can't read how she's feeling worries me. Will our friendship be a casualty of this whole mess?

Mimi, Aunt Nan, Aunt Lucia, and I are sitting in the kitchen when the phone rings. I pick it up. My father is sobbing.

"Dad, what is it?"

Somehow I know instinctively that this is not *the* call. That fear is gone, at least for now.

"It's your mother," he says, trying in vain to contain his emotions.

I wait for him to go on. I look over at Mimi, who is staring at me, clearly terrified. I shake my head, telling her silently that no, it's not what she thinks it is.

"She wants to be transferred to a hospital in Minneapolis," my father says. "I told her it's not possible—not now anyway—and she became furious. She said I'm interfering! She won't talk to me."

I tell Dad that I'm on my way. After I hang up the phone, I share with Mimi and my aunts what my father has just said.

"It is very natural for someone who is sick to take out her anger on the person she's closest to," Aunt Nan offers. Mimi nods in agreement.

"Your mom knows that your dad is the one person who won't abandon her," Aunt Lucia adds.

I'm skeptical. This is all valuable insight for a normal hospital situation. But this is hardly normal. He has already abandoned her once, I think, remembering his two-week class. The possibility of her languishing at Tenacre, pleading to see a doctor, haunts me.

But I also know that if I were lying in a hospital, after being sick and not going to a doctor for nine months or more, it's possible I'd feel angry with myself, and ashamed. And angry at the person who has been my partner in this from the start. Mom knew better than anyone what was happening to her body. She could have left Tenacre. She could have called me. Or Olivia. Or Sherman. She told me to stop calling.

I find my father and Sherman in the ICU waiting room, sitting at the table. Olivia is in with Mom. Dr. White, who will be Mom's surgeon, is also here. He has short-cropped white hair, gentle features, and a kindly manner.

"I told Jo she is getting excellent care," he says to the three of us. "She *does* want to go to Minneapolis. I told her that nobody would advise transferring her anywhere right now, but that it might be possible to move her to an individual room in the Special Care Unit before too long. It will be quieter there, more private, and more comfortable. The noise makes sleeping in the ICU nearly impossible."

I like Dr. White. Everything about him is reassuring: his words, his smile, his unassuming manner. For the moment, he has offered the tiniest glimmer of hope, that Mom may get some peace and quiet.

TUESDAY, AUGUST 12
SPECIAL CARE UNIT

On Tuesday morning, Dad calls from the hospital to say that Mom has been transferred to a single room in the Special Care Unit. We interpret this as a sign of slow but certain improvement. She wanted to be moved earlier, but the doctors said she wasn't strong enough. With this first cause for optimism (and we will take anything, however small), Sherman and I drive into town for a celebratory breakfast. Olivia stays behind to call Grandma, happy to be the bearer of some good news.

An hour later, Sherman and I are back at the house, preparing to leave with Olivia for the hospital, when the phone rings. I pick it up.

"How could you lie to your grandmother?" my uncle Jack asks coolly.

"What do you mean?" I say, confused.

"Telling her that Jo's doing so much better. That she's been moved to a private room."

"She *is* doing better—" I start.

"She is not better. And she's not in a private room. She's been moved to the Special Care Unit."

"She's in a private room in Special Care," I say, "and the doctor only approved the move this morning because she'd stabili——"

"I spoke with the doctor," my uncle says before I can finish my sentence. "He said he's never seen a body in a worse state of neglect. You know, Lucia, prisoners in concentration camps are treated better."

My uncle's voice cuts through me. My mind fixes on the words *concentration camp,* and I find myself writing them onto a notepad.

"We're going to investigate," he continues. "Your grandmother has a right to know what happened. And," he adds, pausing, "the medical center might launch its own investigation. What happened to your mother at Tenacre could be criminal neglect. Her liver is swollen from six months of starvation. She has a tumor in her rectum that may have spread to the lymph nodes."

I write down *tumor* and *lymph nodes*. Uncle Jack must have heard something from the doctor that we haven't. My mind skips over his threat of a hospital investigation to focus on my mother's condition.

"Did the doctor say whether it is malignant?" I ask, terrified. Olivia and Sherman sit motionless at the kitchen table. I turn my back to them so they can't see my face.

"It's malignant," he says.

Malignant. I tilt my head back and stare at the ceiling to contain my tears.

"I thought they couldn't tell without performing a biopsy," I say, raising my voice. "They haven't done a biopsy!"

"They were able to tell from the physical examination; it's malignant. And your mother has a mass in her lungs."

I write the words *mass in her lungs*. I glance behind me to see Olivia's eyes on me. Sherman' s head is down, resting on his folded arms on the table; his shoulders are shaking.

"What happened to Jo at Tenacre is very serious," he continues. "Very. You might be implicated. You, your brother, your sister, your father... You knew for months and denied her treatment. You could be guilty of criminal—"

I hang up the phone.

I turn around and see Sherman's tortured face, but I can't comfort him right now. And I don't want to talk to my sister. If she hadn't called Grandma this morning, and made everything sound like Mom was practically ready to come home...

I head for the bathroom and close the door. Why can't Olivia keep her goddamned mouth shut? Or at least get it right? Olivia wouldn't intentionally mislead Grandma—I know that—but she is capable of letting her own optimism color her report. You can't just rearrange the significance of certain facts because you are hopeful, I want to scream.

There is a knock on the door.

"Loosh?" It is Olivia, speaking softly, cautiously. "Do you want to talk?"

"Not now."

"It's malignant?"

"That's what he said."

"Who?" Olivia asks.

"Uncle Jack."

"What else did he say?"

"I don't want to talk about it."

The silence from the other side of the door tells me my sister is not about to leave it till later.

"He's pissed off because he thinks we—*you*—lied to Grandma."

"What?"

"Come on, Olivia," I say, opening the door. "Maybe you didn't mean to, but when you called Grandma this morning, you gave her the impression that Mom was practically back on her feet."

"I only—"

"Look, what's done is done."

"What's done is done?" There is rage and contempt in my sister's eyes. "Who the hell do you think you are? You didn't even hear my conversation with Grandma."

"Maybe you shouldn't have called her in the first place. If you can't be straight—"

"I *was* straight!" my sister yells back. "And besides, I told Grandma yesterday that if there were any news, I'd let her know. That's *all* I did. So *back off.* Grandma was crying this morning. I was trying to calm her. Don't tell me you wouldn't have done the same. All I said was that Mom looks a lot better than a few days ago. And she *does.*"

"*Sto-op!* Stop fighting!" Sherman pleads with us, through sobs. We return to the kitchen.

"She's going to die, isn't she?" His voice breaks, and he holds his forehead in his palms, his elbows propped on the kitchen table. He seems so much younger than twenty-two, or maybe I just feel so much older than twenty-four. Olivia and I stoop to where Sherman is sitting, and the three of us hold one another.

A few minutes later, the phone rings again. This time it is Dr. Sierocki. I take notes:

- *Tumor in rectum has eroded the wall between rectum/vagina.*
- *Won't know until biopsy whether or not malignant.*
- *Infection in the blood stemming, apparently, from urinary tract.*
- *Lungs appear clear.*
- *Needs colostomy before biopsy. But until nutrition improves, no surgery will be undertaken.*
- *Temperature down, vital signs stable.*

The report is grim, but I am reassured that there isn't a definite malignancy. I am struck by the conflicting messages I've just received. It seems plausible that Dr. Sierocki suspects a malignancy—and may have intimated as much to Uncle Jack—but can't verify it without a biopsy. Maybe there is an understanding among all doctors that allows for a preliminary exchange of information not yet intended for patients or their families.

In the early afternoon, I drive to the airport to pick up Aunt Mary. It is a gray, soggy day.

I need the hour drive from Princeton to Newark to collect my thoughts, to pull back from the rage I'm feeling toward Uncle Jack, and resolve how I will deal with Aunt Mary. I am already on the defensive: it is now *them* versus *us. Them* is Uncle Jack, who has accused all of us of criminal neglect; and Grandma, who has vowed to me she will never forgive Dad; by association, *them* includes Aunt Mary, and Aunt Kay, possibly everyone on Mom's side of the family (with the exception, maybe, of Mimi?). I understand my grandmother's feelings, totally; I don't know if I will ever forgive my dad either. For the time being, though, I have to try to hold these feelings at bay.

Do I—do we—need to contact a lawyer? I realize all this may get much worse.

I know my uncle is not going to see the nuances of how we have come to this point; how Dad, Olivia, Sherman, and I are not a united front. But I also feel this isn't the time to try to explain to him the catch-22 we—Mom's children—faced. Doing so will only aid in the destruction of what is left of our vulnerable family, because Uncle Jack will then see the chasm between Dad and us kids. I can't walk away from us (Mom, Dad, Olivia, Terry, Sherman, and me) because Mom and Dad are still praying together. Maybe there is some benefit in that. I realize, under the gun, that we need to protect the unit we still, barely, make up. So for now, Uncle Jack is our common foe.

I park the car, head into the Northwest Airlines terminal, and wait. I decide I will try to explain what I can to Aunt Mary, but I will not let on about the newly surfaced tension between Mom and Dad; I will keep quiet about that and hope, if Aunt Mary gets wind of it, that I will be led to a solution. *Led.* Christ. I am thinking like a Christian Scientist; all that's missing is the adverb *divinely.*

Aunt Mary emerges from the gate in a black skirt and stockings, a muted pink cotton blouse, and black flats. In one hand she carries an overnight bag, in the other, a trench coat and umbrella. She stands heels together, toes out, like a ballerina, or Mary Poppins, but her eyes lack their characteristic sparkle. Her hair is now silvery white. She sets down her suitcase to hug me tightly. My aunt feels like Mom. I breathe in deeply, closing my eyes. They even smell alike. I can't remember the last time I hugged my mother without fear of crushing her. It's been months since she's hugged me back; she hasn't had the strength. My aunt's embrace feels so good, so familiar and reassuring, that when she lets go, the separation hurts. I hope she will hug me again when everything has played out.

On the drive from the airport to the hospital, I give Aunt Mary the chronology of Mom's illness, starting with the details of Christmas Day. I tell her about Lucia Chase's funeral in Manhattan three weeks later; how, after the nightmarish cab ride home, I asked Dad if we couldn't take Mom to a doctor, or to Lenox Hill Hospital, right down the street. I tell her about Mom's move to Tenacre in January, the day after the space shuttle blew up.

I try to give Aunt Mary a primer on Christian Science, to explain the rationale behind the Church's reliance on prayer over medicine. I quote Mary Baker Eddy from *Science and Health*:

> The dream that matter and error are something must yield to reason and revelation. Then mortals will behold the nothingness of sickness and sin, and sin and sickness will disappear from consciousness.

Then Jesus' Sermon on the Mount from the New Testament Gospel of Matthew:

> Be ye therefore perfect, even as your Father which is in heaven is perfect.

Aunt Mary sits quietly in the passenger seat, staring straight ahead, processing the information without asking any questions. I expected an interrogation, and I am not sure what to make of her reticence.

Mom is surprised when she sees Aunt Mary entering her room. "Why, Mary! What on earth are you doing here?" she asks, as though her sister has flown in from Mars and not Minneapolis.

Aunt Mary looks at me, chuckling and caught off guard by the odd question, and says, "Why, I'm here to see you, of course!"

My mother's eyes tear up. The reason for Aunt Mary's visit is suddenly clear to her. "I'm so sorry for all of this," Mom says.

Aunt Mary reaches for her hand and gives it a squeeze. "It's all right, Jo. We just want you back on your feet, feeling like yourself again."

"How's Mother?" Mom asks, although not cautiously; it sounds more like a chatty question, and I wonder if she is even aware of the turmoil her illness and actions have caused. She hasn't expressed any regret to me. Even though her apology to Aunt Mary hints at an awareness, I am overcome by the impression, not for the first time, that I am in the presence of a child, someone who doesn't comprehend the excruciating reality we all face.

"She's just fine," Aunt Mary says. "Would you like her to come see you?"

"No," Mom says firmly, shaking her head. "No."

Aunt Mary and I exchange glances. Grandma and Aunt Kay will be arriving tomorrow, so this doesn't bode well. But I am relieved that Aunt Mary is witnessing firsthand Mom's behavior. She needs to know that Mom has wanted privacy from the outset. I have trouble understanding how Mom could *not* want Grandma to come, because I have always longed for my mother's presence when I've been under the weather or faced some problem. Once again, I am reminded of the fact that Grandma, at least in her capacity as a former nurse, has no place in my mother's belief system.

When two orderlies come in to change Mom's bedding, Aunt Mary and I go to the cafeteria for a cup of coffee. As we sit facing each other in a booth, stirring our bitter coffee with wooden sticks, I say, "She looks pretty bad, doesn't she?" But in truth I'm relieved that she looks so much better.

"I guess I had prepared myself for worse," she says. There is a long silence.

The fact that we are talking at all is promising. I was expecting Aunt Mary to be angry, but so far, she seems to be listening with an aim to withhold judgment.

"How did this happen?" she asks, shaking her head, downcast. Aunt Mary chews on her lip the same way Mom does when she's deep in thought.

How? I have told her *when*, but I can't explain *how* or *why*. Beneath the chronology of Mom's gradual decline lies a tangle of questions.

Maybe it's because we're here, in a hospital now, but I am struck, all of a sudden, by how truly surprising it is that my parents, and especially my mother, chose the path of Christian Science. Not one of Mom's siblings—not Aunt Mary, Uncle Jack, or Aunt Kay—remained Lutheran once they married (and why is that?). But of the four, Mom's departure was the most radical. She could have become an Episcopalian like Aunt Mary. Mom's conversion to Christian Science had to have been more than a rejection of her parents' mainstream religion and an act of matrimonial loyalty. It must have been a reaction to her father being a doctor. But why?

I don't understand this either: such a dramatic rebellion against the authority of her parents would seem to require a strength of will at odds with what can only be seen as profound acquiescence to another authority in the face of undeniable illness. How are these two reconciled?

Aunt Mary fidgets with her cup, swirling around the one remaining, undrinkable sip of coffee. Does she blame me?

"We talked to you on Christmas Day," she says eventually. There is no tone of accusation or reproach in her voice. I remember how we dispersed to the various telephones in the house to make the holiday phone calls so we could all talk at once.

"What did it feel like to deceive us?" she asks. I can't tell if her question is an accusation or an inquiry.

Like I was a hostage, reciting lines handed to me on a sheet of paper, I think, but I'm not sure how to answer. Looking down, closing my eyes, I shake my head. The regret is unbearable.

On our way back up to Mom's room, we find Olivia, Aunt Lucia, and Aunt Nan sitting in the waiting area. Aunt Nan is knitting. Aunt Lucia has *The New York Times* in her lap, opened to the crossword puzzle, but clearly her mind is elsewhere; she is gazing into space. Olivia smokes.

"Hi," I say.

"Hi, Loosh," Olivia replies, putting out her cigarette. Aunt Nan and Aunt Lucia stand up to greet both of us. Olivia also gets up and hugs Aunt Mary with eyes closed, seeming to relish the comfort just as I did. When she breaks the embrace, I think Olivia is looking into Aunt Mary's eyes for some acceptance, or forgiveness. When she speaks, I realize I have misinterpreted my sister's thoughts completely.

"This has been hell," Olivia declares with a boldness that catches me off guard. My sister's appearance mirrors her words. Her cotton dress is rumpled, her pale face obviously hasn't seen or felt the summer's sunshine, and her dark eyebrows are pinched together by two creases of tension.

"We don't need Uncle Jack's—bullshit—right now."

I look around to see if anyone else is in the waiting room, but we are alone, the five of us.

Aunt Mary looks at me, confused and no doubt startled.

"Maybe it was a pipe dream to think he'd help us, but Lucia called him the other day because we basically haven't a goddamned clue about hospitals and doctors and medicine."

Aunt Nan resumes her knitting, and Aunt Lucia stares at the crossword puzzle.

"You know what he did on Saturday? On Saturday, Uncle Jack called through to the nurses' station, where Lucia was with Mom, and he put Grandma on."

Olivia must not realize that Aunt Mary was there with Grandma and Uncle Jack during the phone call. Maybe I didn't tell her.

"Grandma was sobbing hysterically. Do you know what that was like for Lucia? Why should she bear the brunt of this? And can you guess what Mom was thinking as she watched Lucia on the phone from across the ICU? She thought Lucia was talking to the doctor!

"Then this morning," Olivia goes on, "Uncle Jack called to tell us, among other things, that Mom's tumor is malignant, and there is a mass on her lungs, and that we are all criminals!"

Aunt Mary folds her arms and looks at the floor.

"But guess what? After he hung up, Mom's doctor called. Her lungs are clear. And he doesn't know if the tumor in her bowel is malignant. What the . . . *fuck*."

There is charged silence. I am stuck between my sister and my aunt. Olivia is venting my exact feelings regarding Uncle Jack, but because of our talk in the cafeteria, I don't know if Aunt Mary is really in his camp.

"Olivia," Aunt Mary eventually says, her eyes still on the floor. "Uncle Jack is your mom's brother."

"She's *our* mom," Olivia says, holding her ground.

"Surely you can understand what a terrible shock this has been."

"I just got off the phone with Sherman," Olivia says. "You know where he is? Newark train station. He was on his way to the city to have dinner with some friends. He totally panicked on the train. He called me in hysterics, inconsolable; he couldn't figure out what he was doing, where he was going, or why. Have you or Uncle Jack— have any of you—thought for even a moment what *he's* been going through? Jesus Christ! He's been living here, in Hopewell, all summer! It's sinking in that he may lose his mother."

Olivia's chin begins to quiver. "What do you say to him? What...do...you...say?" She holds her breath and wipes her eyes.

"Liv, is he okay?" I ask.

Olivia nods. "He got back on the train. I told him he should go. That he needs a break."

Olivia turns to our aunt again. "I know it's unfair," she says, "but we can't wait for you, or Uncle Jack, or anyone else to catch up."

Aunt Mary's arms unfold and fall to her sides, and she looks up, first at me, then at Olivia. "I can't speak for my brother. I don't know why he does things the way he does." Aunt Mary pauses, choosing her words carefully. "But he and your father have always been at odds, and...if he's got a problem with anyone, it's with your father...not you. Anyway, I'm here. He's not. I'm here to see Jo, and I'm here for you kids. Lucia and I have had a chance to talk this afternoon."

Aunt Mary looks down again, shaking her head.

"You're right," she says chewing her lip. "I may never understand why this has happened. But I love you, and I love your mother, and I want to help."

Grasping Olivia and me each by an arm, Aunt Mary draws us toward her into a huddle.

"Come on," she says, "we're family."

She holds Olivia and me, trembling, in her embrace. All the pain of the last eight months starts flooding in.

My God. How will I ever live with this?

I want my aunt to hold me and never let go.

The three of us walk down the hall to Mom's room. Peering through the window that separates her room from the hallway, I see that a nurse and two interns are tending to her. Fortunately, the intern who confronted me the other day is not one of them.

Mom's room has a window overlooking a tree-lined street, which today lets in sunlight. There are vases of flowers on the windowsill and on every available surface. Over the past few days, floral arrangements and get-well cards have arrived from old friends and relatives on both sides of the family, in addition to those brought by Olivia, Sherman, and me. There is even a beautiful arrangement from Connie. For Mom's sake, I am relieved to see that someone in the church has sent something.

"How does she look to you?" Olivia asks Aunt Mary.

"I said to Lucia that I had prepared myself for the worst. But I don't know. She looks so...so...resuscitated. Her face has such a glow about it. And there's something about her hair that's so lovely, really," Aunt Mary says.

Over the months Mom's hair has been something to avoid looking at, so matted and flat and colorless, like pale steel wool. It does look better now, somehow, despite the gray. Maybe the nurses here are better with a comb and brush than the staff is at Tenacre.

"But she does look resuscitated," Aunt Mary repeats, now whispering, since the door is open and the nurse and doctors are leaving, "like she was dead."

Dad arrives while Olivia, Aunt Mary, and I are sitting with Mom. I haven't seen him since yesterday. He stayed with Mom overnight, and I passed him in the car on my way to the airport. To my surprise and relief (given how yesterday afternoon Mom wasn't even speaking to him), Mom eventually asked Dad last night to stay with her again, to pray with her. I feel myself softening over the hypocrisy of them reading the Lesson and using Christian Science in the hospital. At least for now. What I care about most is that further confrontations and turmoil be averted. I hope—especially—that Mom's anger at Dad won't surface in Aunt Mary's presence. If it is true that Dad kept Mom from going to the hospital sooner, then the facts will have to come out, and we'll have to deal with it. Somehow. But if, as Aunt Nan and Aunt Lucia suggest, Mom has lashed out at Dad because she feels that she can trust him most (which is also a possibility), then the last thing we need is Mom laying blame on him. I don't know who or what to believe anymore. There are so many angles and layers to all of this, it's dizzying. Right now I am terrified, and angry, that Mom might have just dropped a bomb about our father (or is it only a scare?) and then she'll die, leaving us amid the devastation. Part of me feels pity for my father.

How did this all happen? There must be reasons why Dad was open to Christian Science—just as there were reasons for Mom's vulnerability—although I've never, until recently, given much thought to any of this. Aunt Mary said that Uncle Jack and Dad have "always been at odds," but I wonder if she might have spoken even more broadly, that Dad, on some level, has always been at odds in general: out of place in his family, out of sync with his world.

On the surface, I know Dad was part of a prominent Minnesota family. I've heard it my whole life. But beneath the surface, maybe he was more *apart*. He was only a baby when his parents divorced, and then Ammie quickly married Grandpa, who was always Grandpa to me, never Step-Grandpa. But what was he to Dad? And what must it have been like for Dad to have his own father half a continent away and be raised by Ammie and Grandpa—whom he called Uncle, Unc for short—and who in quick succession had two boys of their own? I remember Dad's testimony about how he was healed of a lifelong stutter thanks to Christian Science. What must it have been like to grow up with a crippling speech impediment? And what caused it?

Aunt Mary, seeing Dad through the window to the hallway, gets up to greet him. I wonder how they will handle the reunion. It occurs to me that maybe Dad avoided being at the hospital for Aunt Mary's arrival. The two hug, but I can't read much from it. Anything less than a hug would be cold. For Aunt Mary, the embrace must feel difficult if not forced, and, for Dad, it is probably sincere; his conditioned response of denial is so basic to his Christian Science thinking: *Man cannot be sick; Man is the perfect likeness of God* includes *Man cannot have conflicts; Aunt Mary cannot be upset with me.* The two speak for a minute, but their conversation is inaudible through the glass. Then they return to Mom's bedside.

I am suddenly filled with apprehension. Everything orbits around my mother. She wields the controls that will maintain our precarious balance, or completely throw it off. Will she turn on Dad in front of Aunt Mary, telling her that Dad kept her from going to a hospital? Or will she dismiss Aunt Mary, as she dismissed us so many times, to read the Lesson?

Mom initiates polite conversation, asking Aunt Mary one question about Minnesota, then Dad another about Hopewell. She wants Olivia to describe her new home in Tucson, which surprises me, and must be a comfort to Olivia. I didn't think their move from Massachusetts to Arizona the month before had even registered with Mom. Every several minutes, Mom closes her eyes and drifts off. We sit there silently, communicating assurances to one another with our eyes, examining our fingernails, leafing through tattered magazines, until once again she joins us. Eventually, Mom asks to be propped up in the bed.

"I'd like to hear the Lesson again," she says to Dad, giving the rest of us our cue to leave.

WEDNESDAY, AUGUST 13

Grandma and Aunt Kay arrived today. I am on my way to the Hyatt to pick up them up, because earlier Olivia met them at the airport, drove them to the hospital to see Mom, then dropped them at the hotel to check in and rest before dinner. Sherman is in Hopewell cooking, which is a first. During the twenty-minute drive to the hotel, I grip the wheel tightly with my left hand and with my right hand stab at the station settings of the radio until I find a song I like.

I am on edge, girding myself for a battle with Aunt Kay, who earlier in the day said to Olivia—in response to my last conversation with Uncle Jack—"Well, you know, Liv, Lucia has a way of listening selectively."

How dare she? I'd like to give her a piece of my mind. I know what I will say too, the moment I get her out of Grandma's earshot: You have no idea, Aunt Kay. And now you're accusing me of lying? Uncle Jack said what he said. I wrote it all down.

I punch the radio buttons again and find Joe Cocker singing "You Are So Beautiful." All of my pent-up, pissed-off, fuck-the-whole-lot-of-you anger dissipates. I am left instead with an unbearable longing. I should pull over to the side of the road until the feeling goes away, or until a different song comes on, but I drive on through, my vision clouded and my head and arms like lead.

I see Grandma and Aunt Kay sitting together on a sofa on the far side of the hotel's atrium. They are an elegant, well-heeled mother-daughter pair, who could easily be meeting for afternoon tea.

Aunt Kay is knitting, and, even from where I stand, I can see her jaw aggressively moving back and forth, chewing gum. My heart races at the sight of her; I realize I am not ready to face her, but she looks up from her knitting, peers over her reading glasses, and sees me. She and Grandma stand and head toward me; we meet halfway.

"Hi, dear," Grandma says, kissing my cheek and pinching my forearm tenderly. She looks terrible: so frail, slightly stooped; the tremor in her hand is very pronounced. My eyes tear again, and I hug her.

I then look up at Aunt Kay, and in my head I hear, *Lucia has a way of listening selectively.* My pulse quickens.

Aunt Kay puts her arm over my shoulder and presses her head to my ear as if she wants to tell me something. Maybe she regrets what she said to Olivia earlier today. I wait.

"Lucia, I've given this a lot of thought," she says, pulling me in close to her. I soften. I turn to face her and offer a partial smile, and she withdraws slightly so our eyes can meet. She has the same ice blue irises as Uncle Jack.

"This has all happened," she says, pausing briefly, searching for the right words, "because your mom is suicidal. It's really a slow death wish."

Oh, my, God. I break away from my aunt before she finishes speaking and pick up my grandmother's bag. I am enraged. I am also worried for Grandma. I hope she didn't hear this. Everyone knows Aunt Kay has the capacity to spew forth her sometimes outrageous thoughts without filtering them first, but nothing has prepared me for this one.

"C'mon, let's go," I say and lead the two of them to the car. I keep a distance between us and open the back door, motioning them both in. We don't speak the whole ride home. I drive recklessly fast, and blast the radio.

I look at my aunt and Grandma in the rearview mirror. They buckle their seat belts and say nothing. I feel omnipotent and vengeful with them in the backseat. I thrill-seek with every hill and bend in the road. For a moment, I worry how Dad might react if I total his car, but then I realize I don't give a shit. I think of the times I drove alone to and from Tenacre, how more than once I contemplated a hasty, impulsive turn of the wheel to veer off into a ditch or hit a tree. At the time, I thought of it only as a way to bring an end to the secret. Even if I didn't kill myself, I'd end up in a hospital bed and draw the Minnesota relatives to Princeton. Then they'd find out about Mom. It wouldn't have taken much courage for a split-second impulse.

Before dinner, Aunt Kay, Grandma, and Aunt Mary are sitting out on the patio. The foot of Aunt Kay's crossed leg taps the air nervously. Both hands cling to the arms of her chair, and I imagine she is holding court, sharing her theories with Grandma and Aunt Mary. Dad appears to be hiding in his study, no doubt doing his protective work. Olivia and Terry sit in the den with the doors closed. When Sherman calls everyone to the table, Grandma, Aunt Kay, and Aunt Mary come in from outside. Slowly, Dad descends the stairs. In the living room, he comes face-to-face with Aunt Kay and Grandma for the first time since their arrival.

Aunt Kay extends a stiff handshake. "Are you off to the hospital?" she asks him bluntly.

"I'm staying for dinner first."

My father bursts through the swinging door to the kitchen, where Sherman and I are putting food on the plates. I look up. His face is the color of beets and he mumbles through gritted teeth, "That Kay, what nerve!" He looks like he may explode at any moment.

I consider telling him what Aunt Kay said about me listening selectively, and Mom being suicidal, but hold my tongue.

It is amazing that we all take seats in the dining room, but we do: Dad at one end of the table, Sherman at the other, in Mom's chair; Aunt Mary, Olivia, and I along one side; and Aunt Kay, Grandma, and Terry along the other. It is customary for our family to join hands before a meal and say grace, but both the grace and Mom are missing.

Sherman, whose culinary ability up until now has been limited to microwave popcorn, has remarkably re-created Mom's standard Sunday fare: roasted chicken, mashed potatoes, bread stuffing, a tossed salad. For dessert, he has made Mom's peach crisp.

At first, the only sounds are the scraping and clinking of silverware against china and water glasses being cautiously replaced on the table after pensive sips. We focus outwardly on our plates, inwardly on the ever-widening, layered, and multiplying rifts: between Dad and Mom's family; Olivia and Uncle Jack; Uncle Jack and me; Aunt Kay and me; between Mom and Dad; between Dad and us kids. The only words spoken are barely audible requests for salt or butter or gravy. Eventually, Dad compliments Sherman's cooking, and everyone enthusiastically voices agreement. Then silence again. Oh, how I—we—could use a glass of wine or two. I consider, for a moment, how odd it must have been—back when we still lived in Minnesota—for my aunts and uncles to come to our house for Christmas Eve dinners every four years, when it was our turn to host. I wonder now if they used to pop a few cocktails *before* heading over, knowing they'd spend the rest of the holiday evening completely, confoundedly sober?

"Did anyone feed the dogs today?" Olivia asks.

"I did," I say. Another lull. The chicken is a little dry. I add more gravy. I think about the wishbones Mom used to save from our chicken dinners, how she hung them to dry on the wrought-iron chandelier in our kitchen in Minnesota, and on the windowsill here in Hopewell. There was always a wishbone to break for any occasion requiring luck: a spelling bee, a hockey game, a pass on cleanup.

"Sherman," Terry offers, barely above a mumble, "want to shoot some hoops in town after dinner?"

Sherman nods. Another pause.

"What's the name of your band again?" Aunt Kay asks.

"The Bureaucrats," Sherman replies, hardly looking up.

The one concern we all share is the one topic we avoid: I wish *she* were here, eating this chicken. I wonder how much longer Mom will be restricted to the intravenous hyperalimentation. I wonder if she will ever sit here with us again. And I wonder when she'll be strong enough to undergo the biopsy.

"So," Sherman asks, "do we know when they're doing the autopsy?"

For an interminable moment of stunned disbelief, everything stops. My forkful of food hovers in midair. Doubting that I've heard right, I look to my sister as I gently set my fork onto my plate. She looks back at me and cracks a smile, pursing her lips quickly to prevent any further response. A puff of laughter escapes my mouth before I can catch it. Then Olivia chokes back a laugh and holds a napkin to her face.

"What?" Sherman asks, confused.

He must be aware of his slip, and too horrified to admit it. It was such an innocent mistake, anyone might have made it. Olivia and I can't help ourselves; the laughter threatens to become the kind you can't stop even if you know you should. I bite my lip and look away and try to think of something else. Aunt Mary is laughing too now, through her nose with her head bowed, chin to chest, her Mary Poppins posture as erect as ever. Terry turns to face Aunt Kay; they smile at each other, then at Sherman sympathetically. Dad wipes the corners of his eyes. Fortunately Grandma, hard of hearing, misses the whole thing.

"What?" Sherman demands again.

"You . . . mean . . . biopsy," I whisper. "You said autop——"

"*I fucking said biopsy!*" Sherman yells. His eyes fill with tears. He stands up and bolts out of the room. We hear the door to the patio slam.

"What . . . happened?" Grandma says.

Dinner is over. As quickly as the laughter has come, it goes, replaced by the deadly silence of collective worry. Terry excuses himself and heads out after Sherman. The rest of us clear the table, even Grandma, despite our urging her to just sit.

I drive Aunt Kay and Grandma back to the hotel. (Aunt Mary is staying with us.) This time, I remain on my side of the yellow line, within the speed limit. In the parking lot, I turn off the engine. Grandma, in the front passenger seat, grabs my hand as I am pulling the key from the ignition.

"You go ahead, Kay, we'll catch up. I want a minute with Lucia," Grandma says.

I stare straight ahead. Aunt Kay gets out of the car.

"Lucia, your mom isn't suicidal," Grandma says tenderly. Her hand trembles, so she grasps mine more firmly to steady it. "She wouldn't do that to you. She loves you very much."

I drape my arms over the steering wheel and rest my head on them. Grandma's hand slips under the back of my shirt. She gently runs her long fingernails along my spine. I am suddenly transported to an easier time, when my grandmother's gentle touch could heal anything.

"This is such a mess," I say, when she stops.

"We all have to try to be good Christians," she says.

She is the only person in the world who can say this to me without provoking a groan. I know the sincerity of her faith, how hard she is trying. The despair in her voice after Uncle Jack put her on the phone still haunts me: "...and tell your father I will *never* forgive him."

> *If ye forgive men their trespasses, your heavenly*
> *Father will also forgive you.*
> —MATTHEW 6:14

FRIDAY, AUGUST 15

Grandma and Aunt Kay's first visit lasts just two days. On their final trip to the hospital before leaving for the airport, Aunt Kay and I are sitting in the SCU waiting room. Grandma wants some time alone with Mom, and Aunt Mary is downstairs on the pay phone talking to her husband, Uncle Brad. Aunt Kay and I have tried to avoid each other as much as possible. But now, we are face-to-face.

To keep from smoking, we both chew gum, Wrigley's Spearmint for me, Nicorette for her. She, like Aunt Nan, has brought her knitting with her. Her needles click away rhythmically. Her blue eyes dart back and forth between a spot in the middle of the room and me.

"I guess I have to believe that, if I were Mom, and I really wanted to use Christian Science, I wouldn't want my kids to interfere," I say. I am reminded, uncomfortably, of the meeting back in April with Mom's practitioner. But I realize too that I am trying to defend my own inaction as much as I am Mom's right to her beliefs.

Aunt Kay's knitting needles stop. She fixes on me over her half-frame glasses. "Don't you believe in rescue?" she asks.

The tone of her voice is not accusing—it is unexpectedly tender and searching—but still, I feel like I've been charged with a crime. Of the three Johnson sisters, Aunt Kay has the most severe features, with a square jaw, a hard mouth, those unforgiving, ice blue eyes. I say nothing, but her question frames the dilemma in a completely new way, and I am thrown off balance.

Of course I believe in rescue.

For the next several days, Dad, Olivia, Sherman, Aunt Mary, and I wait for Mom's condition to improve. Terry, who has returned to Tucson to register for his first semester of law school, is ready to catch the next flight back if necessary. We shuttle between the hospital and Hopewell and divide our time between Mom's bedside, the SCU waiting room, the hospital cafeteria, and the house. Dr. Sierocki informs us that, assuming a continued return of her strength, "Mother" can expect to undergo surgery within the next ten days. (I wish he wouldn't call her that. She's not his mother.) He also tells us that, from now on, to avoid further communication problems, he and the rest of the hospital staff will give updates on Mother's condition only to us: Dad, Olivia, Sherman, and me. Someone (Dad?) must have told him about Uncle Jack.

SATURDAY, AUGUST 16

Olivia and I are quietly sitting in Mom's room. She drifts in and out of sleep. At one point, she asks Olivia to try on the eye mask she had offered me the week before, dangling it like a child might offer her favorite toy in a moment of generosity. Olivia takes it hesitantly, says thank you, and sets it in her lap.

"Mom," I say firmly, "that's just to keep the light out, remember?"

Mom turns her head away from us to face the window and closes her eyes. I feel cruel.

Olivia sets the eye mask on the bedside table, between two vases of flowers, and looks at me. "It's okay, Loosh," she whispers, but I worry that it's not. My mother's confusion scares me, and I don't know how I'm supposed to respond to it. Should I correct her? Does that make it worse? And why is she like this?

I walk up to the nurses' station. I'm still uncomfortable asking questions here—I worry I am being judged—but I approach the desk anyway.

"My mom is saying all sorts of weird stuff," I tell the nurse on duty.

She looks up from her paperwork, and I wonder if I should be disturbing her, but she removes her glasses, suggesting that she will give me as much of her time as I need.

"It's not uncommon for critically ill patients to become disoriented in the hospital," she explains. "It is almost always fleeting."

Almost always does not reassure me. Mom was like this at Tenacre too. And at Connie's house, when she couldn't remember who Bill Cosby was. What if it—this dementia—isn't fleeting but progressive?

"Keep in mind," she continues, "your mom has been in the ICU, where it's hard to distinguish between night and day. Even here, in the Special Care Unit, she's having her vital signs checked, blood drawn, IVs changed, around the clock, disrupting normal sleep patterns. The confusion is totally reasonable."

I feel somewhat better.

Olivia and I wait in silence for Mom to wake up again.

"Liv," Mom says a few minutes later, "it's dripping."

I assume she is referring to the catheter, or the IV bottles.

"I know," Olivia says sympathetically.

"Oh dear," Mom says with more disappointment in her voice than discomfort. "Oh no! It's dripping all over. Drip—dripping all over. Go to the"—she waves a frail and limp arm in the direction of the hallway—"go to the other room . . ."

She is gasping for breath.

"What, Mom?" I ask, heading for the nurses' station.

"Take it out!" she orders. *"Take it out!"*

I stop in the doorway.

"Mom, I know it's uncomfortable," Olivia says gently, "but it has to stay there."

"No," Mom says, shaking her head vehemently. "No! Go to the—the other—"

"Other what?" Olivia asks. Both of us are standing now, examining the IV bags, trying desperately to understand Mom's request.

"The *other room,*" Mom says decisively. "Go to the other room. It's dripping all over. Go to the other room and move all the furniture. Before it gets ruined!"

> *Health is not a condition of matter, but of Mind.*
> —Mary Baker Eddy, *Science and Health*

I am sitting alone with Mom. She is angry with me, has been since I walked through the door.

"Lucia, if you really love me, you'll get me out of here." Her terrified eyes plead with me.

Is she delirious again? Or does she really want to leave here? If so, where does she want to go? Back to Tenacre? Or does she think that's where she is?

"Help me," she weeps. "Help me."

Why couldn't she have said this while she was at Tenacre, when I could have done something?

Later in the day, Aunt Mary, who has returned from Minnesota, is sitting in the vinyl lounge chair on one side of Mom's bed, and I am half-leaning against the windowsill. The closed blinds are blocking out most of the midday light. Mom is sleeping, I am reading a paperback, Nora Ephron's *Heartburn,* which I bought in the gift shop, and Aunt Mary is leafing through *Town & Country.*

"I'm scared," Mom says.

I set my book down and move closer to her so I can hold her hand. I squeeze it gently and search for the right response.

"Are you scared about the surgery?" I ask.

We are still waiting for an exact date from the doctor.

"Wouldn't you be?" Mom answers wryly.

SUNDAY, AUGUST 17

It is a bright, crisp Sunday morning in August, and I am heading out for an early jog when my father calls me into his office and asks me to take a seat in the chair opposite his desk.

"I want you to know that I am going ahead with my association address next Saturday," he tells me.

"You're *what*?" I ask. "Mom's having surgery on Friday!"

"I'll be there when she goes in for the operation," he says, his hands folded in front of him, "but I need to be in New York early Friday afternoon. I'll need the time to...to prepare mentally for my association. Your mom will be pretty out of it after surgery anyway," he adds.

His association is the daylong meeting held once a year for all the students who have ever attended his two-week Primary class. The agenda and purpose of an association meeting are confidential, presumably to protect against the negative thoughts of others.

I am sickened, literally, by what I feel amounts to his complete failure as a husband, a father, a moral being. I am shaking, I cannot believe what I am hearing.

"And you know," he continues, "this coming week I'm really counting on you and Sherman and Olivia to help me out with Mom. I'm going to be very busy."

I am speechless. And I'm certainly not going to help my father out of what he is treating as a simple scheduling conflict.

"I'm really counting on you being out here all week," my father presses.

My mind races. How dare he leave at such a time! What if the surgery is postponed for a few hours? Then he won't even be there while Mom waits to go under. And anything might happen on the operating table.

Sherman was right after all. Several times over the last week, he and Olivia and I had debated what Dad would do if Mom's surgery coincided with his association.

"Don't be ridiculous, Sherman," I had said. "He will cancel. Obviously."

I was totally wrong.

"Lucia," my father continues, "you know I haven't asked much of you . . ."

I almost choke. What he has asked of us is unconscionable.

"Fuck . . . you . . . Dad," I suddenly blurt out. My dad is stunned. I go on.

"Mom is having surgery. Your own *wife* is having surgery, and you won't be there when she comes out of it?" I laugh derisively and shake my head. "You can postpone your association!"

"No I can't!" my father shouts, his face turning scarlet. His clenched fists hit the ink blotter in front of him hard enough to make

a loud thud. The desk shudders, and a pen rolls off it and falls to the floor. "This has been scheduled for a year. I have students flying in from all over the country. Some of them can barely afford their airfares as it is. Some are making big sacrifices to get here."

My father lowers his voice, softens his tone. "Believe me, Lucia, I've given this a lot of prayerful thought, and I know your mother supports me—"

The idea that Mom can support *anything* right now is absurd. "So your students' pocketbooks come before Mom's health," I say coolly, deliberately provoking him.

"That's not true!"

My father begins to cry. He wipes the tears away with his thumb and forefinger, and pauses, trying to collect himself. I wait.

"You think I want to give my address? You think I want to leave your mother's side?"

I think he's a monster.

His voice grows louder with each question. "You kids have no idea how hard this is!"

I laugh scornfully and shake my head.

"You and your beloved *cause*. You're going to heal the world, aren't you?" My voice cracks, and my eyes start filling with tears. There is no longer any filter on my words. I want to hurt my father. "Well, you're doing a great job so far."

"Get out!" he wails.

I don't move.

He looks away and waves his hand, shooing me out the door.

"Get out."

I grip the arms of the chair.

"Tell me something, Dad. If the First Lady were going in for surgery, do you think the President of the United States might cancel a meeting? Postpone a trip? You think he might delay a *summit*?"

"You kids don't understand what I'm—"

"I understand," I say. "I know the real reason you're going through with your association address on Saturday." I get up and walk to the door. "It wouldn't look very good if you had to explain to your students that your wife is dying in a hospital."

I walk out and slam the door behind me.

Friday, August 22

Mom is in the operating room. I am trying to imagine the surgical theater: the bright overhead lights, the beeping, clicking, and sucking sounds of various monitors and instruments; the half-masked faces of the various professionals; the surgeon's brief, muffled orders to the nurse; the whispered assurances of the anesthesiologist. I wonder how accurate my imaginings are, all derived from television and movies. The overwhelming feeling I have, however, is complete frustration. I want to be there, in the room with my mother. I want to see and hear everything for myself. A report from the surgeon might, or might not, be sufficient when it's all over. But what if her heart is pumping away one moment, and then...nothing? What if, at this very moment, they are pronouncing her dead?

Before the surgery, we—Dad, Sherman, Olivia, and I—stood beside Mom in pre-op, waiting for the orderly to come and wheel her away. I held her hand and concentrated specifically on the *feel* of it, its warmth. I wanted to capture the sensation in my memory.

I look around the surgical family waiting room. Unlike the sparse rooms designated for families of ICU and SCU patients, this is more richly appointed, with comfortable sofas and lounge chairs arranged in clusters to provide separate waiting territories and a certain amount of privacy for each party. There are reading lamps instead of overhead fluorescents, and fanned out on low tables are copies of today's papers and current—not tattered and outdated—issues of magazines. There is a wall-mounted courtesy phone in one corner, presumably for incoming calls from surgeons. The room is filled with the soothing aroma of fresh-brewed coffee. Dad, Sherman, Olivia, Grandma (who flew back from Minneapolis for the surgery), Aunt Mary (who, aside from a brief return to Minnesota, has remained here the whole time), Aunt Nan (who drove down from Greenwich), and I are the only people in the waiting room.

The television is on. There is a common effort at courtesy: Dad and Grandma are sharing a sofa, and Olivia and Grandma are smoking together. (Olivia and I have given up hiding our cigarette habit from Dad.) Aunt Nan and Aunt Mary are exchanging bits of news about their children. We all have one eye on the TV, one on the clock. Every once in a while, Dad stands up, walks over to the clock, checks it against his watch, and returns to his seat. He pulls a box of butterscotch candies from his jacket pocket and offers them around.

At one point—way too soon—the courtesy telephone rings, and Sherman jumps up to answer it. The call is for nobody in our group, so we settle back, staring at the television. And we wait.

When I'm not thinking about the operation, I'm revisiting conversations I've had over the last two weeks, with various family members and friends, who have dropped in or called to offer their prayers, their sorrow, their reminiscences and observations. Aunt Nan's daughter Mary, with whom I had brunch back in January, was one of the first callers.

"Hi, Lucia, it's Mary," my cousin said, and I immediately wished I had reached her first. I felt that I owed her that. She asked how Mom was doing, how we all were doing, and confessed that she'd told her mom earlier in the summer (which I already knew). I wanted to apologize to Mary—and did—a blanket apology, without specifics because there was so much I was sorry about. She said how sorry she was too, that she hadn't known what to do. I said that was how we all felt. The conversation was awkward; we stumbled through it.

The last few days have seen the arrival and departure of Uncle Sherm (my father's oldest brother) and his wife, Aunt Claire; and my father's two half brothers, Uncle Nick and Uncle Truck. They have tried to comfort us with old family jokes and anecdotes, shared at the dinner table or in the living room or in the hospital waiting room.

They saved some stories for one-on-one conversations. Each was quick to support Dad and slow to voice judgment about what had happened. But I wondered what they were really thinking.

To me, their visits have felt like pilgrimages, and their conversations have sounded disconcertingly like eulogies—for both Mom and Dad. Still, some of the information intrigues me. Really for the first time, I am viewing my parents beyond their roles as parents: Heff and Jo as children, as teenagers, as young adults, before they gave themselves to Christian Science.

"Your dad used to mix the best martini," Uncle Nick said, eliciting laughter from everyone at the dinner table, including my father, who nevertheless looked uncomfortable with the tribute. Heff Ewing, martini man. I am fascinated and puzzled. I've never seen my father serve alcohol to anyone. In fact, one Christmas, when a new neighbor dropped off a bottle of champagne as a holiday gift (Mom always gave homemade fudge or cookies), my father instructed me to return it, on his behalf, with the polite but firm explanation that, as Christian Scientists, we didn't drink. Reluctantly, I obeyed, trudging through the snow with the beribboned bottle, humiliated.

"I've always felt protective of your father," Aunt Nan confessed to me. "He was just a toddler when Mother and Dad divorced. And then Mother remarried, and had Truck and Nick in quick succession, and, well. . . ."

What Aunt Nan didn't say—what I figured out for myself—is that my father got lost in the shuffle.

"Glamour girl," Grandma had said to me wistfully from Mom's bedside a few days earlier, as we watched Mom sleep. "Jo was always your grandfather's little glamour girl."

I have no memory of my mother's father. I've been told repeatedly that he was a hardworking, respected physician. I wonder how he felt about Mom's religious views. About his son-in-law.

An old college friend of Mom's called me in Hopewell as soon as she heard the news; even she had a story to share.

"Your mom, when she was at Carleton...well, she was one of the Johnson sisters. And were they ever popular! Always had dates. But of the three, your mom was the prettiest. And your dad," she went on, "well, he was a catch. So handsome. And from a prominent Minnesota family. Your father took your mom on a six-week honeymoon through South America."

I was shocked—no, I was jaw-drop speechless—when Grandma told me, in the hospital cafeteria over coffee, about the summer between Mom's sophomore and junior years of college, when she drove from Colorado back to Minnesota with a boy she'd met as a camp counselor. *My mother? On a road trip?*

The reminiscences continued.

"I wasn't exactly surprised when I first heard that your parents had become Christian Scientists," Aunt Lucia said to me in the hospital one morning. "Well...notwithstanding the fact that your mother's father was a doctor. Your great-grandmother—my grandmother—had dabbled in Christian Science. When your dad told me they'd joined the Mother Church, I didn't think much of it. Heff had never seemed particularly ardent about any religion. I guess I never knew the intensity of his conviction....I've often wondered if his Marine Corps days in Korea had anything to do with it."

I had never given much thought to my father's tour of duty. Did she mean he came back from Korea *changed* in some way? And how naïve of me to presume that he didn't. But what did she mean? He became a Christian Scientist because of what he witnessed as a Marine? Or because of what he did when he was in Korea?

"Your mom's always been gullible," Aunt Kay said one day as she was knitting. "Always."

There was a conversation my mother and I had once while I was in college. "If your father had been a rabbi, I'd be Jewish," she said. I was a sophomore at the time, home for a few days, and she and I were debating something, I don't recall what. I do remember, though, how unabashedly, almost proudly she'd uttered the words and how appalled I'd been because of what they said to me about my mother.

"What about *your* beliefs, Mom?" I shot back.

"They *are* my beliefs," she said, as though her position required no defense.

Was my mom's decision to convert to Christian Science that easy? Would she have gone along with any belief system, however extreme? Until Mom got sick, I had thought of my parents as fairly moderate people. What was it about who she was at the point in her life when my mother converted to Christian Science that made her reject everything her family stood for?

Or did she even see it as a rejection? Maybe it was less about faith and more about wanting, above all, to be one with the man she married, no matter what.

Could it be my parents were drawn to each other, and together to Christian Science, because of something that both were lacking in childhood? Is this even a reasonable guess?

I realize there are so many things I don't know, probably never will.

I look over at my dad, who sits watching the television with a butterscotch candy lodged between his teeth and right cheek, and suddenly, I feel like he is a *stranger*. He glances up at the wall clock again, checks it against his watch. What is he thinking right now? Is he imagining his wife on the operating table? Is he still in shock that she is in a hospital at all? Or is he wondering how soon he can—or should, or must—leave for the city, to "prepare mentally" for his big meeting? (It was only after his sisters intervened, and urged him—delicately—to postpone his departure, that he agreed to stay until the surgery was over.)

It is three-fifteen, and Mom has been in surgery for just over an hour. The Authorized Personnel Only door swings open, and Dr. White, the surgeon, walks toward us briskly.

I brace myself. The surgery was supposed to take two hours.

"Mr. Ewing," Dr. White says, extending a quick, businesslike handshake to him, and then to each of us. He folds his arms on his chest. "She's a fighter, that's for sure."

I feel a burden lift from me. She made it through the operation.

"We performed the colostomy. That went well, but then she started hemorrhaging. We got it under control, but there is a sizable tumor in her lower abdomen. We were only able to do a partial biopsy of the surrounding tissue. We had to close up."

Grandma nods in understanding.

My heart sinks.

"How is she doing now?" Dad asks, and I cannot tell if the urgency in his voice has to do with her condition or with his plan to leave shortly for his association. I feel myself tensing all over again.

"She'll be in recovery for maybe an hour," Dr. White says, "but her vital signs are stable. Just as soon as they bring her up to SCU, you can see her. She'll be quite groggy."

"What's next?" Grandma asks, holding her hands behind her back. She is still adept at this sort of conversation. I picture the black-and-white photograph of her, circa 1930, in her crisp white nurse's uniform and cap.

"Let's give Jo the weekend to rest up," Dr. White says. "She should be more comfortable now that the bowel situation is under control. The infection should begin to clear up too."

His voice suggests a glimmer of hope.

"Dr. Sierocki will call you in for a meeting when the results are back. Probably Tuesday. He'll talk to you about the treatment alternatives: chemotherapy, radiation, or possibly a combination of both."

"Is Mom strong enough?" Olivia asks.

"That remains to be seen. Dr. Sierocki is the expert on that. I'll be talking to him about what we found in the surgery, and he'll consider the possibilities and their risks. But she did okay in there," he says, nodding his head. "She did okay. Why don't you get yourselves a cup of coffee, and we'll see you up in SCU in a bit."

It is impossible to reconcile the doctor's encouraging manner with the words *sizable tumor.* Does he mean to imply optimism? Is there any chance she'll be cured? I hold out hope. He wouldn't have mentioned chemo and radiation if they weren't viable treatment options. Would he? People *do* beat cancer.

We are all on hand when Mom is wheeled back up to the Special Care Unit, but it doesn't really matter, for her anyway. She floats in and out of consciousness for the rest of the afternoon and evening, never quite registering where she is, or who we are. We, for the brief spells she is with us, put on our optimistic smiles and squeeze her hand lovingly.

SATURDAY, AUGUST 23
SPECIAL CARE UNIT

The next morning, while Grandma and I are sitting with Mom, the first words out of her mouth are "Where's Heff?"

"He's in New York for his association today," I say, grabbing her hand again. "Remember?"

Mom looks away from me, toward the window, and closes her eyes. I feel Grandma's resentment like a cold wind and wonder if Mom shares my humiliation, shame, and rage.

On Saturday evening, Dad returns from his association meeting.

In the first post-operative days, we all take turns at Mom's bedside while she drifts in and out. When she is alert, we chat, and her spirits are good. The mounting tension between and among us— because of Dad's untimely departure, Uncle Jack's absence, and the decision to restrict the flow of information from the doctor to anyone but Dad, Sherman, Olivia, and me—is not apparent to Mom; we work expertly to keep it below the surface.

Tuesday, August 26

We meet with Dr. Sierocki to go over the findings from the surgery and possible treatments. In keeping with the plan that only our immediate family will have direct access to Mom's doctors, we exclude Grandma and Aunt Mary from the conference. Their exclusion adds to the tension, and I feel torn. On the one hand, they have been left out far too long, and they *are* family. On the other hand, they are in Uncle Jack's camp, or so it feels, and Uncle Jack has added to our troubles, not alleviated them. Still, the policy feels punitive.

The walls of the waiting room of the doctor's office are covered with fake wood paneling, and the carpet is dreary. To compensate for the minimal natural light that three low windows afford, there are several homey-looking lamps with pull chains, on cheap wooden end tables. A coffee table offers the usual assortment of out-of-date magazines: *National Geographic, Sports Illustrated,* and *Ranger Rick*. Framed prints of historic Princeton University adorn the walls.

The four of us take seats in one corner of the room, as removed as possible from the other families. Dad and Sherman sit anxiously on one couch, leaning forward, with their elbows on their knees. Olivia and I sit opposite them.

"Do you think we should check in with the receptionist?" Dad asks sheepishly, meaning "Would one of you tell her we're here?" I get up begrudgingly, annoyed at my father's helplessness, still angry that he didn't cancel his association. I sort of wish Mom's family, or Dad's, had called him on it. The only drama surrounding his absence was my confrontation with him beforehand, which didn't change anything.

Part of me thinks he shouldn't be here now.

Olivia and I walk to the receptionist's window. I am finding it harder and harder not to feel negative about practically everything my father does, or says, or doesn't do or say. And yet, he looks totally defeated. I'm aware of a lingering—even building—sense of pity, a pity that catches me off guard.

After we sign in, we return to our corner, and I open my Filofax to start writing down questions for the doctor.

The receptionist calls our name, and we are led into the doctor's office.

"Let's see now," Dr. Sierocki says, putting on his glasses and opening Mom's file. It must be a hundred pages thick.

"Well, the colostomy was successful. Mother's infection is clearing up. Her vital signs are stable.

"The biopsy," he says, "came back positive. Mother has a sizable cancerous tumor in her lower abdomen. It does not appear to have metastasized to her lungs, lymph nodes, or brain. Everything *upstairs* appears clear from the CAT scan."

"Does that mean it hasn't spread?" Dad asks.

"No, not exactly," Dr. Sierocki says. "It means that it hasn't spread to other regions. But it has begun to affect the bowels and the reproductive region."

"What do we do now?" I ask.

"Nothing *to* do until Mother's strength is back. We're keeping her on the calorie supplements. And we'd like to begin physical therapy. When was the last time Jo walked?" Dr. Sierocki asks Dad, peering over his glasses.

"Uh," Dad says, shifting in his chair. He is sitting on his hands, and his legs are crossed underneath his chair at the ankles, making him look feeble, ineffectual. "It wasn't too long ago. She was walking almost until she left Tenacre."

I wonder if my father is lying. It hadn't occurred to me, until now, that in fact Mom *couldn't* walk. I had assumed, naïvely, that she chose not to, because it was too exhausting. I realize I haven't seen her out of bed, on her feet, for months. Since she was back in Hopewell.

"Her muscle tissue has atrophied considerably," the doctor says, "so I've scheduled brief sessions of physical therapy three times a day."

We all nod. I feel such shame. Now that she is being treated in a hospital, the regret I feel about the responsibility I *didn't* assume for so many months overwhelmingly negates the whole notion of respecting her religious wishes. If we had tried to "rescue" her, to use Aunt Kay's term, Mom might have refused, and died feeling that she had been betrayed. But she is here now, in a hospital. The idea that she might have refused feels impossible. Oh, God.

"That's about all I can tell you for now. Do you have any questions?" the doctor says.

I look down at my Filofax and try to read the list of questions, but my eyes are filled with tears. I can't focus through the blur. All I can think is, *If only we had come sooner.*

"Can it be removed surgically?" Dad asks.

"If the tumor were confined to the colon," Dr. Sierocki says, "then a surgical procedure would make the most sense. But now the entire pelvic region is affected."

"Do you think we should get a second opinion?" I ask. "Like, maybe Sloan-Kettering?"

I hope he isn't offended by the question.

"I always encourage people to get second opinions," he says, allaying my fears, "and in Mother's case, that's already been done. I have consulted with my colleagues in the hospital, and Dr. White—her surgeon—and I confer daily. I think Princeton Medical Center is as well equipped to deal with this case as any of the finest hospitals. But I have some very close colleagues at Sloan-Kettering. If you like, I can put you in touch."

"But what do you think, Doctor?" Dad says.

"It would be a mistake to move her now. Of course," he adds, "anything might happen in the future to make a move to Sloan-Kettering the best option."

"Doctor, have you ever successfully treated someone whose condition was as critical as Mom's?" Sherman asks.

I can feel everyone brace for his answer.

"I've seen some cases far worse than your mother's," he says to Sherman, "and some have had almost miraculous recoveries."

With this tiny ray of hope, Sherman smiles slightly, his chin quivering.

"I can give you a prognosis, if you like, based on statistics of similar cases," he says, looking down at his notes again. He pauses, maybe to make sure that a prognosis is what we want. We wait.

"Mother has a fifty percent chance of living six months."

"As adherents of Truth, we take the inspired Word of the Bible as our sufficient guide to eternal Life."

This is the first Tenet of Christian Science, which appears in *Science and Health,* in the chapter entitled "Recapitulation." I try to break down what it means. *Adherents of Truth* . . . Clear enough: followers of Truth, *Truth* being a synonym for God, because *Truth* is capitalized. . . . *inspired Word of the Bible* . . . That's less clear. It means, I guess, that Christian Scientists don't believe in the *literal* word of the Bible. Since *Word* is capitalized, it means the inspired Word of the Bible is the Word of God. But *inspired Word* . . . Does that mean only parts of the Bible are inspired, and some aren't? Or does it mean the Word of the Bible according to a particular source of inspiration or interpretation? If so, whose? Mary Baker Eddy's? . . . *sufficient guide to eternal Life.* Capital *L*. Life in God. But how sufficient is sufficient? Fifty percent?

When Mary Baker Eddy founded Christian Science, in the late 1860s, in New England, there was no penicillin, no aspirin; there were no X-rays, no radiation or chemotherapy. Surgery was primitive and fraught with danger. One probably stood a better chance of being healed—sometimes—by saying "abracadabra" over and over again than by entrusting one's health to a medical doctor.

Why, I wonder all over again, did my parents convert to a religion founded in Victorian New England by a thrice-married woman who dabbled in hypnotism and mesmerism (whatever that is, I still don't know) and came to believe her life was prophesied in the Book of Revelation? Why do they put their faith in a church doctrine that purports to have an answer for every question? A religion without ambiguity? Why can't they live with uncertainty?

Admittedly, I'm struggling with uncertainty too: 50 percent chance of survival is hard to hear.

I don't feel—nor have I ever felt—the need for dogmas, especially those that require such an enormous leap of faith. My father has all the answers right in his book (or memorized). What is Life? Life is God. Mortal life—which isn't really life at all—is error, nothing. What is God? "The great I AM; the all-knowing, all-seeing, all-acting, all-wise . . ."

A 50 percent chance of living six months?

I go back and forth. Maybe the prognosis is not so grim. Does it mean that half of the people with her diagnosis have lived six months? Will she make it to six months? If she does, then what?

Not unlike my father, I want some truth (but not Truth) I can hold on to.

In the days following Mom's surgery, all of us are amazed to see the dramatic improvement in her condition: physically, the change is almost as pronounced as the difference between her premorbid state upon arrival in the emergency room and her revived appearance after the first twenty-four hours. Her eyes look brighter, her speech requires less effort, she eats eagerly from her tray without assistance, and she even requests seconds on dessert. The physical therapist who comes to work with her three times a day massages and manipulates her limbs and gets her to do strengthening exercises on her own.

It is like having our old mom back. She talks with us enthusiastically about things she's shown no interest in for months; she laughs and jokes with the nurses. I adore the time I spend with her: giving her a manicure, playing backgammon. Even as sick as she is, she exudes a naïve optimism, maybe because she has not heard the prognosis. Fortunately, she hasn't asked for it.

"We're gonna lick this, Lucia," she says. I want to believe her.

The improvement in Mom's condition coincides with a steady deterioration of communication and goodwill between Mom's family and us. The constant presence of relatives, while in some ways soothing, is beginning to make Hopewell feel cramped. Aunt Mary and Grandma are still staying with us, in the twin beds in my room down the hall (I am back in the Nook), but they are increasingly resentful at not having direct contact with the doctors. Our questionable aptitude for relaying accurate medical information strains things even more. Meanwhile, Aunt Kay is back in Minnesota. She calls every evening to talk with Grandma and Aunt Mary but is reticent when any of us kids answers the telephone. She says hello and asks immediately for one of them. Dad won't even attempt to reach for the phone, always deferring to one of us.

Most disturbing of all is the fact that we have not heard from Uncle Jack since the first confusing days in the hospital. The silence frightens us, makes us paranoid. With every passing day, we are more convinced that he is planning to take some sort of legal action. Many conversations between Olivia, Sherman, and me revolve around the question of what that might be. Why hasn't he come to see Mom yet? Has he hired lawyers? Investigators? He looms ever larger and more menacing in our minds.

SATURDAY, AUGUST 30

Grandma, Aunt Mary, and I are walking slowly back to the hospital, arms linked, after a pleasant, late breakfast at PJ's Pancake House on Nassau Street.

In front of the main entrance to the hospital, we see a silver stretch limousine idling, the driver's window open. The driver, dressed in a gray uniform and sitting behind the wheel, is reading the paper. Something about him and the fact that the car is running unsettles me. The sense of foreboding is confirmed as soon as we enter the hospital. I freeze. Uncle Jack is standing at a pay phone in the lobby.

For a moment, I think I am wrong; that can't be him. But then I realize, of course it is. He is a bit heavier, and his hair has turned silver-blond since the last time I saw him, but his height is unmistakable.

Grandma and Aunt Mary said he might be coming next week. What is he doing here now? I wonder if Grandma and Aunt Mary are as surprised as I am, or if they have known all along.

I'm not prepared to face him. I leave my grandma and aunt without explaining and walk past him to the elevator. I don't know if he has seen me. I go straight to Mom's room, my stomach in my throat, but she's not in her bed. I panic. The thought occurs to me that Uncle Jack has transferred her somewhere. Frantically, I run down the hall to the nurses' station. "Where's Mrs. Ewing?" I ask, nearly shouting. "Where's my mom?"

A nurse I've not seen before looks up from her clipboard and smiles. "I wheeled her down to the end of the hall. She's on the day-bed there. It's a nicer view."

I walk more slowly back down the hall, trying to compose myself, but my head is throbbing.

There she is, looking quite peaceful.

"Hi, Mom," I say, relieved. "How are you this beautiful day?" I kiss her forehead and smile.

"Much better," she says. I wait for her to mention Uncle Jack. She doesn't.

Mom stares out the window, preoccupied.

"What's up?" I ask.

She looks into my eyes, and a tear trickles down her cheek, but she is smiling.

"I walked today."

Her words are so unexpected.

"That's great, Mom," I say. I am choked up. I hold her hand, and she looks away from me out the window.

After a long silence, I ask her if she has seen Uncle Jack.

"Yes," she says, smiling again.

"What did he have to say?" I ask as casually as possible.

"To stay put, that these are the best doctors."

The nurse I accosted moments ago comes down the hall to say there is a phone call for me. I know instinctively it is Dad. I haven't seen him at the hospital yet. I wonder where he's calling from.

He is hysterical. Through his gasping and sobbing, I'm able to make out that he encountered Uncle Jack in the hallway.

"I'm gonna get you, Heff Ewing! I'm gonna *get* you!" Dad keeps repeating, mimicking my uncle. "I'm gonna expose this whole thing!"

I feel ill with fear, terrified, and completely torn. I know my uncle's anger could ignite even bigger problems than we already have.

Will he call lawyers? The police? Reporters? At the same time, I understand his fury, even share it.

The pity that so far has kept me from turning on my father is edging closer and closer to contempt.

I tell Dad I have to go, I want to get back to Mom before Uncle Jack does. She's in her room again, settled in her bed, when I burst in.

"What's wrong, Lucia? Are you upset with me?" Mom asks, alarmed.

"Yes!" I answer uncontrollably.

"Why? What have I done?"

What have you done? I grit my teeth and look away. *What have you done?*

"Please, Lucia. Talk to me."

"Everything! This is all your fault!" I say. I am practically shouting at her. "All along, we've done *exactly* as you've wanted. Six whole months at Tenacre! We lied for you. We deceived Grandma, on your...*orders.* And now— Uncle Jack is going to rip us apart. We've kept this from you, because you're sick, but I'm not going to pretend to you anymore! You act as if nothing's *wrong*—like—like you're here...under the same circumstances as any other patient. But who do you think is answering for the fact that, for months, *you* refused to get medical help? Who do you think is taking the blame? All of us: Sherman, Olivia, Dad, me. You could have come here sooner! You chose not to! Bottom line, it was *your decision* to make. Not Dad's. Not Tenacre's. Yours."

I'm shaking. Mom is quiet, but her chin is quivering. She bites her lip.

I suddenly feel that this is what I've been holding in for months— my anger and incomprehension about my mother's passivity, her unwillingness to accept the reality of her situation.

I am totally confused—enraged but also ashamed that I've exploded at her.

"I'm sorry," I say, now desperately. "I'm sorry, Mom."

Uncle Jack, Grandma, and Aunt Mary enter the room.

"Excuse me, I'd like to be alone with Mom," I say to them.

Grandma stares at me, horrified.

"I mean it. I don't want Uncle Jack in here!"

Uncle Jack doesn't move. He stands in the doorway.

"For goodness' sake, Lucia," Grandma says, "he's her brother."

"Get . . . out . . . of . . . here. *She's my mother.*"

I try to push my uncle out. Aunt Mary grabs my arm and his, but violently I shrug her off.

"I love you, Jo," Uncle Jack says.

"Don't cause trouble, Jack," my mother pleads. I hear him agree, though I can feel my mother is as unconvinced as I am.

"Promise me," Mom continues.

"I promise," he says.

Grandma, Aunt Mary, and Uncle Jack leave.

"I'm sorry, Mom."

Mom and I sit in silence.

"I want you to remember this," she finally says. "I love your father. And I love my brother. But they don't like each other. They never have. Your father and Uncle Jack couldn't be more opposite: in their values, in their life's work, everything. Your father"—she looks at me candidly—"has always been jealous of Uncle Jack, but he'll never admit it. Jealous and intimidated. And your uncle? He doesn't like your father because he can't understand him. And he can't control him."

Mom grabs my hand and holds it in hers. "You know how much I love your father. I love my brother too."

She squeezes my hand and asks me to find my uncle. "I want you to be a peacemaker," she says.

Blessed are the peacemakers: for they shall be called the children of God.

On one level, this directive is a fitting one, and nostalgic, reminding me of when Olivia and Sherman and I were kids, bickering over the usual sibling stuff. On another level, I almost find it contemptible. Here she is, invoking the Beatitudes when she's the one who has brought this all on. If she weren't in this hospital, with a horrible prognosis, I might dismiss the request outright. But my mother strains to sit up and leans toward me with considerable effort to kiss me. I concede.

I go off to find my uncle.

He isn't in the SCU waiting room, so I take the stairs and head to the cafeteria, where I find Aunt Mary.

"Come here, Lucia," she commands. "Sit down. I am appalled at what you've done. Your uncle has come here to see his sister. He has every right."

Again my rage takes over.

"He may have come here to see Mom, but he has also come here threatening my father. Is he going to sue Dad? Sue us?"

Aunt Mary looks away.

"Did you think he'd greet your dad with open arms?" she asks quietly.

Grandma walks in, heading straight for me.

"Lucia—you are the cruelest person in the world. Imagine! On your mother's deathbed!" She turns away from me in disgust.

"Where's Jack?" she asks Aunt Mary.

"Making a phone call."

"Mom wants to see him again," I say coolly, hardly a peace offering.

I leave the cafeteria.

I walk back up a flight of stairs and notice, for the first time, the hospital chapel. I enter and take a seat in the second pew.

I let go a full sigh, and, with it, everything else comes. I cry for so long, and so hard, my head is throbbing.

At some point, I realize I am not alone in the room. A hand is rubbing my back. I assume it is my grandmother's until the person speaks.

"Did you hear some bad news today?" an unfamiliar woman's voice asks.

"No." I don't turn to look at her.

"Is somebody you know a patient here?"

"Yes."

I can't answer more fully because I am gasping for air.

Eventually, I calm down enough to begin to tell the woman about everything: Mom, Dad, Christian Science, Tenacre. All I see of the woman are her feet. I guess from her no-nonsense shoes that she is in her fifties. I've been half-sitting in the pew, half-kneeling on a prayer bench. When I finally turn to face her, I notice a name, followed by "R.N." on a pin on her lapel. She tells me she is the head nurse of the hospital.

"It sounds like you have a lot to deal with," she says. She presses her hand firmly on my shoulder.

"You know, you couldn't have brought her here against her will. Or at least, legally, we couldn't have taken her."

We sit in silence for a few more minutes, until I have calmed down.

"I'll be on duty all weekend," the head nurse says, "so if you want to talk some more, come find me."

I leave the hospital to buy a new pack of cigarettes. The stretch limo is still idling at the entrance as I turn and walk toward Nassau Street. When I look back again, I see Aunt Mary kissing Uncle Jack good-bye. He gets in the car, and it drives away. He passes by me, but I don't look up, and he doesn't stop.

WEDNESDAY, SEPTEMBER 3

I have returned to work. Olivia is in Tucson and will probably come back when Mom starts chemo or radiation. Sherman hasn't decided yet whether to register for classes this semester. On the one hand, things could go on like this for a while—months even—and he needs to finish his undergraduate work. On the other hand, if Mom's condition worsens, he won't be able to concentrate, and his studies will suffer. I can go back to the office, and catch up on a backlog of work, and if I have to leave, the Condé Nast personnel department will send German *Vogue* a temp. I can hop on a train at a moment's notice.

Grandma and Aunt Mary flew back to Minneapolis on Sunday, the day after Uncle Jack's visit. I haven't talked with any of Mom's family since their departure.

THURSDAY, SEPTEMBER 4

Mom continues to get stronger. I talked with her on the telephone today. It is almost possible to imagine that she is calling from home, not from a hospital bed. She's been moved out of Special Care and into a private room.

FRIDAY, SEPTEMBER 5

I am back in Hopewell. Mom has returned to the Special Care Unit, because the doctors believe she has some sort of intestinal blockage. They have hooked her up to a gastrointestinal pump to alleviate pressure in her abdomen. It doesn't appear to be working, though; her gut is horribly distended, so swollen it is hard. The pump is sucking green stuff out and makes an awful gurgling noise, but for some reason, her belly continues to grow. She is in a lot of pain. Dr. White has scheduled emergency surgery for tomorrow morning. He calls it "mostly exploratory." Olivia will stay in Tucson until after the surgery, when Dr. White will know what's causing the blockage. Sherman will come home for the surgery. Aunt Kay and Uncle Bear fly in tomorrow. I'm nervous about their visit; things are still strained between us.

Ham is here. We managed to track him down in Paris, and he caught the first flight back. If there is tension between Dad and Ham, neither one is showing it.

SATURDAY, SEPTEMBER 6

Dad, Ham, and I are waiting in the pre-op area with Mom. After a nurse introduces herself and checks Mom's vital signs, she disappears. We are the only people around. Apparently, on Saturdays the operating rooms are used only for emergencies. There is a line of prep stations, each with its own dangling blood pressure monitor and partitioning curtain. I am shivering at the sterility of the place, or maybe it's cold in here. Putting on the mandatory surgical clothing and mask, I fantasize about being my mother's doctor. When I see her head swathed in the green cotton cap, I am surprised by how pretty she is, even now. I'm proud of her courage—she is calm—but I also feel, what an incredible waste. This didn't have to happen.

I hold Mom's hand. When our eyes meet, I try to cover my sadness with a wink.

"Where's Sherman?" she asks.

"He's on his way back from the city. He'll be here in about an hour. Olivia's in Tucson. A phone call away.

"I love you Mom," I say, kissing her forehead.

"I love you too, Lucia.

"Come here," she says, reaching for my hand again. "We're gonna lick this thing," she says.

Sherman is sitting in the surgical family waiting room when we get there. He stands, approaches me, and gives me a hug. Then he bursts into tears. He grips Ham's hand to shake it but ends up with his head buried in Ham's shoulder.

In the waiting room, we watch TV again. It is the final weekend of the U.S. Open. Dad sits with his Christian Science books in his lap, peering intermittently over his reading glasses at the television, then returning his focus to the opened books. Moments later, his chin bobs to his chest and he awakens with a jerk, or snoozes for a few minutes, sighs, rolls his head back, and awakens self-consciously.

Dad is still a handsome man. His silvering hair lends him a distinguished, patrician air. I think about how his outward appearance belies his inner self, much in the same way the Church's appearance masks its real nature. My father, when dressed casually, wears old Levi's with loafers and golf shirts. When he dresses for church or a trip to the city, he wears a bespoke suit, pressed shirt, tie, and an old Burberry raincoat. Outwardly, he personifies the Establishment without even trying. The Church, especially through the *Christian Science Monitor,* works hard promoting an image of itself as a credible, established, legitimate, mainstream institution. Most people have no idea what is concealed behind the veneer of its grand city church edifices, the prime-located suburban churches and Reading Rooms, and the impressive Boston headquarters designed by I. M. Pei. Every few years the media jump on the story of a child of Christian Scientists who dies from something horrible, and treatable—a bowel obstruction, diabetes, meningitis—because he or she has not been given medical care, and then the Church puts on a full-court press with its First Amendment lawyers. Eventually the story dies, the controversy blows over.

For reasons I don't fully understand, and may never, my father needs the security of a way of life that leaves nothing to doubt— at least in its teachings—a belief system that tells him exactly what to think, not how to think. I have theories about the root causes of his conversion: an unhappy childhood marred by divorce in a privileged but fractured family; the psychological damage of being sent away to boarding school too young; the minimal contact with a wealthy, remarried, and geographically remote father (the granddad I met only twice before he died and I was thirteen); the invisible scars of combat in Korea. Christian Science gives my father connectedness, relevance, purpose. But the more I look for clues and causes and reasons, the less important to me they become, for now anyway. After more than half a lifetime of circumstances, many of which were beyond his control, my father has become who he is, a person of immense complexity. Do I know for sure that, given the same set of circumstances, I wouldn't also be ripe for a theology as controlling and rigid and absolute as Christian Science?

I'm more puzzled by my mother.

I have no memories of her father, whom we called Bops. He died of a heart attack when I was very young. Once while Grandma and I were talking in the hospital, I asked her what he was like.

"Oh, he was a marvelous man," Grandma said, "a dedicated physician. His patients always came first."

Did that mean his family came second? What sort of a father and husband was he? I vaguely recall hearing that, during World War II, he enlisted as a physician, leaving Grandma with four children under the age of what? Eleven, maybe? And during those war years, Aunt Kay almost died of scarlet fever—or rheumatic fever?—and had a long convalescence. Could any of these factors have played a role in Mom's conversion?

I wonder what my grandfather thought of his daughter's rejection of medicine. Did he roll his eyes, like a cattle rancher might behind a vegetarian daughter's back? Did he try to dissuade her?

Did he worry for his grandchildren's welfare? Were there ever arguments between my mother and her father about Christian Science?

If he were still alive, might things be different?

I look at the clock. Mom has already been in surgery for an hour and fifteen minutes.

"Sherman," I say.

"Yeah?" he replies, not taking his eyes off the tennis match.

"Aunt Kay and Uncle Bear arrive today. Do you know when?"

"Sometime this afternoon."

I catch myself chewing on the inside of my mouth. Aunt Kay and I haven't really spoken since before Mom's first surgery.

She and Mom couldn't be more different.

When I was in college, Aunt Kay and I developed a special closeness, sharing confidences and opinions and cigarettes at a time when my relationship with Mom wasn't faring so well. In my opinion, the way I lived my life was none of my mother's business, even when I practically forced the details on her. I remember once asking Mom about birth control, and she denounced my immoral behavior (which I was quick to point out was monogamous, at least) using street slang; I accused her of being puritanical.

I could talk with Aunt Kay about anything, and I could smoke cigarettes with her, which made me feel accepted as an equal. She had a voracious appetite for books and ideas; she collected contemporary art. She had a really cool, modern, nontraditional house. She wasn't afraid to speak her mind, which, most important, wasn't my mother's. I would fly to Minneapolis for long weekends and return to Hopewell for a day or two, making parenthetical comments about the great conversations Kay and I had. I would refer to her as *Kay,* without the *Aunt.* Mom would sit down at the kitchen table, with a full cup of coffee, ready to chat; I would pour myself a cup and disappear to my bedroom, closing the door.

I wish I could have a do-over.

I look around the waiting room. Sherman is stretched out on the couch, Dad is slumped and snoring, and Ham is—remarkably— asleep sitting perfectly upright in a chair.

He opens his eyes and motions me to come over. Before this, the last time I saw him was at my high school graduation.

"I wonder what's taking so long," I say.

"Sometimes it just *does,*" Ham says, clearing his throat. "They may have found something that needs correcting."

He pauses. It seems like he wants to say something but is hesitant. "You know, your father and I haven't spoken in a long time," he says.

I nod.

"I'm afraid I hurt him."

We sit for a moment in silence.

"I'm sure you heard that I left the Church," Ham says.

Again I nod, but I hadn't actually heard. So that was why Dad wouldn't let us call Ham when Mom first went to Tenacre. I wonder if he knows that I'm not a Christian Scientist.

"I withdrew my membership," Ham says. "A number of years ago, I started having trouble with my shoulder. It was very painful, and I was making no progress." He lowers his voice to a whisper and glances over at Dad to see if he's still sleeping, "But quite frankly, I also noticed that all these Christian Scientists in their fifties and early sixties were just dropping. Like flies, for God's sake! And nobody would even talk about it. Well, I think your father felt very rejected by my decision. And now . . . this. I'm devastated, I'm sure you know that."

Ham shakes his head in disbelief.

The telephone rings. I jump up to answer it.

"I would like to speak to a member of the Ewing family," a woman's voice says.

"I'm one of the daughters," I say. I look around to see Sherman, Dad, and Ham all alert and listening.

"Dr. White just came out of surgery and—"

"Is she okay?"

"He didn't give any information, except that she's in recovery now until her vital signs stabilize. He'll meet you shortly in the ICU conference room."

The door opens, and Dr. White appears.

"Mr. Ewing, Lucia, Sherman," he says, shaking our hands. I'm impressed that he remembers our names.

The doctor takes a handkerchief from his pocket and pats the back of his neck. I know he has bad news.

"Well," he begins, "she endured the surgery quite well,

considering her situation. But I wasn't able to do much once we got in there. There's very little blockage of the stomach."

But I thought the surgery was *because* of a blockage.

"The problem is considerably more serious," Dr. White continues. "The tumor has developed quite rapidly in the last two weeks. Since her first surgery, it has literally mushroomed."

The cup of my hand goes to my mouth.

"Now the tumor is engulfing the entire pelvic region, exerting extreme pressure on your mother's system."

"Is this the sort of thing that can be removed surgically?" Dad asks.

The doctor replaces his handkerchief in the breast pocket of his lab coat and shakes his head no.

"Chemotherapy?" Sherman asks.

"She's too weak to undergo the kind of stress chemo entails. I doubt radiation would even be possible now."

Dad sighs, and his eyes fill. We all stand there, speechless.

"The next three days are critical," Dr. White says.

We make phone calls to Tucson and Minnesota. Olivia takes the first flight back to Newark.

Dad, Sherman, Ham, and I sit in Mom's corner of the ICU. She is hooked up to a respirator. At regular intervals, the machine causes her chest to heave abruptly outward while a blue plastic tube resembling a vacuum hose collapses in a white plastic box beside her bed. Mom's neck is swollen and distorted to accommodate the life-sustaining pipe. I hold her clammy and unresponsive hand. Suddenly, I'm aware of a commotion. When I look up, I see that Dad and Aunt Kay are hugging, speaking to each other. Uncle Bear stands behind them in the doorway, viewing for the first time his sister-in-law's condition.

Aunt Kay motions me over to her. "Lucia," she says, pulling me toward her. "I am so sorry."

She hugs me tightly, and then pushes me away to arm's length and rests her arms on my shoulders so that she can look at me while she's speaking. "I've done a lot of thinking over the last few weeks," she says.

I lower my gaze to the floor and brace myself for the next bomb to drop.

"There are a lot of things that won't ever make sense. But I love you," she says, shaking my shoulders slightly. "And we'll get through this. Together."

She pulls me back into a strong embrace.

In the evening, we all go to dinner. Afterward, Dad, Ham, and Sherman drive home; Uncle Bear goes to the hotel; and Aunt Kay comes with me back to the hospital. We check in at the nurses' station to see how Mom is doing. The nurse tells us that Mom has been weaned from the respirator, is breathing on her own, and is sleeping.

The waiting room is empty except for us. Aunt Kay pulls out her knitting.

Her tone is direct. "You know, Lucia," she says, "when I'm upset about something, I say things before I think them through."

She starts to knit, and the needles click rhythmically.

"Uncle Jack is the same way, only he tends to *do* things without thinking them through."

Aunt Kay's blue eyes move to the far corner of the ceiling.

"I'm sorry about some of the things I've said," she says.

"I'm sorry too."

"And Uncle Jack," she goes on, "he's not going to cause any trouble."

I feel my shoulders relax.

"You probably don't remember this," I say, "but you taught me the word *agnostic* when I was in second grade."

Aunt Kay smiles.

We sit in silence, except for the clicking of her knitting needles, while I smoke.

"Do you think your mom ever had any doubts about Christian Science?"

I shake my head no. It isn't until I've replied that I remember what Mom said shortly after arriving at the hospital. "I should have come here a long time ago. I wanted to, and your father knows it." I decide not to mention it.

"She wasn't unhappy," Aunt Kay says, looking into my eyes. "Don't forget that."

And suddenly, I picture my parents dancing alone to Tony Bennett in the common room at Tenacre, and I know it is true.

One of the residents finds me in the waiting room.

"Your mom's awake. She said she'd like to see you."

"Hi, Mom."

"Hi, sweetheart," she says softly.

Mom closes her eyes. She seems content just to have me there. She is lying perfectly still, except for the barely perceptible flickering of her eyelids. Several minutes later, she opens her eyes again.

"Can you go find Gomer for me?" she asks.

"Huh?"

She shuts her eyes and drifts back to sleep. She must have been hallucinating.

After a few minutes, she opens them again. "Gomer and I," she says with a look of anticipation, "we're going to the Bermuda races."

*DEATH: An illusion, the lie of life in matter; the unreal and
untrue; the opposite of Life... Any material evidence of
death is false, for it contradicts the spiritual facts of being.*
—MARY BAKER EDDY, *Science and Health,* Glossary

Hope is strange. For a long time I thought—no, I think I really
knew—that my mother would die. Yet when Dr. White said that the
days following the second surgery would be critical, I nevertheless
ended up in Manhattan, back at work. I believed there was more time.

My mother died at 2:15 in the morning on September 9, 1986,
a Tuesday, three days after her second surgery. Olivia was by her
side. At 2:00 A.M., the ICU nurse said to Olivia that she might want
to call Dad, that he should come quickly. Mom was already gone by
the time he got there. My father said two things to Olivia: that he'd
hit a deer in the road on his way to the hospital and "I can't understand why—*why?*—your mom couldn't have stayed at Tenacre and
spared me this."

At the time of Mom's death, I was asleep in my apartment. I
think I always knew I would be. There had been so many sleepless
nights when I lay alone in my bed, waiting for it. But that night—or
early that morning—somebody ringing the buzzer woke me up. I
looked at my clock radio: 4:27. It was still dark outside.

At first, half asleep, I thought that the visitor downstairs was a
drunk, so I tried to ignore the rings, but when they wouldn't stop,
I climbed out of bed and went to my window overlooking Third
Avenue. "Hey you," I thought I'd yell, "knock it off..."

But before I had even opened the window, I saw two people
leaving the entry to my building, heading for the pay phone on the
street corner.

Oh, no. No.

It was my father and Aunt Lucia. I opened the window and
yelled.

"Come up!"

Mom is dead. Mom is dead. Mom is dead.

I was completely unprepared for the finality of death. *Mom is dead.*

Olivia had wanted to be with Mom when she died, and she was; she had wanted her lasting memory of Mom to be peaceful. Not having wanted to see her dead, I remember her at her living worst. Sometimes I have vivid dreams in which she is still horrifically sick, still angry with me. Occasionally, she won't even talk to me.

But once I had a dream in which I found her, happy and healthy, living in a suburb of Pittsburgh, married to an orthopedic surgeon.

Because Christian Science asserts that what we experience as life on earth is an illusion (because matter is not real), Christian Science churches do not perform holy rites at life's milestones of birth, marriage, and death. If Christian Scientists want to have a church wedding, they must go elsewhere and find a minister, since there are no Christian Science clergy. Likewise with funerals. So two days after my mother *didn't die,* we held a service in Hopewell's Baptist church, to "celebrate Life" (with a capital *L*), but not *her* life. There was no printed order of service. There were no eulogies. There was no reference to my mother's personality, or to anything she had ever done or said. No mention of the wishbones that used to hang in her kitchen. No sharing of anecdotes—like the time my six-year-old cousin Teddy threw a snowball at her car and to his surprise she got out, chased him down, and stuffed a snowball down the back of his snowsuit, laughing mischievously. No mention of the unmanageable giggles that endeared her to her children, like the time we attended the Christmas Eve service at the Anglican church on Virgin Gorda, and, as the old British minister sermonized about the Virgin birth, the open-air nightclub next door blasted the disco song "Bad Girls." Not a word about her interest in art, or even her commitment to her church. In fact, the service had nothing to do with Joanne Ewing, except for the fact that she had been a Christian Scientist, and the readings were passages from the Bible and *Science and Health.*

That day, the Baptist church in Hopewell was filled with Christian Scientists and non–Christian Scientists, family and friends. Mimi contacted my closest friends from boarding school and college, and many of them attended. For the Christian Scientists in the sanctuary, the service was probably beautiful. For me, it was at moments pointless, at other moments enraging in its purposeful avoidance of acknowledging my mother's life, her final agonizing months, and her death.

I remember sitting in the second pew between Sherman and Olivia. For some reason, we left the front pew empty. Maybe because we didn't want to face the reality that we were at our own mother's service. Dad was seated on the other side of Sherman. I couldn't imagine what was going through his mind. It occurred to me that he might have been the only one of us who felt no guilt at all for what had happened: his church's doctrine could explain everything. He had never compromised his beliefs, whereas I, at least, had never fully stood by mine. To his thinking, Mom's death was the result of her inability to demonstrate her God-given perfection. And certainly, he could argue that there is no death, that his wife had simply gone on to another plane of existence.

I was ill at ease to see Mrs. Hannah—the Christian Science practitioner from Minnesota to whom my parents had turned for all of our childhood bumps and scrapes and charley horses—stand before the congregation and start reading the Scientific Statement of Being: "There is no life, truth, intelligence, nor substance in matter..."

As I was leaving the church following the service, I overheard a Christian Scientist friend of my mother's whisper to another Church member, "She should never have gone to the hospital." I wanted to shake the woman, hard. I was baffled. Did she honestly believe that Mom would have lived had she stayed at Tenacre? Or did the woman only view Mom's transfer to the medical center as a betrayal, or even bad publicity?

I thank God that my mother did in fact go to the hospital; that I was given a month to be with her; that she died with a diagnosis, and with her family around her. Sometimes I wonder if she went to the hospital for *us*.

Afterward, people came back to our house. It was a beautiful fall day, sunny. Family and friends gathered inside and out, in the screened porch, in Mom's Bird Room. It was surreal: never before had so many people been to the house. But I wanted everyone to leave. I snuck away for most of it and hid in the Nook, waiting for it to be over.

Once people began leaving, Mimi and her dad, my uncle Brad, arranged to take my friends and me to the Tap Room at the Nassau Inn in Princeton. There, we sat talking, oddly, more about workaday things than about Mom. It could have been a birthday outing or a girls' night out, except that it was midafternoon, midweek. Our waiter asked us what the special occasion was, and one of my friends, without missing a beat, said it was a shower. I was so stunned, I laughed. Then we all did. I was profoundly grateful for the company of these friends, most of whom I hadn't seen or spoken to for so many months.

Two days later, we buried Mom in Lakewood Cemetery in Minneapolis, the same cemetery where her father was buried. It was a private ceremony, for family members only, except for Mrs. Warner, another Christian Science friend—the one with the big house, seven kids, and the annual Christmas sing-along. Dad had asked her to select a reading. Again, there was no mention of Jo, and the readings were from the Bible and *Science and Health*. Uncle Jack did not attend. He had chosen not to be at the service in Hopewell either. In fact, Olivia and Sherman and I didn't see him again until a few months later, when we were all—minus Dad—back in Minneapolis for Grandma's eightieth birthday. For a while I hated my uncle for not showing up. But eventually I came to feel that by staying away he was, in his own way, keeping his promise to Mom not to cause trouble. Over time, I began to see my uncle's anger and mine as not that far apart.

The last thing my mother ever said to me was "Gomer and I, we're going to the Bermuda races." I had hoped for something personal, maternal, loving. To Sherman she had said that whatever he chose to do in life, he should give it his very best. For a long time after her death, I felt robbed by the inconsequential nonsense of those parting words to me. In fact, her words were so random that I quickly forgot them, and would have lost them forever had I not scribbled them down in my journal.

Occasionally, I find comfort in believing that Gomer was, in Mom's private, dying world, my father; and that she, with a look of happy anticipation, was going somewhere warm, and sunny, and healthy. With him.

part three

In April 2001, nearly fifteen years after my mother's death, my father passed on. We never learned the cause of death. For a long time I assumed, because of his gradually debilitating symptoms, that he had developed ALS, Lou Gehrig's disease—an irony, I suppose—a disease for which there is no medical cure.

A couple of years ago, I had to go to Philadelphia for the day, and, before returning to New York, I made a detour through Princeton and Hopewell. I decided to go back to Tenacre. I got out of my car and walked down the footpath past the white clapboard administration building and toward South Hall Extension. The place looked smaller than I had remembered, and the buildings and landscaping were in need of attention. It reminded me not at all of a small liberal arts college, minus the students—the way I had perceived it when my mother was there. My heartbeat quickened as I neared the front entrance to South Hall Extension. I opened the door and walked in. There was nobody at the desk. I could hear a television blaring down the hall, and I saw the familiar portrait of Mary Baker Eddy. I closed my eyes and willed myself to stay a few moments longer. Then I left. I never encountered a single person, which was a blessing. I don't know what I would have done or said.

Next I drove to Hopewell and turned in to my parents' old driveway. I hadn't been there in more than ten years. Rolling slowly down the bumpy road, I came face-to-face with half a dozen deer. I stopped the car and watched them casually move on. Before reaching the bend in the road, I turned back. I decided I didn't need to see the house.

In early September 1987, my father called to announce that he was getting married. I froze. "Do you remember Heather?" he added. He sounded far too chipper for a husband in mourning. It had not even been a *year.* Heather? I racked my brain. A Christian Science nurse—the daughter of a neurologist and a psychologist?—who had been my mother's friend back in London. She possessed a meekly pious air, was about fifteen years younger than my mother, and had wide-set eyes that crossed asymmetrically, so that it was difficult to know when she was making eye contact. If my mother was Angie Dickinson, Heather was...? To tell the truth, there was no movie star equivalent. Dad told me that, almost like a sign from God, a letter from Heather had arrived while Mom was at Princeton Medical Center. Heather regretted that she had lost touch with both of them and wanted to reconnect; thus began a quiet correspondence. She had known nothing of Mom's illness. A trip to Europe late that fall, billed as a visit with Ham, had turned out to be a courtship of sorts.

Dad had called to see if Sherman and I would join the two of them for a celebratory dinner on September 9. Olivia was in Arizona, so she was spared the invitation but not the announcement. I literally trembled. September 9 was the one-year mark of Mom's death. My father's timing couldn't have been worse. I declined the invitation, on principle, and because I was still grieving. However, I dutifully met them for dinner a few weeks later, just as I had dutifully met my father for dinner every Tuesday that first year, thinking that he was alone. When he dropped this bomb on me, at first I was offended, then, gradually, relieved.

In the years immediately following my mother's death, my sister, my brother, and I each picked up the pieces of our lives and independently put them back together. Sherman bottomed out with an addiction problem shortly before his twenty-sixth birthday. Since then, with the help of a rigorous recovery program, he has maintained continuous sobriety for more than twenty years. He is a singer-songwriter, lives in Brooklyn, and has a thriving dog-walking business in Manhattan. Olivia is a social worker and a mother and lives in Minnesota with Terry and their son.

Sherman and I enjoy a close relationship, but Olivia and I have had less contact. Geography has made it easy for my sister and me to be apart; our history has made it hard to be together. I hadn't seen Olivia in almost ten years when, during the summer of 2008, she called to say she was coming with her son to New York City to see Sherman and would I like to meet up. We had a lovely dinner in the East Village. Olivia's hair had turned silver, she now wore glasses, and she had become elegant in a Gloria Steinem sort of way. I don't know why, but in the hours leading up to our reunion, I had felt very nervous. After dinner we linked arms and walked to a nearby club to hear Sherman's band play.

I am a full-time mom, living in New York with my husband and four very active children, two of whom have chronic eczema, food allergies, and asthma. We joke, occasionally, that our family is the loss leader at Oxford Health Plans; rarely a week goes by that we do not have a trip to the pediatrician, the dermatologist, the pulmonologist, or the emergency room. A few years ago, our middle boy, Truckie, was hospitalized with a severe concussion. He went over the handlebars on his bike and—helmeted, fortunately—was thrown headfirst into the pavement. I sometimes marvel at the incontrovertible fact that my Christian Science childhood avoided these kinds of excursions to the doctor. Admittedly, my parents converted to Christian Science after we had received most of the childhood vaccinations. Still, I never had a strep test, and none of us ever needed stitches. We never took Tylenol or aspirin or an antibiotic. (Well, that may not be entirely true. When my daughter, Ellie, was a toddler, I was giving her some bitter-tasting antibiotic that I had hidden in her baby food when suddenly I flashed back to my bout of chicken pox. Was there crushed St. Joseph's aspirin for children mixed in with the apple-sauce Grandma had spooned into our mouths? Had Mom taken us to our grandmother's house knowing that Grandma might do this?)

When I married my husband, David, in 1990, my father walked me down the aisle of an Episcopal church in Greenwich Village and gave me away in an elegant, traditional wedding. Members of both his family and my mom's were present; a second cousin on my dad's side was one of the two ministers officiating. Given the shattered state of my immediate family, the wedding was every bit a fantasy, painting a nearly perfect image for anyone who didn't know our history. My father paid for the whole thing except for the liquor, which my husband and I took care of. The only misstep was when my father asked that Heather be the last person escorted down the aisle before the ceremony commenced. I balked—this role was reserved for the mother of the bride, not the bride's widowed father's second wife—and I had wanted my mother's absence to be felt, to be honored. In the end, I acquiesced, because I didn't want to be the cause of an ugly scene.

During the first year of my marriage, I needed an emergency appendectomy; a month later I was hospitalized again, for post-surgical peritonitis. Had my appendix burst when I was a child, I would not have survived.

My father was the first person to visit us in the hospital in March 1993, when our daughter, Ellie, was born. He and Heather greeted each birth with flowers, baby clothes, and an engraved silver cup from Tiffany & Co. While our relationship remained strained, I was unwilling to sever the tie to my father. I wanted some semblance of an extended family, and for my children to have at least one maternal grandparent. For my father's part, he loved to visit his grandchildren and would meet us for lunch at a nearby diner every six or eight weeks. He and Ellie would share a milk shake, sipping from two straws out of the same frosty aluminum cup. To her delight, he'd magically pull his thumb off his hand and stick it back on. He played peekaboo with our second child, Dwight, and I marveled at how absolutely normal the scene looked.

After one of these luncheonette rendezvous, probably in 1997, I noticed that my father was limping. I wondered if perhaps he had turned his ankle. I didn't ask him about it because I knew he wouldn't give me a straight answer. The next time we got together, several weeks later, he was already seated in our usual booth when we arrived, and it wasn't until he kissed Ellie and Dwight good-bye and turned to walk down Third Avenue that I noticed the limp was more pronounced. I felt instantly ill, unsteady on my own feet. I rushed home, pushing Ellie and Dwight's double stroller frantically, and called my husband in a panic.

The next time I saw my father was the last time he ever met us for lunch at the diner. Again, he was seated in the booth before we got there. Ellie got her own small milk shake; he ordered a Diet Coke, and when the drinks were brought to the table, he very slowly brought the glass to his lips, cupping it in both of his hands.

Oh, God.

When my mother died, I swore I would never go through such an ordeal again; I wouldn't allow myself to ever get that close to my father. I had very minimal contact with him during his illness, but it was my father, not I, who severed the tie. In fact, he and Heather had begun their withdrawal from our family long before any illness was apparent. First they sold the house in Hopewell, then the apartment on Seventy-seventh Street and moved twenty blocks south, to an apartment on Sutton Place. I was invited there only once, while they were renovating. When my father's illness had progressed to the point where its existence was indisputable (at least to any non–Christian Scientist), he and Heather moved to an old farmhouse in Rhinebeck, New York, further removing themselves from us. Sherman and I worried. Olivia didn't, or wouldn't show it. She grew remote. Pressing our father and Heather for an invitation, my brother and I drove up to Rhinebeck one afternoon for lunch. It was a chilling visit, reminding us of our mother's illness. We exchanged awkward, forced chitchat punctuated by long periods of silence. The visit confirmed our fears: our father was confined to a wheelchair with a blanket over his legs. He didn't eat. We never saw him use his hands.

Several months passed without any contact at all. Sherman phoned me one day to say that he had tried repeatedly to call the house in Rhinebeck but there was no answer. A few days later, he reported that the phone had been disconnected.

The next morning, David and I got in the car and set out for Rhinebeck, an hour-and-forty-five-minute drive. I wondered where Dad and Heather could possibly be. Could they have fled Rhinebeck without telling us? Could he have died without our being notified?

At their house, David got out of the car and walked up to the front door. I sat in the passenger seat, too shaken, too nervous to move. The curtains on all of the windows were pulled closed, and there were some yellow UPS delivery notices stuck to the front door. David rang the bell several times. No response. Then he walked around the periphery of the house and came back to the car to say that he could hear some music coming from a window in the basement. He returned to the front door and rang the bell again, and then started pounding the door with his fist. He knew there was someone home.

"Heather?" he hollered. "Heather!"

My heart raced.

"I know you're in there! But your phone has been disconnected and Sherman and Lucia have been trying to reach you."

David pounded some more.

"Heather, please open up!"

Nothing.

"If you don't come to the door, I'm going to call the police."

I was alarmed at my husband's bold threat, but suddenly, the white lace curtain on one of the windows flanking the front door moved. I saw a hand. David moved toward it, and there was an exchange of words, but I could hear only my husband's end of the conversation.

"Heather, we'll leave as soon as we see Heff."

The door remained closed.

"Please let me in so I can see him. I need to know that he is in there, and that he is all right."

Heather said something more, and David looked back at me, shrugging his shoulders, before walking around to the side of the house, to a basement window. After several minutes, somebody opened it from inside.

"Heff," David said loudly enough so that I could hear, "we are here because we couldn't reach you. Your phone has been disconnected, and Sherman and Lucia were worried."

David went down on his knees—God bless him—and moved closer to the window so that he could hear better, then pulled back suddenly. Getting up to his feet again, he said, "No, Heff, that's not why we're here."

David walked back to the car, shaking his head in disbelief.

"He thinks we're here for his money."

We drove home.

David said my father had looked "pretty bad." The vague description carried for me a haunting sense of déjà vu.

One night, probably in 1998, after David and I had returned from a dinner, there was a message on our answering machine from Aunt Nan. She said to please call when I got the message, no matter how late it was. My head spun. I dialed the number, my hand trembling. It was nearly midnight. She answered immediately and told me that she'd gotten a call from Heather. Dad had been taken by ambulance to Albany Medical Center. Heather had told Aunt Nan that he did not want any visitors.

Albany Medical Center. My gut reaction was stunned disbelief, followed quickly by vindication: He has gotten what he deserves. Then outrage: How dare he?

I hardly slept that night. I pictured my father in a hospital bed. To capitulate, he must have been close to death. Was he in a coma? On a ventilator? Would I ever see him again? As the night went on, my anger receded, and I resolved that I would go see him. Maybe there was an opportunity here, not only for his health to be restored but for our hearts to heal as well.

In the morning, David and I got in the car once again, this time to drive up to Albany, 150 miles north. We found my father at the medical center, semi-reclined in a bed, with Heather by his side. His breathing was labored, but he was not on a ventilator, and he was alert. At first, he and Heather acted pleasantly surprised to see us, as though our being there, and their being there, were perfectly normal. It reminded me of Aunt Mary's first visit to Mom at Princeton Medical Center. I went along with the charade but worried that at any moment it might end, and then what? We sat quietly with Dad for several minutes. Then Heather asked if we'd like to walk with her to the cafeteria for something to eat. After a snack and some unilluminating conversation, we returned to Dad's room. He mumbled that he would like a few words alone with Heather, so David and I moved into the hallway, and I went to find the nurses' station. I wanted information. I felt like an undercover cop. I had to feign casual inquisitiveness, so the nurse would think that I was just looking for an update. She glanced at my father's chart and said he was recovering well. I wanted to ask how long he'd been there; I wanted a diagnosis and the prognosis, and to find out how long a recovery we might expect.

Before the nurse could say more, Heather appeared and told her curtly, in her lofty British accent, that I was not to be given any information on Heff Ewing and that we were not welcome here. Then she turned on her heel and disappeared back into my father's room.

David walked toward me. Through gritted teeth and tears, I told him what had happened. We decided that he would try to reason with my father. He went back to the room. My father grew very agitated.

"Look, Heff," David said, his patience tested, "I took a day off from work to drive up here because your daughter was worried about you. But if you want us to leave—if you don't want Lucia here—just say the word."

"I don't want Lucia here."

I left the hospital, shaking, with my husband's arm over my shoulder, holding me close, guiding me back to the car. I was a grown woman, yet I felt newly orphaned and powerless.

We heard nothing from Heather or my father for several months. I was going through a stack of mail one day when I found a U.S. Postal Service notification card, the kind one normally sends to magazine publishers to alert them to a subscriber's change of address. On it, in Heather's handwriting, was an address in Lakewood, Colorado, a suburb of Denver.

Colorado?

Sherman and Olivia got the same postcard.

In April 2001, Heather left a message on our machine saying that Dad had "passed on" peacefully in his sleep.

He was sixty-eight years old.

At the time of his death, I was very pregnant with our fourth child and could have used my condition as an easy way out of attending the memorial service. But I felt I should go. My obstetrician permitted me to fly.

David and I flew to Denver with Sherman. Olivia chose not to attend. The night before the service, there was a small dinner, during which Heather invited people to share their memories. I listened to my father's siblings come up with funny anecdotes from their childhood, as though they had been glory days. David held my hand under the table. Toward the end of the meal, I read a brief statement I had prepared, and barely got through it. It was not a eulogy. It was neither poignant nor pretty. It thinly veiled my anger at the waste of it all. I recounted how, when I was a child, my father used to make French toast on Saturday mornings before riding with us on the ski bus. He had been a ski instructor. On family vacations when we were very small, he had always brought his camera with him and took beautiful photographs. He was fully engaged. *What had happened?* I was shaking. I half-expected Heather to stand up, like an attorney, and call out "Objection!" but she did not react.

I wasn't sad about my father's death. I didn't miss him. But I missed my mother terribly. And being eight months pregnant with our fourth child, I felt the enormity of her absence from my life, and her grandchildren's lives.

The next day we congregated at a funeral home. There, I was surprised to see a man my parents had known in London whom I had met a few times. John Somebody. A church member and handyman at Hawthorne House, if I remembered correctly. He shook my hand heartily and spoke effusively of how much my father had meant to him, as a friend and a Scientist. He said something about how supportive Heff had been of "the center." I thought it was an odd thing for him to say, but he spoke as though the center was a subject with which I was familiar. I filed the comment in the back of my mind. Another man I didn't know handed out programs printed with the order of service. I bristled. My mind flooded with memories of that other service, at the Hopewell Baptist church, where there had been no programs.

I didn't bring a program home from Denver as a keepsake, but I vaguely remember—or did I dream this?—that on one page of the folded, white, ribbon-bound program was an image of a Bible and *Science and Health,* overlaid with a white dove. On another page, there was a photograph of my father. During the brief service, people I didn't know read passages from the Bible and *Science and Health.* They sang hymns from the Christian Science Hymnal, but I didn't sing along. Halfway through one hymn, I sat down, holding my very pregnant belly as an excuse. The service included a Marine Corps honor guard, which made me wonder again about the unknown, unknowable legacy of my father's tour of duty.

For someone who strove during his life to deny the reality of death, the program, the service, and the honor guard all felt incongruous and hypocritical, but no more so, I realized, than his reading glasses, or his stay at Albany Medical Center.

Six weeks after my father died, Charlie, our youngest, was born. Heather sent an engraved silver cup from Tiffany, with an enclosure that said: WITH LOVE, DAD AND HEATHER.

I wondered for years why it was that Dad and Heather had moved to Colorado at a time when my father was clearly bedridden. It could not have been an easy move, and had seemed utterly random and out of the blue. While I was surfing the Internet one night, I remembered what the man at the funeral home had said to me about Dad and his support of "the center." On a whim, I Googled "Christian Science Center Denver." What popped up shocked me.

Christian Science Endtime Center
www.endtime.org

End-time theorists were (and are) Christians who believed that, in accordance with prophecies in the biblical Book of Revelation, the Second Coming would occur at the time of the Millennium, and, in a Rapture, all Christian faithful would ascend, with Jesus, into heaven. As a student at Brown, I had written a paper about nuclear millennialists, who believed that this end-time would be brought on by a nuclear exchange. End-time theories had never been taught by my Sunday school teachers, but I did remember, vaguely, that some Christian Scientists believed that Mary Baker Eddy and Christian Science were the fulfillment of a prophecy in Revelation. I was stunned. I hadn't remembered my father espousing any millennialist notions. I called Sherman and told him to get online. Together we tried to remember when it was that Dad and Heather had moved to Colorado. We were both fairly certain that those change of address cards had arrived sometime in the spring or summer of 1999.

Another memory came back to me, but it too was fuzzy. During one of the last holiday seasons that my father was alive, he started calling me. It was very puzzling. After more than a year of no conversation whatsoever, he was now dialing my number every Sunday evening, just to chat for a few minutes. At the time, I had mulled over two possibilities: one, he was trying to rekindle a relationship with me; the other, that he was close to death and wanted to make amends. He had sounded very frail. But now a new theory surfaced, and its merit hinged on the question of when those calls had come. Was it during the last month of 1999? Had he believed that Armageddon was imminent? I wished that I had still kept a journal back then. An entry might have provided a clue.

Over the years Aunt Mary and Aunt Kay have stayed in touch with Sherman, Olivia, and me. Aunt Kay calls to chat from time to time, and Aunt Mary never misses a birthday. At Christmas, each of them sends a box of presents for us, and for their sister's grandchildren, in an effort to fill in some small way the bottomless void left by our mother.

I have had very little contact with Uncle Jack. Until September 2010, we never spoke about what had happened in 1986. Our encounters were limited primarily to small talk at family weddings and funerals. For me, these meetings were exercises in anxiety. If I spotted my uncle across a room, my heart raced, but he always greeted me warmly with a bear hug. Frequently he said, with an extra squeeze, in a hearty, reassuring tone, "Blood is thicker than water."

When Grandma died in November 2001, she was buried next to Bops's grave in Lakewood cemetery, and in accordance with her wishes, Mom's ashes were transferred from an obscure gravesite to one beside her parents; the plot belonged to Uncle Jack, and he gave his blessing for the reinterment. For Sherman, Olivia, and me—and, I suspect, for all of our mother's siblings—this "relocation" was a comfort. (We were required to get permission from Heather to move Mom's ashes, because unbeknownst to us, she and Olivia were legal co-owners of the plot. This felt terribly uncomfortable, and wrong. I called her, angst-ridden and offended that we should need her approval, but she was willing—eager, even—to help.)

Maintaining ties with my father's family has been fraught with ambivalence. On the one hand, I have longed for some connectedness, and at times have thought to circumvent my father's place on the family tree, to establish my own bonds with his siblings, because they are good, decent people. I will always be grateful for Aunt Nan and Aunt Lucia's calming presence during the final, tumultuous month of my mother's life. On the other hand, sometimes I feel uneasy and resentful that their remembrances of my father don't jibe with mine.

Through Facebook and with Christmas cards I keep in touch with several of my cousins on both sides of the family, and I get together with a few of them. Facebook allows me to peek in on their lives and see their children's faces and recall the very happy times we had together as kids.

I spent more than two decades working on this memoir (with various drafts idling for long periods of time) and almost as many years grappling with the question of whether—and with whom—I could share it. Losing my mother was painful, and writing about it was difficult, but probably in part because my siblings and I were silenced for so long, the more time passed, the more strongly I felt that the story needed to be told. I recognized, however, that if a book were to be published, a spotlight might be cast not only on me, but on my aunts, uncles, Sherman, and Olivia as well. While I could determine my own readiness to tell the story, my family would be denied that choice. I worried that even though I endeavored to portray each member of my immediate and extended family fairly and honestly, some might take issue with their characterizations in the book—nobody more so than my uncle Jack. I also worried that both sides of the family might read the account as an indictment of them, which has never been my intention. Despite these fears, I went ahead. I found an agent, who found a publisher, and I signed a contract.

In September 2010, Sherman and I flew out to Minneapolis. When I called Aunt Mary and Aunt Kay to say that we were coming out and that I wanted to meet with them about the book (which I had told them about earlier in the summer), they responded with their usual warmth and enthusiasm, offering us a place to stay and planning a dinner. The calls were as comfortable and comforting as ever. But it took two days before I could dial Uncle Jack's number.

I got his answering machine. On his outgoing message, I heard the familiar raspy voice.

"Hi, Uncle Jack, this is your niece Lucia. Greenhouse," I said, searching for the right words. "Sherman and I are coming to Minneapolis and would love to see you."

I left my cell phone number.

He called the following day, Wednesday, the day before we were flying out. He could not have been kinder, and sounded genuinely happy to hear from me. But his warmth made me feel worse, not better. We agreed to meet him at his house on Thursday afternoon. Sherman and I would call him when we landed.

I hung up the phone and took a deep breath. I felt sickened and scared. I knew that his portrayal in the book was not altogether flattering. But neither was mine.

I decided I would talk everything through with Sherman en route to Minneapolis, but as luck would have it, Delta misplaced the seating chart for the plane, and the flight was full, so we ended up eight rows apart. During the bumpy takeoff, I was reminded of another flight to Minneapolis twenty-four Septembers before, when we returned to bury our mother's ashes. Sherman and I had sat on either side of the aisle, holding each other's hand through much of the flight.

We entered Uncle Jack's address into the rental car's GPS, and fifteen minutes later stopped in front of a charming house with a manicured lawn. It was very different from the lakefront mansion in Highcroft where my uncle had lived with Aunt Helen and the four cousins. I tried to still my nerves with a deep breath.

The front door opened almost before I had lifted my finger from the buzzer, and there stood Uncle Jack, all six foot seven of him. He gave us each a bear hug, and a brief tour of the exquisitely appointed downstairs of his home. He told us, beaming, that Judy, his second wife, was an interior designer. There was a floral arrangement on the kitchen counter and a dish of roasted pecans on the coffee table in the sitting area. On every surface I noticed beautiful framed photographs of the cousins I hadn't seen in years: Harry,

Sargent, Steven, and Annie, with their spouses and children. He identified each of them, his voice full of pride. He asked us if we would like something to drink, saying that Judy was on her way but was running a bit late. We took seats in the family room.

Uncle Jack asked Sherman about his dog-walking business and his music. He asked me about Ellie, Dwight, Truckie, and Charlie—their ages, current grades, and interests—and about David's work. My head started to hurt. We talked a lot about sailing and a little about fishing, and as the time ticked away, my headache grew worse. Judy joined us, and I wondered how I would segue to the topic that brought Sherman and me to Minneapolis. I began to wonder if Uncle Jack already knew why Sherman and I were here. Was he avoiding the subject intentionally?

I looked over at Sherman, and I could tell he wondered how—or even if—I would ever broach the subject of the book. Then he said, "Did you know Lucia's been writing?"

Uncle Jack must have thought Sherman said *riding*, because he started to tell us about our cousin Harry's wife, who was an accomplished equestrian.

I glanced at my watch. It was five-thirty, and we were to meet Aunt Mary, Uncle Brad, Aunt Kay, and Uncle Bear at Woodhill Country Club at six-thirty. If I remembered my Minnesota geography, Woodhill was a good twenty minutes away.

"Uncle Jack" I said, "I actually came here with a specific purpose." I glanced at Sherman. "I don't know whether you're aware of this, but I've been writing a memoir about growing up in Christian Science. And about what happened to Mom."

There was a long pause, as I tried to choose my next words.

"When I got the call from your mom…"—Uncle Jack started, as though we were well into a conversation about her, instead of at the beginning of one that had been on hold for nearly a quarter century—"… I don't know how she dialed me, but it was late one day—she asked me to come out to Princeton, to bring her back to Minnesota. I got on a plane the next morning. And when I saw her at that place—"

"Tenacre?" I asked.

"That's right, Tenacre."

"You saw Mom at Tenacre?" I asked, stunned. I looked at Sherman, who appeared to be equally shocked. That meant that Uncle Jack had known about Mom's illness long before I called him from the Emergency Room, which made no sense.

"No, wait a minute," he said, correcting himself. "She was at the end of a hallway, lying on ... it wasn't a gurney, and it wasn't a hospital bed—"

"It was a daybed of sorts," I interjected. "She was there, lying in the sunlight. That was at the hospital."

"That's right. She was at the hospital. She was waiting there while her room was being cleaned. I asked Joanne if I could examine her. She said yes. I lifted the sheet and turned her gently onto her side. There was a ... a ..."—my uncle hesitated—"literally a *hole*." At this he made the shape of a circle with the full circumference of his thumbs and forefingers, and his hands trembled slightly. "An *ulcer* from a bedsore that had been festering for months."

I felt my chest heaving as I took a deep breath.

"She was lying in a puddle of *feces*," he went on. "There was no wall between ... her vagina and bowel. The cancer had completely eroded it. There was nothing but a ... a ... *void* where her bowel should have been."

I closed my eyes and tried to expel the image from my mind. My uncle sounded shaken, as though it had happened yesterday. He was both expert witness and grieving brother.

"Your father came walking down hall," my uncle said. "I wanted to kill him." A cloud of anger moved across his face. "Not kill him," he corrected. "But I would have beaten the crap out of him, except that he ran away."

I told Uncle Jack about my father's call to me right after that; how he had repeated my uncle's threats hysterically: "I'm gonna *get* you, Heff! I'm gonna *get* you! I'm gonna expose this whole thing!"

My uncle nodded. It occurred to me that if my father hadn't run away, things might have taken an even more tragic turn.

"I left the hospital and drove to Ten Mile," Uncle Jack said. Ten Mile Lake was the name of the lake in northern Minnesota where Grandma and Bops had had a cabin; Uncle Jack, Mom, Aunt Mary, and Aunt Kay had spent their summers there as children.

"You mean, Tenacre," Sherman said.

"Yes, that's right, Tenacre."

"I needed to see the place. When I got there, a nurse approached me, and I asked her about Joanne. You know what she said? She said that Joanne was fine until just before she went to the hospital. She said that she and Heff loved to dance, and did so every night, right up until she left."

I remembered my own conversation with one of the Tenacre nurses, and the image she described of my parents' dancing.

"Let me tell you," Uncle Jack went on, "your mother was bedridden for months. She couldn't walk, and she sure as hell couldn't dance. That afternoon, I contacted an attorney in Princeton. I told him about Joanne and said I wanted to investigate."

Sherman and I waited.

"He said I could fight this all the way to the Supreme Court, but I wouldn't win."

Uncle Jack looked down at his hands, pressed together finger to finger.

"Your Mom was always stubborn," he said, looking up. "You know, she and I had big arguments about Christian Science for years. I remember one Thanksgiving—"

"Are you sure it wasn't Christmas Eve?" I interjected.

"Oh, there were many of these arguments, with your mom *and* your dad; your dad especially. Anyway, she'd talk about Christian Science healings, and I'd send her copies of *The Lancet* and *The New England Journal of Medicine*. I'd say, Joanne, look at this." Uncle Jack's right forefinger jabbed his left palm, as though he were still holding the publications in his hand. "This is scientific data. Not your anecdotal accounts of 'miracles.'"

"But she was so stubborn," he went on. "Eventually, she told me to back off. So I did."

Uncle Jack's expression changed from frustration to a smile.

"Your mom was beautiful. You know that? When she was a teenager, she had these *legs*. And a killer body."

Decades ago I might have taken offense at his plastic surgeon's critical eye, but now (as a forty-eight-year-old mother of four with the body to prove it) my uncle sounded to me more like a nostalgic older brother who adored his little sister. He mentioned the time Mom showed up in Grandma and Bops's driveway with the fellow camp counselor who'd given her a ride back from Colorado; how he (Uncle Jack) had felt so protective of her and towered over the poor guy, staring him down, interrogating him. We all smiled at the picture he painted.

Driving to dinner, Sherman asked if I was okay. My head throbbed, the base of my skull was cramping, and my eyes hurt. I felt overwhelmed. I wanted to get home to my family.

"I haven't told him about the book deal yet," I said, as we drove up Woodhill Road. "He still doesn't know."

Dinner took the same course as our conversation at Uncle Jack's house, with two hours of chat about cousin Ted's upcoming nuptials, Aunt Kay and Uncle Bear's travels, golf and fishing stories, and questions about our lives in New York. My mother's siblings and their spouses all looked wonderfully healthy, even Uncle Brad, who I knew was frailer at ninety than he appeared. How would I ever steer the conversation where it needed to go? Uncle Jack told the story of a Sunday afternoon back in the seventies. He and his boys were watching TV in the den when he got a phone call from the Vikings' trainer. Fran Tarkenton had sliced his face open during a game and had requested that Uncle Jack come down to stitch him up. He raced downtown and put twenty-six stitches in the Viking quarterback's cheek.

"If you'd done half that many he might have gotten back in the game," Uncle Bear said with a smile.

"I did twenty-six, and he *did* play the rest of the game. Can you believe that? He got right back in there. And we *won!*"

The waitress brought two chits to the table, one for Uncle Bear to sign, and one for Uncle Brad. Dinner was over, and I hadn't done what I needed to do. People started pushing their chairs back, when Aunt Mary spoke.

"Just a moment. I know Lucia has something she would like to discuss," she said. Even after all these years, her posture was as erect as a ballerina's. Her manner was almost businesslike, but she tilted her head to one side and smiled at me encouragingly. Everyone remained seated. I looked once again to Sherman.

I said I'd been writing a memoir about growing up in Christian Science, and about what happened to Mom. Aunt Kay and Aunt Mary nodded. "It's going to be published next summer."

Judy, who was sitting to my right, squeezed my forearm and congratulated me warmly. But it made me feel worse, not better.

"I guess what I want to say, first, is that I feel very strongly that Mom's story be told. But I am pursuing this with mixed emotions. I have made this decision based on my own readiness, while you have not been given the same choice. You haven't asked to be part of the story, but you are. And for this, and for any stress this may cause you, I am sorry. I have lived with regret about the way things unfolded. It is regret, not guilt," I said, shaking my head, but as the words came out, my eyes flooded with tears. When I looked up and saw Uncle Jack, I thought—for the millionth time—about what might have happened had I defied Mom and called him sooner. "I know our hands were tied," I added, with more conviction than I actually felt. I hurt all over. I was sorry about the book, but more than that, I was sorry about everything.

Uncle Jack spoke. "Lucia, Sherman," he said, looking at both of us and speaking very slowly, "I want you two, and Olivia, to know that I don't blame you now—nor have I *ever*—for your mother's death. She made her choice."

His words were almost too much to bear.

After midnight that night at the hotel (we had declined Aunt Kay's offer to stay with her, anticipating, correctly, that neutral ground would feel safer), I sobbed quietly into my pillow so that Sherman, in the adjoining room, wouldn't hear me. In the morning, I woke up before dawn, wrecked. I lay in bed and replayed in my head, over and over again, my uncle's statement: *I don't blame you.*

Sherman and I drove back to Wayzata for breakfast with Uncle Truckie, our father's half brother. On the way, we talked about the meeting with Uncle Jack and dinner at Woodhill. Sherman told me he was very proud of me. If he had said as much the day before, I would have come undone. I thanked him for being there with me.

We were met at the door by Uncle Truck, Aunt Adrienne, and their son, little Truck (who was now more than six feet tall, in his forties, and married with two kids). My son is named for Uncle Truck, with good reason: he is smart, grounded, fun-loving, and handsome. Over the years, I have seen my uncle infrequently, but he has sometimes called me out of the blue to check in, and occasionally—especially after he retired and had more time on his hands—we've spoken at length.

We chatted for a while about their grandchildren and my kids and Sherman's music before I told him about the book. He immediately started talking about Dad.

My father, he reminded me, had been a Marine, and several years after he went through boot camp, Uncle Truckie followed in his footsteps.

"Just before I left for Parris Island, which is the camp for Marines on the East Coast, your father came to see me. He told me that basic training nearly destroyed him and he wasn't exaggerating. Hell, it almost killed *me*, and I was six-two and athletic. But your dad told me that far worse than the physical ordeal was the brutal taunting he had endured for his speech impediment. I can only imagine what he went through. Then, he shipped out to Korea. I was too young for Korea, and too old for Vietnam. But he was right in it. He had troops dying to his left and right."

"He never mentioned that," I said, surprised. "In fact, when I asked him, he said he never saw combat."

"And he told me," Sherman added, "that all he did was break eggs and sweep. Break and sweep, that's what he said."

"Your dad told me that the only good thing that came out of Korea was that he was cured of his speech impediment."

My eyebrows went up. "Well, he may have said that, but he wasn't cured then."

My uncle was adamant. I told him about Dad's testimony at church, how he credited Christian Science with that healing. "And we can assure you, Uncle Truck, he stuttered when we were kids."

Uncle Truck also told us that recently he had been reunited with his half sister, Jane. He couldn't have known the significance it held for me.

I vaguely remembered that Grandpa had had a kid—or two?— from an earlier marriage.

There had been three, my uncle said, but one had died as a child. He had never known these half siblings. After Grandpa divorced his first wife, the children from that marriage remained with their mother. He and Uncle Nick never spent time with them on vacations or holidays, nor did these children ever really know their own father.

"Anyway," Uncle Truck said, "we met up. And I gotta tell you, it was the oddest thing, to meet a grown woman, my half sister—as close to me genetically as your aunt Nan or aunt Lucia—except that *this* woman *looked* like me."

I realized then that my father's childhood wasn't the only casualty in his family's history. There was other collateral damage.

Late Friday afternoon, Sherman and I drove to Red Wing, a small town fifty miles south of Minneapolis, to see Olivia and Terry, and catch their son Hoka's varsity football game under the lights. When

I had called Olivia, several months before, to tell her about the book deal, she had been reticent, and bitter, in part because she'd heard about it from someone else first. I wanted things to be okay between us.

We arrived at their house just as they were leaving for the football game. I got a glimpse of my sister's life, which was so different from mine, living within the supportive culture of the Native American community. I had brought her some gluten-free foods from back east. (I'd learned that she, like I, followed a gluten-free diet); she gave me a bag of wild rice and some homemade maple-sugar candy.

Sherman and I sat on the bleachers with Olivia and Terry and cheered every time our nephew ran onto the field. In the two years since I had seen him, Hoka had become a strapping, six-foot-four sixteen-year-old. His team won in a big upset.

In the morning, Olivia drove to Minneapolis for an early breakfast with Aunt Mary and Sherman and me, and when Aunt Mary got up to leave, Sherman walked out with her to run an errand.

"I'm sorry, Liv, that the news of my book upset you, and that you didn't hear about it from me. I had planned to tell you when the contract was signed."

Olivia took a sip of coffee from her mug.

"Can you tell me what else is bothering you?" I said. "I know there's more."

"I just want you to know," she said, cautiously, "you, Sherman, and I—we had three very different sets of parents. Your story's not mine."

"I know," I said. But her words stung like an accusation. I had to resist the temptation to feel I was being attacked. After all, there was truth in what she said. I thought of how she had joined the Mother Church at age twelve—the only one of us who did—in what I've come to see as an attempt to gain our parents' love; a love that she understood, long before I did, was the conditional sort.

"And the happy childhood I read about in that draft you sent me ten years ago?" she went on. "Well, that wasn't my childhood."

"I know that too. Liv, I don't want you, or anyone, to think I'm speaking for you. We were silenced for so long, all three of us. It's taken me years to do this. But I don't want my voice to rob you of yours."

Sherman returned to the hotel coffee shop just as Terry and Hoka arrived. We said warm good-byes, and the four of them—Sherman, Olivia, Terry, and Hoka—headed over to Target Field to take in a Twins game, with tickets from Aunt Kay and Uncle Bear. I left for the airport, eager to return to my family.

I am a worrier. I tend to see doom behind every door and a crisis lurking around every corner. I have anguished for months—years even—over the risks of publishing this story. To this day, the specter of mental malpractice lies in wait. Will the result be injury to Sherman or Olivia, or to one of my aunts or uncles? My mother had cancer when she was fifty. If I tell this story, might the same happen to me? Sometimes, it is hard to conceive that anything good can come of it. But I feel I am as ready now as I will ever be.

In part because of the dogmatic way I was raised, in which there was an absolute answer for every question, I am more comfortable muddling my way through matters of faith. For a while after my mother died, I attended a socially liberal, liturgically traditional Episcopal church; the church where my husband and I eventually married and my second cousin Lucia—*Lu-chee-ah*—was a minister. (She had introduced herself to me in Hopewell the afternoon of my mother's service, handed me her card, and said, "Look, I wouldn't blame you if you never set foot in *any* church, ever again. But if you find yourself in the neighborhood, or ever want to talk...why don't you keep this in your wallet.") I finally got to indulge my childhood longing for stained-glass windows, kneeling cushions, choirs, and communion. But eventually, I realized that I didn't believe the Nicene Creed any more than I believed the Scientific Statement of Being, so I couldn't in good conscience recite it. Now I attend, when I can, a nondogmatic, liberal, urban church, for its beautiful music, thought-provoking sermons, and calming sanctuary. In the company of my fellow congregants, I recite two lines I can live with:

In the freedom of truth and in the spirit of Love
we unite for the worship of God and the service of all.*

* The Unitarian Bond of Union, which is the Ames Covenant with inclusive language.

acknowledgments

In April 1988, I walked into my East Village studio apartment and found the red light on my answering machine flashing. I hit Play and heard the voice of a guy named David, whom I had met in the Hamptons nearly a year before. He'd heard that I had finished writing a book and was calling to take me out for a drink to celebrate. Two years later, I married the guy, and twenty years after that I am finally writing the acknowledgments for *fathermothergod*—the same book, sort of, after several drafts and many years on and off the back burner. I owe my greatest thanks to him, for acts mundane and wonderful and everything in between; for his forbearance, comfort, devotion, intellect, and, perhaps most of all, his sense of humor.

I am indebted to my editor, Sydny Miner, at Crown, whose enthusiasm for my story, encouragement, wisdom, compassion, gentle prodding, and deft use of a pencil (and Delete button) transformed my manuscript into a real book. Thank you to Kimberly Witherspoon of Inkwell Management for offering to look at my manuscript two decades after we first spoke about it, for getting editors to read it, and for holding my hand while she worked her magic. Without Kim, this manuscript might still be unfinished in various files scattered throughout my hard drive. Thanks also to my extraordinary writing teacher, Joelle Sander, and my esteemed colleagues in the Art of the Memoir class at the Writing Institute at Sarah Lawrence College, who will go unnamed except for Inge Hershkowitz, who is an inspiration to everyone who knows her. To the late Richard P. Brickner of the New School; Greg Pagano, M.S.W.; Annette Rotter,

Ph.D.; and the late Rev. Forrest Church. To my dear friends Susan McGovern, Laura Sillerman, Erica Gourd, Susan Gibbs, Christina Clifford, Nancy Lauritzen, Betsy Swindell; my brother, Sherman; and my daughter, Ellie; for reading one of a number of penultimate drafts. To Deirdre Carmody Millones, who read the earliest draft and has cheered me all the way to the finish. At Crown, I would like to thank Sydny's assistant, Anna Thompson, cover designer Laura Duffy, interior designer Lauren Dong, senior production editor Tricia Wygal, and copyeditor Susan Brown, as well as Matthew Martin and everyone else there who supported this book. At Inkwell Management, I would like to thank Kim's assistant, William Callahan. Thanks to Terri Riendeau for assistance with a chronology question. To Adrienne Rogers, M.D., for guidance with medical concepts. To Rita Swan, for her close reading of the manuscript, and to her organization, CHILD, Inc. (Children's Healthcare Is a Legal Duty, Inc.) for its ongoing effort to fight for repeal of the religious exemption laws that allow parents to deny medical care for their children on the basis of faith doctrines. To Meredith Manning and Richard Cooper for assistance with legal terms. To Bobby Friedel and Brooke Greenberg. To my friends whose love has sustained me over the years: Ebit, Kath, Meredith, KJ, Boatie; Elise; Pam, Melissa, Susan, Anne; Laura, Mary, Silda, and our dear, much-missed friend the late Connie Hays. To Gus, Deneze, Stephanie, Amber, Wendy, Bella, and Gemma. To the Rye Free Reading Room, the Greenwich Library, the Stonington Free Library, and the New York Public Library; and to Arcade Book Sellers, of Rye, New York. To Google. To the people whose support and encouragement have never failed me, even if my memory to include them by name in these pages has. And finally, to Ellie, Dwight, Truckie, and Charlie, who are God's greatest blessing (and who have always called me a writer).

questions for discussion

1. How successful would you say the author was in conveying the doctrine of the Christian Science Church, starting with a child's point of view?

2. As a young girl Lucia thinks about the dichotomy between Christian Science and the real world as being like the Venn diagrams she's seen in her math class and wonders if the two realms overlap at all. Does this dichotomy apply to your own religion or that of others? Does it apply to other conflicting aspects of a child's life?

3. What were Lucia's parents' motivations in embracing Christian Science? Lucia's grandfather and uncle were prominent physicians. What are possible explanations for her mother's rejection of medicine?

4. Has there been a time in your own life when you've had to make an extremely difficult choice between adhering to your own beliefs and respecting those of close friends or family members? How have you dealt with that conflict?

5. The Christian Science Church has often been viewed as a more-or-less mainstream—if small—Protestant religion. What was your understanding of the church, and how has that understanding changed?

6. Freedom of religion is a fundamental principal of American democracy. Are there limits to the free exercise of religion? Should there be?

7. Lucia and her siblings had been raised in the Christian Science Church and indoctrinated as children. Even though they never fully embraced Christian Science, its grip on them remained tight, even paralyzing. But the same cannot be said about some of Lucia's other family members who remained silent after they learned about Joanne's illness. What kept them from acting? Filial loyalty? Religious tolerance? Fear?

8. What would *you* have done, had you been in Lucia's shoes?

9. Where should the line be drawn between personal choice and legal interest (such as assisted suicide)?

10. At one point Lucia says that her grandmother may be the only person capable of forgiving her father, and only because her grandmother's faith dictates it. What role has forgiveness played in Lucia's life and that of her family since the events of 1986?

11. Do you think Lucia loves her parents?

12. What is the lowest point in the story?

13. Regardless of one's feelings about Mary Baker Eddy's theology, she was an early feminist who founded a religion and started the *Christian Science Monitor*. What is her legacy?

14. What do you think attracts people to Christian Science?

15. What is the difference between a religion and a cult?

16. Lucia's sister, Olivia, said to Lucia near the end of the book, "I just want you to know, you, Sherman, and I: we had three very different sets of parents. Your story's not mine." Is Olivia's comment a universal truth?

17. Sibling dynamics around family secrets are always complicated. How is what happened in *fathermothergod* similar or dissimilar to the way families handle other secrets, such as alcoholism or other addictions?

18. Which character in *fathermothergod* do you most identify with, and why?

For more information, visit LuciaGreenhouse.com, facebook.com/luciagreenhouse, and twitter.com/luciagreenhouse.

interview with lucia greenhouse

Q: **How old were you when your parents became Christian Scientists? Did you attend church with them regularly?**

A: My parents converted to Christian Science before my earliest memory, so for me, my family's religion was something immutable, constant. For my parents, however, their conversion marked what could only be described as a radical departure, especially for my mother: her father was a doctor, her mother had been a registered nurse, and her brother was a plastic surgeon.

To hear them tell it, my father was first introduced to Christian Science as a boy during World War II, when his family was living in Fort Worth, Texas, where his stepfather was stationed in the army. My grandmother—whose own mother had "dabbled in Christian Science" earlier in the century—enrolled my father in the local Christian Science Sunday school when my father began having terrible recurring nightmares.

Many years later, when my sister, brother, and I were small children, our parents "turned to Christian Science" because a pediatrician said that my brother "had weak ankles and bad asthma, and might never lead an active boy's life." Within a few days of contacting a Christian Science practitioner, Sherman was "healed." As a child, this family lore was for me unquestionable truth.

I attended Christian Science Sunday school every week without fail. While my cousins, who were not Christian Scientists, got to plant bean seeds in Dixie cups and watch them sprout at the Episcopal Sunday school, we studied the weekly Bible lesson, whose subject might be "Love" or "God" or "Probation After Death." The most daunting of all Weekly Bible Lessons was "Ancient and Modern Necromancy, alias Mesmerism and Hypnotism, Denounced." It came up in the cycle of Bible Lessons twice a year, and each time it did, our Sunday school teacher spent the better part of the hour trying, in vain, to parse its meaning for us while we struggled, with glazed eyes and fidgety fingers, to pay attention.

Wednesday evening testimony meetings were a "special treat" that ended with a trip to Baskin-Robbins and a later bedtime.

Q: **You got chicken pox as a child. What did your parents tell you was wrong with you? How did that square with what you had learned in school about germs?**

A: Did I get chicken pox? According to my parents, I did *not* get chicken pox. The itchy blisters were *error*, an illusion, unreal, like a mirage: the image of water shimmering in the arid desert. And the spots, which we were told weren't itchy—even though they itched like crazy—were likewise not contagious, because there was no such thing as contagion. (Curiously, though, my sister's non-bout preceded mine by several days.) What my parents were telling me didn't square with what I was learning in school and on television (Lysol kills germs, but I knew there was no such thing as germs). Over time I began to question these contradictions, but not as a young child. That I ended up with only a few spots, and my sister suffered with significantly more, was evidence to me only that my understanding of Man's God-given perfection was greater than my sister's.

Q: **Your father was a Christian Science practitioner. What is a practitioner?**

A: When a Christian Scientist is faced with a problem (for example, an illness or injury; unemployment; a shaky marriage), instead of paying a visit to a doctor or a therapist or minister (there are no clergy in the Christian Science Church), he or she will engage the services of a Christian Science practitioner, who will pray for a healing on the patient's behalf. He or she (Christian Science was an early, equal opportunity calling) will suggest readings from the Bible and the Church's textbook, *Science and Health with Key to the Scriptures*. He or she will counsel the patient on ways to better understand man's true nature as the perfect Child of God, which cannot be sick. Together, they may sing hymns from the Christian Science hymnal. The fees for being treated by a Christian Science practitioner are determined by the individual healer, but range, generally, from $15 to $75 per day.

   The mission of Christian Science, according to the Church, is to restore the healing practices of the early Christians. Christian Scientists eschew medical care, so the role of a Christian Science practitioner is perhaps best understood as analogous to the role of a medicine man in certain tribal societies, with a few notable differences: the cost of treatment by a Christian Science practitioner is tax deductible, and a note from a Christian Science practitioner can, in some jurisdictions, excuse a "patient" from jury duty.

Q: **I was surprised to learn that there are Christian Science boarding schools. Why don't Christian Scientists just go to regular boarding schools?**

A: Christian Scientists are fully integrated into mainstream society, so they *do* go to regular boarding schools, and public schools and private schools. But there is also the option of a Christian Science education. For three years I attended Claremont, an all-girls boarding school for Christian Scientists outside of London, England, with my sister; my brother attended a nearby Christian Science boarding school for boys called Fan Court. My sister also studied at Principia, a coed Christian Science boarding school in St. Louis, Missouri. Principia College, in nearby Elsah, Illinois, is an accredited four-year liberal arts college for Christian Scientists.

In my memoir, *fathermothergod,* I remark about the extraordinary fact that in my three years at Claremont, I do not recall a serious illness or accident among the student body. There was not a nurse on campus or a doctor on call (but there was ready access to Christian Science practitioners). I do not remember stomach viruses or even nasty colds scourging the dormitories.

However, the same cannot be said about Principia College. In 1985, there was an outbreak of measles on the campus, and three people died. The same year, there was another outbreak of measles at a camp for Christian Scientists, and while there were no deaths, the threat to public health was real, as the outbreak in both cases occurred among an unimmunized population.

Q: **You describe being gradually cut off from your mother as she grew increasingly ill. And your father also limited access to her. Why?**

A: In Christian Science, there is a concept known as "mental malpractice," which stipulates that the negative, evil, or ignorant thoughts of one person can negatively impact the health of another. For this reason, when a Christian Scientist becomes ill, it is common practice that he or she removes himself mentally and physically from the company of others, especially those who are not sympathetic to Christian Science. My mother spent several months at Tenacre, a Christian Science Nursing Facility in Princeton, New Jersey. At first, we were allowed to visit. As my mother grew sicker and sicker—despite the fact that she was being "treated" by another journal-listed Christian Science practitioner and teacher in addition to my father—my brother and sister and I were allowed less and less contact with her. Phone calls were restricted. Eventually, our visits were curtailed altogether, as we were thought to be part of the problem, a cause of our mother's illness.

Q: **Your uncle Ham was also a Christian Scientist. But then he left the faith. Why?**

A: A favorite "uncle" of mine, Ham Lynch, was brought into Christian Science by my father, when I was about eight years old. Some ten years later, Ham withdrew his membership when he noticed that relatively young Christian Scientists— fifty- to sixty-year-olds—were "dropping like flies," yet nobody would discuss it. His departure from the Church drove a wedge between Ham and my parents.

Q: **What is it about Christian Science that is so attractive to some people? Do you have any theories?**

A: I often ask myself what explains the appeal of Christian Science to educated, intelligent people today. How is it that Henry Paulson—former chairman of Goldman Sachs and secretary of the Treasury charged with bringing our country back from the brink of fiscal ruin—believes in the fundamental precepts of Christian Science: namely, that "there is no life, truth, intelligence or substance in matter..." and that "matter is unreal." The fascination with Christian Science at the end of the nineteenth century makes some sense. Mary Baker Eddy's "discovery" of this *science of Christian healing* came at a time when the culture was abuzz with the power of the mind, hypnotism, and the like. (Hypnotists and mesmerists crisscrossed the countryside of New England like traveling salesmen.) Transcendentalism, also a product of New England, had made its appearance just decades before. And, of course, medical science was still quite primitive. The first X-ray image of a human body part was not taken until 1895, in Germany, and the discovery of penicillin was still a quarter of a century away.

While the Church does not make public information about the size of its membership, it is widely believed to be dropping precipitously. Comparing the number of branch churches listed in the *Christian Science Journals* of twenty-five years ago to the listings today is one indication of a church in decline, as is the number of journal-listed practitioners. But the websites of the Church paint an entirely different picture.

Interestingly, while the number of branch churches in the United States is falling, Christian Science has made some inroads in other parts of the world. For example, there are three new Christian Science boarding schools in Africa, which makes me wonder if there hasn't been a calculated shift on the part of the Christian Science headquarters to focus on developing countries, where quality health care is not readily available. Here in the United States, the Church has attempted to position its methods as an alternative to traditional medicine, along the lines of acupuncture or homeopathy. Its lobbying arm has aggressively pursued the inclusion of Christian Science treatments in Obama's health care plan.

But why, when I recently attended a Wednesday noon testimony meeting at the Mother Church in Boston (the Christian Science Headquarters), did I find that young, vibrant, articulate adults, men and women of all ethnicities, were well represented in the congregation? One reason is that the main offices of the *Christian Science Monitor* are right across the street, and while Church membership is not a prerequisite for employment, many Christian Scientists do work there. But as I sat and listened to the service (which, given my history, might have unnerved me but surprisingly didn't: the service was an oasis of tranquility and silence in the center of bustling Boston), it occurred to me that the Church may be hoping, and positioning itself, for a new interest in a "low cost" alternative to medicine in this current climate of economic uncertainty.

Printed in the United States
by Baker & Taylor Publisher Services